CIVIL WAR
COMMANDO

William Cushing and the Daring Raid
to Sink the Ironclad CSS *Albemarle*

JEROME PREISLER

REGNERY
HISTORY

Regnery History™ is a trademark of Salem Communications Holding Corporation

Regnery® is a registered trademark of Salem Communications Holding Corporation

ISBN 978-1-62157-679-2
ebook ISBN 978-1-62157-761-4
LCCN: 2020011270

Published in the United States by
Regnery History
An imprint of Regnery Publishing
A Division of Salem Media Group
300 New Jersey Ave NW
Washington, DC 20001
www.RegneryHistory.com

Manufactured in the United States of America

10 9 8 7 6 5 4 3 2 1

Books are available in quantity for promotional or premium use. For information on discounts and terms, please visit our website: www.Regnery.com.

For my wife, Suzanne

In a word, I would not take any risk of being entangled upon the river, like an ox jumped half over a fence, and liable to be torn by dogs, front and rear, without a fair chance to gore one way or kick the other.

—*Abraham Lincoln*

CONTENTS

BILL COONS

Chicago, 1847

Later in life, Will Cushing would insist his name was "Bill Coons." Though it was not the boy's real name, his older brother Alonzo sometimes called him that with affection. And Lon was his hero.

The nickname originated long before the Cushings lived in Chicago. When Will was barely old enough to walk, his family lived near a narrow river crossing where the Cushing boys would go diving in the summer heat. Raccoons were plentiful there, stealing right up to the cabin, always snooping around where they didn't belong. Like Will, nothing scared them off—not fire, not loud noises, nothing. Even the smallest cubs were unafraid of the water, swimming with playful ease as they searched for fish and crabs.

On one warm summer day, Will had watched his brothers leap bare-chested off the footbridge. Impulsively he copied them, thinking he would swim the way they swam, the way the raccoon cubs swam, as if born to it.

But the moment he hit the water, he felt himself going under. The harder he struggled to stay afloat, the deeper he sank. He flailed, kicked, and splashed. Water gushed into his nose and mouth, filling his throat so he couldn't breathe. If not for Michael, the eldest of the three brothers, he would have drowned. But Michael swam over in a hurry, got hold of him, and brought him over to the riverbank. He gasped for air in the weeds that rose almost to his chin, Michael and Lon slapping him between the shoulder blades to clear his throat and lungs.

When their mother heard the commotion from the cabin and rushed out to find Will coughing up water, she was both relieved and upset.

Relieved because she could tell he would be okay. Upset because it was not the first time that he had acted without regard for his safety and almost been seriously hurt...or worse, she thought.

Bill Coons, like the raccoons where the Cushings once lived, had a habit of getting into things, sometimes way over his head.

Now the cabin and the river were far away. The coons, too. Here in the city of Chicago—the third place Will had called home in as many years of life—the dangers of following his impulses were different. He was always under adult supervision and had very few opportunities to indulge his boundless curiosity.

But today, unexpectedly, he had a chance. His half-sister Rowena was babysitting him when he noticed she had left his side, either to fix a meal or to tend to Mother in her sickbed. The rooms his family occupied were tiny and boxlike, and the other tenants were mostly sailors and shipyard workers, men whose rough, booming voices were heard through the walls at all hours. None were married or had children, and Will was without a single playmate. Bored and restless, he slipped out from under Rowena's nose and wandered off.

A slight, blue-eyed tot, he could not have explained why he took his father's stovepipe hat from the rack beside the door. Maybe he had a vision of him wearing it in his mind.

"Doctor Cushing." That was how Father introduced himself to others. Tall, dignified, and handsome, he was a man of proper bearing and authority. Respected by everyone, he always wore the finest clothing, like the honored gentlemen who would assemble on the waterfront to

christen new ships before they set sail or cut ribbons for the buildings going up one after another along the great lake's muddy banks.

Will had noticed that those men also wore top hats.

He carried the hat downstairs with him, his short legs taking the steps awkwardly, one hand on the rail. Had he worn the hat on the stairs it would have slipped down over his eyes to blind him, and he might have tripped and fallen.

Walking out the front door, he shuffled onto the street and turned toward the bustling harbor, drawn to the piers and expansive water beyond. Around him husky dockworkers milled around horse-drawn carts loaded with timber, coal, grain, and other crated and barreled freight. Bare-chested and sunburned, the men shouted at each other in loud, barking tones as they hoisted the weighty containers from their shoulders onto the flatbed wagons. Their gruff voices sounded like those he heard through the walls of the rooming house, and some indeed may have been its tenants.

Undistracted by the commotion, the boy walked toward the busy quay. The harbor was crowded with barges, tugs, and full-rigged merchant ships, their steam whistles blowing and their paddles churning in the water. Some might have wondered what he was doing out there alone, but his calm determination may have led people to assume an adult was nearby. A child who strayed from his parents' side usually panicked or showed some sign of distress.

Will did not appear lost or frightened. Instead he looked determined as he shuffled out onto the pier, his eyes fixed on a steamboat pulling away over the water. He did not know where the ship was going any more than he had consciously known his destination when sneaking out of the house. He only understood that the boat was on a voyage to some faraway place.

Its smokestack chuffing sootily into the breeze, the vessel moved toward the harbor entrance, tossing up a long white wake of foam that ran back to its vacated berth like a twisted rope. Will gazed after it, mesmerized, his father's top hat wobbling on his head. He'd put it on as he stepped out onto the pier, holding its brim so it would not slip over his eyes.

He could see everything well in front of him.

The steamboat. The water. They went, and they went, and they went. And they also seemed to be calling for him to go with them.

On impulse, Will hurried to catch up to the ship, moving forward with a herky-jerky toddler's trot. He wanted to reach the boat before it pulled out of sight. Reach it and climb onboard.

By then he was standing at the edge of the dock. Water splashing at the piles beneath his feet, he stared wistfully out at the departed steamboat. Someone began shouting behind him, but he paid no attention. In a minute, the boat would be gone, vanished, leaving him behind.

Will made up his mind. Without a flinch of hesitation, ignoring the alarmed shouts, he leaped past the end of the wharf into the emptiness above the water and plunged into the deep, cold currents of Lake Michigan. It would not be the last time he instinctively and impulsively risked his life answering adventure's call.

PART I

BOWLING ALONG UNDER A GOOD BREEZE

CHAPTER ONE

A GOOD SHIP

On the quarterdeck of the USS *Plymouth*, William Barker Cushing looked up into the night with open astonishment. The sky above had split in two. Half was clear and calm, the moon and stars bathing the Atlantic's mirrored surface with their radiance. The other half was a solid, pitch-black band of clouds. Driven by a furious wind, they were spooling out in the *Plymouth*'s direction.

She rose and fell on the building chop, a staunch old gunboat on her final practice cruise. Upon her return from Europe, she was to be replaced by the recently overhauled USS *Constitution* for the benefit of the Naval Academy's next class of young gentlemen—assuming there was another class.

It was Tuesday, July 3, 1860. In one day, America would celebrate its eighty-fourth year of independence. But questions about the future were rampant among the midshipmen. As the *Plymouth* set out on a journey that would take them close to four thousand nautical miles from home, Will had been acutely aware of the political tempest threatening to divide his county like the ominous sky overhead. The slavery debate...Calls to rebellion...Fear of the inevitable rise of a Southern confederacy...

Will was no deep political thinker, but he hoped his countrymen would avoid the worst.

A lightning bolt seared the air. Another. Will blinked, dazzled, glancing around the deck. Then he turned his face to the wind. In the near distance, waves were rearing up over the water like humpbacked giants angrily stirred from the depths.

His heart filled with awe. He had been at sea before as a third-classman and stood on the deck of the rickety school ship *Preble* as a forceful squall came whirling across the Chesapeake Bay. Heavy weather was nothing new to Will. But the sight before him was more terrifying—and strangely majestic—than any he had ever imagined.

Again, lightning flashed, briefly casting the men on deck in silhouette. Minutes ago, Boatswain Miller had called his second alarm of the night. He'd sounded the first hours earlier, while the crew was in the mess abusing their stomachs with a typical supper of hard tack and salt horse. A galley fire had broken out, shooting flames into the funnels. Reacting at once, the veteran blew his whistle to summon the men up top. If the canvas sails caught fire, they would rapidly turn the ship into a floating pyre, the flames spreading from one mast to the next until all were ablaze.

He had another reason to be quick. The ship's barometer readings had shown a high-pressure front coming on, a storm warning, and the middies had not wanted to find themselves simultaneously battling fire *and* the elements. As they scrambled toward the rigging, they activated the pumps and smothered the flames with seawater.

The fire was extinguished before it had done much damage, and the young sailors returned to their tasteless meals with a collective sigh of relief.

Afterward, Will wrote of the fire to his beloved cousin Mary Edwards, trying to lighten his account with humor. He quipped that he had no objection to fireworks "in their proper time and place." A patriotic Fourth of July display, preferably on dry land, would have been appropriate, he wrote. But it had seemed somehow *un*patriotic to set them off a day too soon in the middle of the ocean.

In truth, it was a narrow escape. With the emergency past, however, Will turned in for few hours' sleep.

He got precious little of it. At midnight, the boatswain's whistle sounded again, its shrill tone jolting him awake.

"*All hands heave ship!*" Miller ordered bluntly.

Will had sprung off his hammock and dressed. As one of almost thirty first-class midshipmen aboard, he took shifts in charge of the deck and fulfilled that duty with the poise of a seasoned officer, ordering the sails gathered and secured before the heavy weather blew in.

At his post near the ship's stern now, Will heard the wind's growing moan and saw the clouds roiling more thickly in the halved sky. The men had gone hard to their tasks, responding to his commands without hesitation. An upward glance revealed that the spars were bare as the "leafless trunks of tall, slender pines," their lifted sails vanished "as if by magic."

Will barely had time to notice this before the storm overtook the *Plymouth,* a menacing parade of swells at its forefront like Neptune's troops charging to war.

Lashed by the rain, shouting above the roar of the wind, Will ordered the middies hurriedly to fashion lifelines from coils of rope. Soon a huge, white-crested wave crashed down on the ship, tossing her precariously to one side. The men held onto the ropes for all they were worth, the deck at a sudden tilt, their heels scuffing for purchase on its drenched, foam-slicked boards.

The aging sloop-of-war had seen her best days, and Will knew she might not outlast the gale, but he felt no fear in his breast, not the slightest tremor. Some men wish to become president of the United States, but his only desire was to lead the crew of a good ship.

Not that dying was his intention, ever. Will looked forward to graduating the Academy, serving as an officer aboard a warship, and visiting many foreign shores. A man could not be happier than when he was bowling along under a good breeze at fourteen knots. And should the ocean wash him from the *Plymouth*'s deck tonight, he would go down knowing he'd experienced one of the Lord's true wonders.

•   •   •

On the second day of the gale, a seam opened in the ship's wooden hull, and she began taking on seawater too rapidly for the bilge pumps to handle. Soon the hold was inundated, and the men could not locate the hole in the calf-deep water. The ship's laboring pumps creaked, groaned, choked, and eventually failed.

Craven consulted with his officers. Many had endured worse leaks in their careers and lived to tell of it. But coupled with the rough, high seas, it was putting the ship in extreme distress. Unless the men found the source of the leak, they would have to make for the nearest harbor—a dicey proposition. They were a thousand miles from land and captives of a changeable but persistent wind.

Although the officers downplayed their concerns, the young men sloshing through the flooded hold understood their predicament. But luck was with them. After searching high and low for spare parts, the ship's carpenter managed to repair the disabled main pump—or at least get it working well enough to keep the vessel afloat.

Independence Day was soggy and unsettled, but the storm's grip on the sloop gradually weakened. By July 6, the remnants of the wind sighed off to leeward, leaving the *Plymouth* drifting in an eerie, dead calm. When a breeze at last swelled her sails, it elicited three cheers from the middies and a merry racket from the drum and fife boys.

Overall, the *Plymouth* upheld her stalwart reputation. The worst storm damage was a split topsail which Craven, ever the dedicated instructor, turned to beneficial use by having his midshipmen practice sending up a new sail. The *Plymouth* had come through the storm in creditable shape, and the same held for Commandant Thomas T. Craven, his officers, staff, and the 115 acting midshipmen of the Academy's first, second, third, and fourth classes.

By Cushing's personal log, it was 8:10 a.m. on July 17 when the ship's lookout spotted land, calculating it to be three points off the starboard bow. Drawn by his excited shouts, Will and the rest came topside for a glimpse. Some forty miles away, an enormous mountain soared eight thousand feet into the air, its upper reaches blurred by a "strange looking" cloud column. As Will gazed over the rail, he watched the white fluff break away to reveal a wide crater at the summit.

The cloud was no true cloud, then. His ship was east of Mount Pico, the tallest mountain in the Azores archipelago—and a dormant volcano. What Will had seen was superheated vapor escaping its caldera.

He would always remember the sight with perfect clarity. The great fuming peak was nothing like those near his hometown of Fredonia, in western New York. It stirred his fancy and sense of adventure.

As the *Plymouth* drew closer to the mountain, Will noticed tiers of cultivated vineyards on its slope, their leafy green grapevine trees nourished by the rich lava soil. Further off to starboard was the slender length of São Jorge, another island in the Azores cluster. But the *Plymouth* was headed the opposite direction, around the southern edge of Pico Island into the five-mile channel separating it from Faial.

At 5:00 p.m., after twenty-two days at sea, the training ship lowered anchor off the busy commercial village of Horta. The United States Naval Academy's current crop of midshipmen had reached their first port of call.

•   •   •

An American consulate had existed in Horta since President George Washington ordered its official establishment in 1795. But its geographic importance to the States hearkened back to the Revolutionary War, when Portuguese-governed Faial became a waypoint for colonial envoys traveling to friendly European nations.

Shortly after the *Plymouth* entered port, Charles William Dabney, the second of three successive Dabneys to hold the American consulship in the Azores, came huffing and puffing over the side to extend his august welcome. A health officer followed the stout, grey-haired, walrus-mustached diplomat onboard and cleared the crew to go ashore, but as it was already late in the day, their leave was held up until morning.

The midshipmen waited impatiently. The summer practice cruise had been an intense, wearying, and stressful challenge. While at sea they had been schooled in all aspects of navigation and command. They had plotted the ship's position and course by dead reckoning and celestial observation and were tasked with setting, furling, and maintaining the sails. They had manned the helm, practiced the use and upkeep of the guns and ordnance, done target practice and drilled in infantry swordsmanship, learned anchoring and rescue-at-sea techniques, and rehearsed countless other aspects of practical seamanship. Besides all this, they had performed the most menial of sailor's chores from scrubbing the deck to washing and stowing their own hammocks.

As morning broke over the deck, Will pushed up to the gangway with the other blue-jacketed middies eager to explore. Straight off the quay, he and two shipmates used their meager spending money to hire guides and mules for a tour of the lushly beautiful countryside. Then they pooled more of their remaining funds—possibly even sold off their spare clothes and sextants—for the coinage to order dinner for six at a hotel, intending to double up on their portions when they returned from their trek into the hills. For the first time in weeks, they looked forward to a decent meal.

Will could have explored the islands all day. But Dabney was hosting the *Plymouth*'s officers and first-classmen at his summer home, and he was not about to snub the invitation. The Dabneys were a family of status and influence, and Charles was famous for his elegant soirees.

For Will, an afternoon at the consul's lavish estate would be a pleasant change of scenery and atmosphere from the hardships of life at sea.

•   •   •

Charles Dabney's remarkable fortune derived from a wide and diverse range of commercial ventures. These included the export of Pico wine from his family-owned vineyards and the transcontinental shipping of oranges, figs, whale oil, and other products native to the Azores. Charles had also opened a shipyard to service and repair the cargo vessels that stopped at Faial in the course of doing trade with the islands—a shrewd move, since it also kept his family trading enterprises literally afloat.

Arriving at Dabney's estate Will was introduced to Mrs. Dabney and her two nieces, who took him on a pleasant stroll around the hillside grounds. Besides relishing feminine hospitality after weeks aboard a Navy ship with only men, Will found the sprawling citrus groves, shaded gardens, and twittering songbirds enchanting.

"Never were birds or men so favored before," he enthused.

Of proud old New England stock, Charles Dabney was more than just a third-generation diplomat and enthusiastic raconteur. Above all, he was the custodian of his family businesses, his mansion, "the hub of American enterprises" in the Azores. The possibility of Southern secession and outright civil war between the States held worrisome implications for the Dabneys' commercial interests. At his home with his guests from Annapolis, the consul would have engaged in at least passing conversation about the widening schism between North and South, a crisis brought to a head by the 1860 presidential campaign, with antislavery candidate Abraham Lincoln carrying the Republican Party banner.

It is not surprising that he found Will Cushing interesting. Despite his impoverished upbringing, Will had a respectable family pedigree. Zattu Cushing, his paternal grandfather, had established one of the first steamboat lines to ply Lake Erie and was one of the founders of his hometown in northern New York. Will's maternal ancestry, like Dabney's, could be traced back to the original Pilgrims and had produced many illustrious relatives. His cousin Commodore Joseph Smith was chief of the Bureau of Navy Yards and Docks and oversaw all government naval construction, making him one of the most powerful men in Washington. His uncle Francis Smith Edwards was a native of Dunkirk, New York, just up the road from Fredonia, and was elected to the House of Representatives in 1854. Only serving a single term (he was defeated in his reelection bid), he returned home to practice law, keeping many connections in government.

While Edwards and Smith were both strong influences on Will, it was Edwards who lived nearby and had kept a steady, watchful eye on him since childhood. Having lost his father, Milton Cushing, when he was five, Will came to view Edwards as a benevolent paternal figure, the only constant and reliable male presence he had known known since his father's death.

Not that Milton had ever been a rock of stability. Chronically frail, he was a man who had never found his place in life and meandered through it without a true sense of direction or self. Hiding behind airs and graces, he would introduce himself to people as "Dr. Cushing," though he never practiced medicine or earned a college diploma. After dropping out of Hamilton Literary and Theological Institute in 1820, Milton had traveled to Ohio from his hometown of Fredonia, worked in a relative's dry goods shop, then borrowed the funds to open his own store. But he proved a poor manager of his earnings. When the shop did not earn a profit, he moved again, obtained a loan for another store, fell into serious debt, and once more closed his doors.

It would be his last stab at shopkeeping. With his second wife, Mary Barker Smith Cushing, Milton piled his family and belongings into a horse-drawn carriage and rode off across the prairie to Wisconsin Territory. His first wife, Abigail, had died of tuberculosis, and there were five children in the wagon—two from this first marriage, and three from his marriage to Mary.

The tiny wilderness settlement of Delafield near the winding Bark River had no post office and only a single tavern, where the trappers who came to hunt for raccoons stopped on their way to distant points. One of Milton's brothers had bought him a cabin on two hundred acres of land, expecting repayment later. Beyond the easy reach of creditors and process servers, the Cushings hoped to lead a profitable and quiet existence on their farm.

William Barker Cushing was born at the cabin on November 4, 1842, but would be uprooted before reaching his second birthday. No more successful as a homesteader than as a seller of dry goods, Milton saw his family fall into poverty and near starvation during the harsh frontier winter. By the summer of 1843, he had secured a position as a justice of the peace in Milwaukee, probably on account of his claim that he practiced medicine. The city's growing communities were receiving physicians with open arms, and his family name might have helped him avoid having to present the proper credentials to government officials.

But for unknown reasons the situation didn't last. Within a year, the Cushings had left Milwaukee and found themselves crammed into a rundown boardinghouse near the Chicago waterfront. Will and his siblings lived next door to transient sailors, longshoremen, and poor widows, and the hallways reeked of stale tobacco and alcohol.

In Chicago, Milton's health declined. He suffered from various ailments, including tuberculosis it was said. Around the fall of 1846, he traveled to Vicksburg, Mississippi, at the offer of a nephew, who had convinced him the warmer southern climate would improve his condition. Will was four years old when he saw Milton don his impressive stovepipe hat, straighten it carefully on his head, and walk out the door, forever.

Milton Cushing's final migrations were as vague and disjointed as the rest of his life. On his way to his nephew's home, he stopped in Ohio and Wisconsin, perhaps to settle some of his debts through the sale of the Wisconsin property. Then he took a riverboat to Vicksburg. But within a couple of weeks he returned to Ohio, where two of his brothers resided. Burning with fever, gripped by a violent cough he had been treating with a popular—and highly addictive—opiate-laced cold remedy, Milton checked into a riverside hostel and died there. He was forty-six. He had written Mary only once since leaving her and the children to fend for themselves.

Almost penniless, Mary followed her late husband's body back to Fredonia, where his family lived. The town had grown large around

Zattu's stately old home, and his descendants were some of its most prominent citizens—doctors, attorneys, druggists, and storekeepers. What little financial help Mary received from them was more out of obligation than generosity, and the children lived on "pudding and molasses" for months. Relatives on *both* sides—Smiths and Cushings— suggested Mary put them up for adoption, but she managed to keep her household together, bringing in money as a seamstress. Eventually she opened a small elementary school for some of the town's wealthier children, where she derived the calculated benefit of being able to educate hers among them.

Will never forgot his mother's hardships, or, in his explosive temper, forgave the Cushing's parsimony. He could be chivalrous and charming to female friends and relatives. He showed kindhearted loyalty to boys who were weaker and smaller than himself, once even defying an adult's order not to visit a friend, Harpswell, who had fallen ill with tuberculosis. But his impoverished youth had left him with a volatile, savage temper, and he often fought older, bigger boys in town, beating them mercilessly at the slightest provocation. Later in life, older men in authority would continue to rouse his temper.

With Mary struggling to make ends meet, the Cushing children worked to help bring money into their home. Milton Jr. was a clerk at White's grocery and drug store, Howard mixed inks as a printer's devil at the local newspaper, and Alonzo and Will brought cattle out to pasture early mornings before school. Industrious, Will spoke often of buying Mary an expensive satin dress and other gifts as repayment for her sacrifices.

He was far from equally responsible in the classroom, where he gained the reputation of a troublemaker. At ten years old, while attending Miss Julia Moore's Select School, Will formed a group of boys who called themselves the Muss Company and appointed himself their captain. Slipping out from under the nose of his teacher, he would convince them to climb over the school's low board fence and join him in playing pranks around town—at times influencing the normally well-behaved Alonzo to tag along. Once when he and his friend David Parker were made to stay after school as punishment for a classroom stunt, Will convinced the other boy to make a break for it. As they dashed for the fence, the teacher ordered some of the older boys to chase them. Halfway over the fence, Will turned to throw a kick at one of the boys, fell backward, broke his arm, and wound up getting it set at the office of his uncle, Dr. Squire White.

Mary eventually grew concerned about Will's future. When he was fourteen years old, she asked her brother Francis, then serving his term in the House, to help keep him out of trouble. He obliged, finding the boy a coveted spot as a congressional page.

But Washington, D.C., in those days was no quiet, taming environment. The Capitol building was still under construction, and the Mall was best described as "a chaotic jumble of shacks, industrial buildings, and unpaved roads." The narrow, muddy streets spoking off it were crowded with saloons, brothels, and gambling houses.

Will lost no time getting acquainted with both sides of the city, running messages on the House floor by day, and leading his fellow pages into the seamy red-light districts after dark. He was, nevertheless, conscientious about his duties. Although political speeches and posturing bored him, he paid attention to the underlying issues. He heard many heated slavery debates and knew of the savage caning on the Senate floor of Massachusetts abolitionist Senator Charles Sumner by South Carolina Representative Preston Brooks.

Charles Dabney would have appreciated Will's familiarity with Washington at his reception for the *Plymouth*'s first-classmen. A handsome, well-mannered officer in training with close ties to the city's inner circle, he was conversant in a wide range of subjects.

As the function ended, Dabney presented Will with a basket of his choice native oranges, dispatching a servant to carry it back to the *Plymouth* for him. He was flattered by the gesture—and now ready for his first decent meal in weeks. After leaving the estate, he and his friends went straight over to the hotel where they had ordered dinner and devoured every last morsel the landlady set out on the table.

"She never took six dollars with a greater consciousness of having earned them," Will recalled contentedly.

With the *Plymouth* setting sail for Cádiz that same evening, he "took a last look at the narrow streets, the houses with their red-tiled roofs, and the churches, and then went down to the boat."

But there was one last stop to make. During the previous year's Mediterranean cruise, when he sailed as an underclassman, he had begun to develop a fondness for curios, buying his brother Alonzo an authentic meerschaum pipe that became one of Lon's prized possessions. In Faial's harbor that evening, he followed suit with a hurried detour to an anchored whaling ship, buying a whale's tooth for himself and an elegant hand-carved whalebone cane for his Uncle Francis.

As it turned out, Cushing never did give Edwards the cane. It dropped from his hand one day when the ship was at sea, splashing overboard into the warm equatorial currents. He could not, of course, know where the flowing Gulf Stream waters would bear it or whether it might finally sink to the ocean bottom or drift up onto the sands of some faraway beach.

But in his solitary moments, he wondered about it.

●   ●   ●

On September 3, 1860, two months to the day after the *Plymouth*'s close encounters with fire and storm in the Atlantic—and four months after she made sail for Europe—the sloop-of-war dropped anchor off Hampton Roads in the Chesapeake Bay.

Her summer cruise had ended sooner than expected. When local health officials in Spanish Cádiz imposed a prolonged quarantine on the crew and students, an impatient Craven had gone underway without putting anyone ashore and then skipped a planned trip to Madagascar due to severe wind conditions. Brief port calls in Madeira and Tenerife had preceded his orders to sail home ahead of schedule.

Will made the most of the ship's final two stopovers. On one, he plucked a bit of seaweed out of the water, pressed it flat to dry, and slipped it into an envelope with a letter to Mary. It was a small memento, but he wanted to share a physical piece of his voyage with his beloved cousin.

Overall, he rated the voyage a success. He had seen most of the foreign places he'd hoped to visit, savored his first taste of command, and come through perilous circumstances calmly and coolly.

Back in the States, Commodore Craven made the most of his ship's early return by holding three weeks of extra seamanship drills on the Chesapeake—a decision met with quiet grumbling by the middies. Anchored just offshore from Hampton Roads, a fashionable vacation area, the young men gazed with longing at its busy hotels and restaurants, their mouths watering at the sight of outdoor tables piled high with fresh fruit, seafood, and other delectables.

But for all their mutterings of complaint, the first-classmen felt a collective sense of pride and accomplishment. The cruise behind them, they were set to begin their fourth and final year at the Academy on October 1. As one midshipman put it, their weeks at sea had taught them "sympathy with the life and endless work of the sailor" and "the *camaraderie* of the older officers and men...which bound them together with loyal attachment to country and to each other."

As the *Plymouth* finally slipped from the wide-open Chesapeake into the Severn River, the late summer sky was an endless run of blue, the water sparkling like polished crystal in the sunlight. Swept with the joy of being home, Will Cushing and his classmates were optimistic that they would graduate with full honors come June of the next year.

They could not have known how far the shadow of impending civil war loomed over the Academy's walls.

CHAPTER TWO

THE BLOOD OF THOUSANDS

A borrowed pen in hand, using a sheet of his classmate's paper, Will sat writing by the dormitory window as a grainy winter dusk settled over the Annapolis grounds. It was December 17, 1860, a Monday evening, and Christmas was barely a week off. He had planned to enjoy the holiday visiting relatives, as he'd done the previous two years while at the Academy—his first Christmas was spent with Uncle Francis and his wife at their old Washington residence, and his second, in 1859, with Commodore Smith's family in nearby Arlington. But this year the Academy's superintendent, George S. Blake, had ordered a blanket denial of leave to the midshipmen.

Blake was up-front about his reasons. Set to replace the *Plymouth* as the Academy's practice ship, the USS *Constitution* was anchored on the Severn at the northeastern side of the campus. The forty-four-gun frigate was one of the Union's oldest commissioned vessels, a floating symbol of its history and naval might. Captain Blake wanted the ship—and the arms, ammunition, and gunpowder stored in the yard—guarded against Maryland secessionists should their state break away from the Union.

He would not chance letting the *Constitution* become the first ship of war to have the flag of a new Confederacy hoisted onto its mast.

Blake's other major concern was the school's proximity to Washington, D.C. The Academy's grounds stood on the site of a fort built during the War of 1812 to protect Annapolis harbor from British invaders. If captured by a rebel militia, it would be a logical base of operations from which to launch raids against the capital city. Blake had warned the Navy Department of its vulnerability, but the troops he requested for its defense had not yet materialized. It left him with only his students—mere boys, as he expressed, and some of them citizens of secessionist states—on hand to repel an attack.

Mild-mannered and advanced in years, Blake showed an almost paternal concern for his inexperienced midshipmen and was loath to place them in harm's way. But boys or not, they would be ready to hold their ground and keep the *Constitution* safe...or burn her to cinders to keep her out of rebel hands.

An oppressive mood hanging over the campus, Will felt drained of any holiday cheer as winter recess approached.

"Men are arming in every portion of the State; all the banks have suspended; the blue cockade may be seen in every nook and corner," he had written Cousin Mary on December 12. The cockades, or secession badges, were ribbons worn on the uniforms of secessionist militiamen and, lately, Annapolis students from the South. "Midshipmen are every day resigning. Each Southerner has orders to resign as soon as his State secedes.... Matters cannot be improved except by a miracle, and unless that miracle happens, the 'Ship of State' which has been so long on a lee shore, must go down, carrying with it the Naval Academy...."

Will was not being overdramatic. Lincoln's victory in the November election had sent divisive tremors through the Academy's student body. Southern middies gathered secretly in their barracks after dark, huddled over muted lanterns to read newspaper reports of the national crisis and speak freely of their conflicted allegiances. Fistfights and shouting matches had erupted between Northern and Southern boys on campus, mirroring outbreaks of violence at rallies and town meetings throughout Maryland. In neighboring Virginia, tensions had flared out of control the year before when a group of slavery abolitionists, led by John Brown, seized the military arsenal at Harper's Ferry. Although the raid was suppressed in a couple of days, it led to the proliferation of armed militias sworn to defend the state's sovereignty against an imagined invasion of federal troops.

As Will's classmates chose sides, he did the same, reluctantly. Although his Quaker family had opposed slavery, he did not have strong views on the issue, other than loyalty to the Union.

"If it comes to blows between North and South, I will shed my last drop of blood for the State of New York," he declared to his cousin. "If this place does break up, I will get my graduation papers. If it does not, I will get them all the same."

The normally verbose Will only penned a brief note to Mary that gray December afternoon. Running out of time, daylight, and labored optimism, he began to jot down his closing lines, sending his regards to her parents and other family members.

That was when a gaudily clad figure outside the window caught his eye. In his ostentatious red uniform, the young man strolling past the dorm was laughing and carrying on as if he did not have a care in the world.

Will abruptly stopped writing and gazed down at him. With Superintendent Blake's permission, the Maryland Guard of the 53rd Militia had been conducting drills on campus for months. Going by the exotic-sounding name *Zouaves*—a French word for the ferocious Berber tribesmen who fought with the Foreign Legion—the volunteers wore red-trimmed jackets over scarlet-and-orange plaid shirts, baggy scarlet trousers, and flat-topped scarlet kepis.

Will knew the Zouave had arrived from the state's eastern shore, where secessionist passions ran deep. He cared nothing for their ostentatious uniforms and supposed its color represented "the blood of thousands of Northerners to be slain in times to come."

His preconceptions may have been rooted in mistrust; he disliked sharing the school grounds with any outsiders regardless of politics or fancy uniform. There were, he knew, Zouave companies that had pledged their support for the Union—including the Chicago Zouaves, who marched the streets in full regalia and touted themselves as the best-trained military outfit in the nation. But Will had years of naval officer's training under his belt and took pride in being an Annapolis bluejacket. As he wrote at the conclusion of his letter:

"June is only six months off, and I am going to graduate."

•   •   •

A courtly, fastidious French immigrant and much respected educator among his academic peers, Edward Roget—nicknamed "The Don" by the middies—had become the bane of Will's existence over the course of the semester. He found Roget's hairsplitting classroom manner pompous and superior, while the professor saw Will's disinterest in his studies, cocky attitude, and affinity for practical jokes as hallmarks of a chronically poor, disruptive, and contemptuous student.

Their bad blood stemmed from an incident early in the school year, when, in Will's eyes, the professor was excessively critical of one of his recitations. Will felt it was a deliberate attempt to embarrass him in front of his classmates and decided to retaliate. To him, you were either friend or enemy, and the line had been drawn.

Will got his first measure of revenge against the professor by mimicking Roget's European accent and genteel mannerisms in class, producing snorts of laughter from his fellow students. There was also a rumor that he later victimized Roget with one of the Academy's hoariest practical jokes, the so-called bucket trick, which involved balancing a pail of cold water atop the partly open door of the professor's quarters. As Roget stepped through the door, the bucket tipped over and left him a dripping mess in an expensive Italian bespoke suit.

While drenching Roget did not make the official records, Will was certainly guilty of other repeated misbehaviors. The Academy's conduct regulations were plain: a midshipman with two hundred demerits against him faced automatic expulsion. Will had already piled up 158, putting him at the top of his class for waywardness and horseplay. His cited offenses included fighting, disorderly conduct, disturbing class in quarters and recitation rooms, card playing—a breach of regulations that resulted in his temporary suspension—and "a highly improper communication" to the school's chief disciplinarian, Commandant of Midshipmen Christopher Raymond Perry Rodgers.

None of these citations curbed Will's shenanigans or deterred him from taking cruel shots at Roget. He enjoyed his humiliation.

In mid-October, Will pushed Roget's tolerance to the limit. Partway through a lesson, Roget noticed Cushing drawing a picture in his textbook, occasionally glancing up at the professor like a sketch artist at his subject. Taking the bait, Roget strode over to Will's desk, checked the book, and saw a cartoon of a jackass. Beneath it were the words: *Drawn from life.*

Roget realized he'd been duped. But with the rest of the class watching, it was too late to back off. Wanting to save face, he pointedly asked Will if he had intended to ridicule him.

Cushing denied it but said he might have been daydreaming when he drew the animal.

The professor wasn't buying the excuse. "Oh? Then what was your object in looking at me so frequently?"

Will fixed his blue eyes on him.

"To observe if you were watching me," he replied.

Once again, his cutting humor drew laughter from around the classroom, but this time he had pushed Roget too far.

Two days later, he reported Will to Commandant C. R. P. Rodgers for disruptive behavior. Rodgers passed his complaint on to Superintendent Blake in an official report, alluding to yet another, unspecified, episode of insubordination against an Assistant Professor Hopkins. His frustration clear, Rodgers wrote that he had "kindly and gravely" addressed the Hopkins incident with Cushing, who ignored him.

"It is desirable that this young man's misconduct should be checked, for his talent for buffoonery renders him a source of trouble at recitations," he concluded.

Meanwhile, Will kept flouting the Academy's disciplinary rules. In this, he had plenty of company in Annapolis and might have escaped punishment, if he'd only known when to ease off. In those days enforcement of the rules was lax, with the mild-mannered Blake mostly ignoring his students' antics, and the middies taking full advantage of his leniency. School policy allowed them to leave campus after study hours and return before 10:00 p.m., signing in and out of a liberty book that the watchman presented to Blake each morning. But even at that late hour, the action in the Prince George Street bars was barely starting. For the students, a long night out in Annapolis proper meant evading the designated watchman, his book, and the superintendent's curfew.

The quickest and simplest way to leave the grounds undetected was to scramble over the Fort Severn wall on the harbor, across campus from the main gate and guardhouse. The middies would climb it alone or in small groups and then meet at Rosenthal's Saloon or another watering hole, where they kept the wine and champagne flowing for local chorus girls until closing time. Eventually they would steal back onto campus and move the revelry over to their dormitories and barracks.

Just as he had been as a congressional page, Will was quick to learn the ropes and was not to be outdone when it came to finding ways to slip off campus without detection—or "Frenching it."

The students' furtive means of reentry was the exact reverse of their escape. With the first rays of sunrise, they would circle back to the fort wall, "going around the end of it, which was in an unfinished and ragged state, and protruded into the end of the bay." Taking off their boots and rolling up their trousers, they negotiated the slippery stones along the shore with their arms outstretched for balance—no small feat after hours of heavy alcohol consumption. A spill on the rocks was much less likely to get anybody hurt than falling from atop the wall in a boozy stupor.

By the midshipmen's accounts, these antics were all in good fun and the furthest thing from serious transgressions. But the campus watchmen must have differed. One of them owned a large black Newfoundland that he let roam the school grounds overnight. He had trained it to go after wall-jumpers with fangs bared. Upon returning from one escapade in town, Will had no sooner hopped the wall than the dog came after him, growling and snapping its massive jaws. Will managed to escape unhurt, but the dog got the seat of his pants.

The hard-drinking roughnecks who labored in the shipyards were no admirers of the Academy's officer trainees either. They thought them arrogant and entitled and didn't much like their showing up in dapper blue uniforms to compete for the attention of pretty young women. With middies wandering into some of the town's seediest dives and alcohol fueling tensions and jealousies, some share of stool-hurling, window-crashing bar brawls was inevitable.

Overall, the midshipmen were fortunate to enjoy Blake's generous, see-no-evil permissiveness. But Rodgers had none of his tolerance. A square-shouldered, blue-blooded, aristocratic veteran of the Mexican-American War, it was his job to strengthen and enforce the school's disciplinary policies. When a dozen midshipmen stole across his back-yard flower garden dressed as ghosts in white sheets, he did not find it amusing and grew determined to rein in their impertinent behavior.

Will's long list of infractions and clashes with his language instructor caught Rodgers's stern attention. Despite overall high marks in seamanship, his recklessness and insolence at a time when his country was coming apart at the seams exhausted Rodgers's patience.

Reports of Will's behavior found their way to Superintendent Blake, who sent him a cautionary letter on December 28, warning that he was in danger of expulsion. He had by then accumulated 168 demerits, of which, Blake reminded him, "forty-five have been removed in the hope that you may amend your conduct." Blake was bending over backward for one of his middies by wiping out over a quarter of his demerits. He went on to specify several of Will's more egregious offenses and concluded with an admonition that "if two-hundred demerits are accumulated against you, I shall report you to the department and recommend your dismissal from the service."

Will could not have failed to understand the severity of the warning. Given his unfaltering determination to become a naval officer, he should have taken Blake's admonition to heart.

Instead, he found reasons to ignore it.

CHAPTER THREE

TEARS OF MEN AND ANGELS

Gilbert Elliott was only sixteen years old and working as a banker in his mother's birthplace of Norfolk, Virginia, when opportunity struck. The town was a busy commercial center, the bank run by family connections, and his post as a cashier considered excellent preparation for a career in finance. But sometime in 1860 Gilbert received a job offer that would bring him back to Elizabeth City, North Carolina, where he had grown up, near the narrowing of the Pasquotank River.

He could hardly refuse. The man who had made the proposition, William F. Martin, Esq., was a longtime family friend and one of the community's most prominent individuals. He had a thriving law practice in Elizabeth City, and he owned a shipyard in Deep Creek, Virginia, at the northern extreme of the Dismal Swamp Canal. A lieutenant in the volunteer Home Guards, the militia he had helped organize ten years earlier, Martin was a respected figure in Democratic political circles and a vocal champion of states' rights.

The issue sharply divided the people of North Carolina. Politically, the state had pro-Union Democrats, pro-secession Democrats, and loyalist Whigs—all of whom would have been disappointed had they looked toward outgoing President James Buchanan for direction. As discord over the slavery question moved the country toward civil war, Buchanan toed the vague political line that a state's withdrawal from the Union was illegal, but the Constitution did not empower the federal government to *stop* a state from choosing to secede.

Outspoken William Martin showed no such indecision: he was firmly behind Southern self-determination on slavery and owned slaves himself that worked as shipbuilders and carpenters in his Deep Creek yard. As he would insist in dozens of debates, speeches, and newspaper editorials, secession was not his preference for North Carolina. But he had concluded that any attempt by federal authorities to interfere with slavery or wage war against a secessionist state would amount to an act of treason.

With Abraham Lincoln's March 4 swearing-in just a few months away, the nation was approaching a critical juncture. Long before Lincoln campaigned for president, he had strongly disapproved of the Kansas-Nebraska Act of 1854 that gave individual states the power to decide whether to allow slavery within their borders. "No man is good enough to govern another without that other's consent," he asserted. "I say this is the leading principle—the sheer anchor of American republicanism."

Believing open conflict inevitable, Martin committed to preparing for Elizabeth City's defense before the president-elect took office in March. But the militia he'd co-founded—recently rechristened the *State Guard*—was far from ready. Of its original officers, only Martin was still alive; many of the others had been advanced in years and since died of illness or old age. Although Martin would lead the forty-nine current members through regular weekend drills—sometimes having to remind them participation was obligatory—the group most often donned their yellow-trimmed blue frock coats on celebratory occasions, when they paraded through town alongside the Musical Club's brass band. They even had a spirited theme song for the festivities; at a volley from their rifles, the crowds of men and women outside the city courthouse would launch into a merry jig called the "Home Guards Quickstep."

Martin knew he would have his hands full turning these cheerfully ornamented holiday paraders into a crack military company. And this was on top of spending his weekdays serving the legal needs of his clients and soliciting orders for the shipyard he had inherited from his father and grandfather.

Juggling so many commitments, Martin finally sought help with the pileup of administrative tasks and clerical work at his home office on East Church Street. He needed more than just a competent law clerk. The various tasks associated with his shipyard's daily operations required his assistant to be highly intelligent and a quick learner, someone whose upbringing, education, and temperament had prepared him for a diverse and challenging set of responsibilities. He also had to be trustworthy enough to serve as a part-time custodian at the family residence. Martin shared a large Federal Greek Revival home with his aging mother, and his increasingly hectic schedule made the property's upkeep difficult.

The attorney was convinced he'd found his assistant in George Elliott. Their families had ties going back decades, and he knew the youth to be of exceptional upbringing. Gilbert's late father and namesake had been Martin's friend and colleague, a fellow member of the North Carolina bar who had the brightest of legal minds. His maternal grandfather was Charles Grice of the renowned Camden County Grices, a merchant and shipbuilder whose fleet of canal boats had once ranged up and down the Pasquotank and led to the founding of Elizabeth City. Indeed, Martin and his brother James, an Army officer with a distinguished service record, had taken seven-and-a-half-year-old Gilbert under their wing after his father's untimely death at thirty-eight and would eventually pull strings to secure his nomination to Annapolis without even mentioning it to him. Gilbert was grateful upon learning of their support—a recommendation to the Naval Academy was no small kindness—but he chose a different path. The construction of ships interested him, sailing aboard them not at all. He was resolved to follow in his father's footsteps as a financial attorney, and his job as a cashier had been a way to learn the banking industry and gain valuable contacts.

The invitation to join Martin's firm, then, perfectly aligned with his long-term goals. It offered him a chance to be mentored by one of North Carolina's top attorneys, while giving him hands-on experience running a shipyard—a family trade for generations. As an added benefit, Elliott did not have to lose any time seeking room and board. He would move back to his mother's Elizabeth City home at Main and Elliott Streets, only a stroll from the Martin House.

By the time fall arrived, Gilbert had enthusiastically thrown himself into his duties as a law clerk, freeing Martin to handle other vital business affairs and step up the training of his militia.

The end of the year brought the Secession Convention in South Carolina and a Christmas Eve manifesto out of Charleston laying out the reasons for the state's decision to quit the Union. It concluded with this paragraph:

> We, therefore, the People of South Carolina, by our delegates in Convention assembled, appealing to the Supreme Judge of the world for the rectitude of our intentions, have solemnly declared that the Union heretofore existing between this State and the other States of North America, is dissolved, and that the State of South Carolina has resumed her position among the nations of the world....

As a mild, wet November gave way to the icy winter of 1860 and chimney smoke puffed into the North Carolina nights, the people of the state were torn about their prospects. In homes and meeting halls, disunion was the subject of constant questioning and debate. Was South Carolina truly a sovereign country, as its leaders declared? If so, what were the implications for its neighbors? Would postal deliveries continue between loyalist states and those that seceded? Cross-border travel? Open trade? And the national currency...would it hold any value in the breakaway states? Or was each state now intending to issue its *own* legal tender and rate of exchange?

Gilbert Elliott's views on such matters are unknown. Being of a diligent, conscientious nature, he focused on his duties as a law clerk and would have looked to lower the stacks of paperwork on his desk well before looking to take up arms against the North.

But his employer's position was no secret. As an elector for his political district, Martin had in 1851—the same year he and others established Elizabeth City's militia—helped draft a series of Democratic Party resolutions on the subject of slavery and the federal taxation of slaves:

> If our northern brethren continue the aggressions of which we have heretofore had so much cause to complain, we claim it as a right, as it will be our duty, to meet such aggressions, even with force, should it be necessary, *let the consequences be what they may.*

Along with most of North Carolina's elected officials, Martin had long ago drawn a line in the sand. With tensions now rising across America, it was only a matter of time before that line was crossed. And before Gilbert Elliott's life changed forever.

●　　　●　　　●

As reported in the December 15, 1860, edition of the *Baltimore Sun,* the first midshipman to resign from Annapolis over secession was Francis W. Thomas. A member of the third class and a South Carolinian, Thomas was in the middle of the pack scholastically and owned a perfect conduct record with not a single black mark against him. He returned to South Carolina the day his name was struck from the register. Before the end of January 1861, seventeen more midshipmen from Southern states had dropped out of the Academy.

One of the most widely admired was Sardine Graham Stone Jr. of Mobile, Alabama. The son of a veteran steamboat captain, Stone ranked second in general order of merit behind his New Yorker friend, William T. Sampson. When Stone resigned on January 31, his path was already set. With the help of influential relatives, he was appointed a lieutenant in the Mobile customs office. He later became a navigating officer in the Confederate Navy.

His final night on campus was a melancholy affair. A young man of sixteen, the popular, mutton-chopped Stone was taking leave of friends with whom he had roomed, drilled, and sailed for the past three years.

William Cushing was among the thirty-six first-classmen to gather outside the barracks for his sendoff. There was none of the usual banter as they lined the walkway in the chilly evening darkness. They were saying goodbye to one of their fellows, knowing they might soon stand on opposite sides of a great conflict. It put the group in a somber mood.

Tall and straight-shouldered, his uniform trimmed with gold lace, Midshipman Sampson linked arms with Stone at the front of the procession. As cadet adjutant, Sampson was responsible for middies' discipline and had been less tolerant with the Southern boys in recent days. Once, while walking past a small clique, he heard one loudly assert that if Washington were attacked, Northern troops would not be allowed to march through Baltimore to protect it.

"Well then, the North will March *over* Baltimore," he said with proud confidence. "Or the place where it stood!"

A group of Northern middies within earshot took Sampson's words as a rallying cry, realizing "for the first time what it would mean to us if war really came, and the safety of the Republic were at stake."

Sampson and Stone's parting took a different tone; they were close friends, their relationship built on mutual respect. The middies started toward the campus gate from their quarters, walking in a slow, decorous procession. Ahead were the superintendent's home, the officers' housing, and the residence of Commandant Rogers. At their rear, behind Fort Severn and the practice batteries, the grounds sloped down to the wharf and the dark band of the river.

As they crossed the parade grounds, the cadets raised their voices in chorus, mouthing the words to a popular sea shanty, with its theme of parting and separation across a wide gulf.

> Farewell and adieu to you Spanish ladies,
> Farewell and adieu to you ladies of Spain,
> For we've received orders for to sail for old England,
> But we hope very soon we shall see you again.
>
> Now let every man toss off a full bumper,
> And let every man toss off a full bowl,
> And we'll drink and be merry and drown melancholy,
> Singing here's a good health to all true-hearted souls....

The group was nearing the Commandant's house when the front door swung open.

"What is this rioting on a Sunday night?" Rogers demanded to know from his entryway. He was surely remembering the time the boys had cavorted through his garden in white sheets, making a shambles of it.

Sampson was respectful. "No riot sir," he explained. "We are only bidding our classmate goodbye."

The commandant's severe features relaxed, and he stood quiet for a while.

"Go on, gentlemen," he said at last, and withdrew into his home.

The midshipmen resumed their march to the gate, passed through with a few words of explanation to the guard, and then walked on to the single-track railroad spur at Academy Junction. Before Sardine boarded the train to Baltimore and its connecting lines, they all made pledges of brotherhood and enduring friendship, exchanged tearful embraces, and perhaps smoked a peace pipe in Indian fashion, as was the vogue on campus in that bleak period. With each puff of the pipe, as the resignations mounted, came solemn promises never to spill each other's blood with the sword or gun.

Those pledges would prove more easily made than kept.

CHAPTER FOUR

THREATENED CATS LIVE LONG

F ort Sumter, South Carolina, was one of four military strongholds built to defend Charleston Harbor (the other three being Fort Moultrie, Fort Johnson, and Castle Pinckney). Situated on a mudflat off the harbor, Pinckney was closest to Charleston itself. At the time, the small, round masonry structure was used primarily as a lighthouse station, with a lone ordnance sergeant watching over its token gun battery and powder magazine.

Further down the main shipping channel, facing the harbor from its southwest side, Fort Johnson on James Island stood as a shabby, abandoned, and defenseless relic of the War of Independence. At the southeastern side of the channel entrance, on Sullivan's Island, the crumbling Fort Moultrie was similarly derelict. But it was the only garrisoned military works in the harbor, occupied by two skeleton companies of sixty-one enlisted men and seven officers, along with thirteen members of the regimental band—far short of the three hundred men needed for proper defense of the fort. The group was all that remained of a larger contingent that had arrived back in July to conduct repairs and improvements.

Standing in the middle of the channel, Fort Sumter cast the most imposing reflection over those troubled harbor waters. Designed for three tiers of guns—135 altogether—its five outer walls rose sixty feet into the air on an artificial island of Maine granite and enclosed a large parade ground and three-story masonry barracks.

Like Johnson and Pinckney, Sumter remained unmanned until adoption of the secession ordinance. The obligatory sergeant-custodian was joined by about a hundred civilian engineers and slave laborers sent to finish construction of its walls with no troops assigned to guard them. Federal bureaucrats believed the North and South would, in the end, resolve their differences without hostilities, which accounted for the lack of a military detail.

Figuratively, the bureaucrats were wearing blindfolds. Even before Lincoln won the White House, South Carolina's bellicose Governor William Gist had rumbled about seizing the forts for his state. Instigated by Gist and other government officials, the people of Charleston grew increasingly antagonistic toward Fort Moultrie's bluecoats—especially the Northerners—making them feel vulnerable to assault. General Abner Doubleday, stationed there since the summer of 1860, would learn that cannons were secretly placed downriver at the channel's mouth to oppose the passage of any vessels bringing reinforcements and supplies.

The unanimous 169-vote ratification of the Ordinance of Secession on a cold December night unleashed a wave of celebratory excitement throughout Charleston City. Inside Institute Hall, the convention's president, David R. Jamison, had read the document aloud from beginning to end before an auditorium crowded with state legislators. As he spoke his last word, a reporter from the *Charleston Mercury* observed they "could contain themselves no longer, and a shout that shook the very building, reverberating, long continued, rose to heaven, and ceased only with the loss of breath."

On the streets outside, elated cheers arose from the three thousand Charlestonians who had poured from their homes to take part in the momentous celebration. Militiamen paraded through town, firing their rifles into the air while holding up their state's palmetto flag—or a new version of it, emblazoned with rattlesnakes and the words *Hope, Faith, and Southern Republic*. At the esteemed military college The Citadel, Southern artillerymen blasted defiant thunder from their cannons as the loud clanging of church bells echoed out over the channel.

Across Charleston Harbor, meanwhile, Fort Moultrie's commander Major Robert Anderson felt understandable trepidation. The state had declared itself a sovereign power, and those who would fight for it were, in his mind, no longer secessionists. Now they were simply *rebels*.

A man of stern, quiet authority, the dark-eyed, gray-haired Anderson felt a profound heaviness of heart. Born in Kentucky fifty-five years before, he owned several slaves on a family plantation and was assigned to Moultrie largely because the Army felt his Southern background would help overcome local animosities. But as a loyal Union soldier, he focused on the safety of his men and guarding the harbor, not his Southern roots. Convinced South Carolina's leaders would try to seize Fort Moultrie as property of their "free and independent nation," Anderson made repeated requests for reinforcement and equipment, all denied by James Buchanan's Secretary of War John B. Floyd, which left his troops in naked peril.

Shortly before Christmas, Major Anderson decided to move men and their families to the larger, more defensible Fort Sumter, but he shared his intention with only a handful of officers. He was aware of the "widespread disaffection" among Southern federal troops and had not been at Moultrie long enough to trust his own staff.

He was also conscious of the patrol boats in the harbor tracking his little garrison's movements. As he worked on evacuation plans, Anderson kept the bricklayers working at the fortress walls with their picks, trowels, and hammers. He would do whatever he could to prevent spies on the boats from relaying useful intelligence back to Charleston.

"As a preliminary," recalled Doubleday in his memoir, "[Anderson] directed the post quartermaster, Lieutenant Hall, to charter three schooners and some barges, for the ostensible purpose of transporting the soldiers' families to old Fort Johnson, on the opposite side of the harbor, where there were some dilapidated public buildings belonging to the United States. The danger of the approaching conflict was a good pretext for the removal of the noncombatants. All this seemed natural enough to the enemy, and no one offered any opposition."

On December 26, Hall ferried Fort Moultrie's forty-five women and children to Fort Johnson, on Jones Island, aboard boats loaded with provisions *and* disguised military supplies for the troops. As a participant in the subterfuge, the commandant's instructions were to keep passengers on their vessels with the excuse that he was having trouble finding quarters for them. At a prearranged signal—the firing of three flare guns—Hall was to turn the boats toward Sullivan's Island.

Around nightfall, the boats moved on toward their real destination, releasing their passengers on the wharf outside Fort Sumter's north wall. Soon afterward at Moultrie, in the glow of a full moon, the garrison slipped through the main gate, walked a quarter mile to three concealed longboats, and rowed off to join their families. A rear guard stayed behind to man the cannons, a precaution in case the Southern watch boats opened fire on the evacuees.

The crossing was carried out without incident. Once the troops arrived at Sumter, a small detachment of men returned to Moultrie to assist the rear guard in carrying out the rest of Major Anderson's orders.

Instructed to destroy anything the rebels could put to good use, they hammered steel spikes into the big guns, set fire to the guns' wooden carriages, and finally chopped down the flagstaff so the South Carolina state flag could not be hoisted in place of the Stars and Stripes. By 8:00 p.m., their mission accomplished, they paddled a mile across the channel to join their comrades and families on Sullivan's Island.

The departure from Fort Moultrie was complete and its entire garrison installed within Sumter's stronger, higher, and better-armed walls.

But they were hardly safe or secure.

•   •   •

Will Cushing began 1861 in a funk.

There were several reasons for his gloomy state of mind. He was in poor health, his energies sapped by a stubborn hacking cough and upper respiratory congestion reminiscent of his father's ailment. He was also disheartened by the mounting number of student resignations and the growing cheerlessness on campus. As North and South waited to see if a compromise on slavery could be reached, it was unclear whether the Academy would hold together long enough for Will to graduate...or even endure as an institution till winter's end.

Soon after New Year's, Will asked for a week's emergency leave to care for a "favorite aunt," who he informed Superintendent Blake was "ill and lonely" in a Washington hotel room. Blake knew his cousin, Commodore Smith, lived in Washington and assumed the aunt was Smith's wife. Given the unsettled times, he may have also assumed Smith was on urgent government business, away from Washington and unable to look after his wife. At any rate, he was sympathetic to the request and granted it at once.

Will left the Academy on January 7 but did not return by week's end. Instead, he sent Blake a request to have his leave extended another seven days. His relative was still in need of care, he explained. The compassionate superintendent again consented.

Another week passed, and Will did not show up on campus. Then Blake received a third message from him. It said he had contracted his relative's illness and would be back as soon as he was able.

That proved to be a full twenty-four days after his original leave began. Blake would have understood had Will been sick. But whatever he was doing during his prolonged absence—a time when students were hitting their books in Annapolis to study for midterms—Blake found out he was not with Commodore Smith's wife.

Will would soon pay the consequences.

•　　•　　•

January brought great hardship to Fort Sumter's transplanted garrison. On the night of their arrival, General Abner Doubleday had found the island stronghold "a deep, dark, damp, gloomy-looking place, enclosed in high walls, where sunlight never penetrated." It looked like a prison and soon began to feel like one.

From the first, the troops and their families endured bitter deprivation. An inventory of their provisions, taken after a cold, rainswept New
Year's Eve that foreshadowed a long, stormy winter, revealed they had
only a month's store of cooking oil, very few candles, and no soap. They
had too few warm blankets and were short on food, medicine, and
ammunition. Surrounded by water on all sides, blockaded by South
Carolina's rebel government, the isolated soldiers were unable to receive
their military pay, and the Charleston merchants, whose shops they had
once frequented, were refusing to extend credit.

Worse, the fort's defenses were further from completion than originally
supposed. There were no gun batteries to repel flank attacks, since only
seventy-five of the one hundred forty heavy guns ordered for the upper tiers
were delivered by Secretary Floyd's War Department. The second story
embrasures on the walls couldn't close and were covered instead with flimsy
wooden boards. "Three or four blows of an axe would have made a broad
entrance for an escalading party," Doubleday wrote.

Meanwhile in Charleston, public resentment toward Major Anderson
and his men reached a fever pitch. South Carolinians considered the bluecoats an occupying force and vehemently clamored for their expulsion.

Determined to prevent supplies from reaching them, Governor Gist
put the fort in a chokehold. The same day Anderson ordered his inventory, he observed a battery of cannons being installed at Morris Island,
about a half mile west across the water. The New Year's Eve squall had
not moved off, and a fierce wind was blowing as cadets from The Citadel arranged the guns, sandbags, and ammunition on the high bluffs
commanding the channel.

Anderson noted the cadets' construction and responded with his
own preparations. "All is activity within the stronghold; the men
engaged in strengthening defenses and mounting guns, the women in
arranging the quarters," wrote the wife of one of his company.

As the blockade tightened around Sumter, the major sent a flurry of
communications to the United States War Department asking for more
troops and supplies. The situation inside the fort was growing more
desperate by the day.

Late in the first week of January, the Buchanan administration finally responded, ordering a twenty-one-gun sloop-of-war to sail from Fort Monroe, Virginia, with reinforcements and provisions. But those orders were abruptly rescinded, and a civilian paddle steamer was dispatched in place of the warship. Winfield Scott, the Army's commanding general, decided the appearance of a fighting vessel outside Charleston Harbor might ignite the overheated passions of Southern rebels and lead to an act of war. The smaller, unarmed steamer was less likely to be seen as a direct threat and had the advantage of being more maneuverable in the narrow main channel. With luck, it could slip up to the fort at night, drop off its men and freight, and leave without drawing attention.

Unfortunately, it was noticed by hostile eyes before it even set sail.

On the morning of Saturday, January 5, 1861, a telegraph went out from the offices of the *New York Herald,* a popular newspaper headquartered in Manhattan. An employee at the *Charleston Mercury* received the dispatch and relayed it to South Carolinian government authorities.

Its sender was Dr. Alexander Jones, a North Carolina native and veteran commercial reporter with the *Herald*. Though he would deny it later to a grand jury, he was a Southern spy.

Jones had learned that a mercantile vessel, *Star of the West,* was leaving her Lower Manhattan berth at dusk, and the hurried preparations for her departure had aroused his sharp interest. There had been a bustle around the ship Friday morning and afternoon when longshoremen at the dock had loaded her up with enough coal and freight to visibly lower her draft in the water. Also, the captain was John McGowan, the retired commander of a Revenue Marine cutter and one of the best pilots in the port of New York. He was known for chasing down smugglers and tariff dodgers in the harbors and bays close to shore.

Why was someone of his stature and ability hired to man the helm of a sluggish commercial freighter?

Jones wanted to know. As a newspaperman, he had heard the widespread rumors that the War Department was seeking civilian steamships to bear reinforcements to Southern forts, and the *Star* was made-to-order for that purpose. A 228-foot-long Vanderbilt steamship, she had plenty of stowage room for cargo and was at her Warren Street slip after completing U.S. mail runs to New Orleans, Savannah, and Panama.

Curious, Jones paid a visit to the Mercantile Building on Wall Street where he looked through recent customs filings. His suspicions were confirmed; the federal government had chartered the steamboat that same week.

The secret wasn't exactly kept under a tight lid. On Friday night, the ship's crew, drinking in the smoky riverfront bars on South and West Streets, crowed to anyone in earshot that they were bound for Charleston and expected to take on federal troops in the night. McGowan and his officers had not yet told them their destination, but a fair number of crates had their endpoint clearly stenciled on the outside: *Fort Sumter, South Carolina.*

On Saturday, the buzz around the docks grew louder. Curious eyes had noticed unusual movements of harbor steamers between the Brooklyn Navy Yard and Governor's Island, where the Ninth Infantry recruits were garrisoned.

At sunset, the *Star* left her wharf near Battery Park and sailed quietly into the Bay of New York. As night fell, she reached the waters off Staten Island, where a smaller steamship approached her in the darkness. McGowan ordered his men to heave to and dim the lights.

The *Lockwood* carried two hundred troopers and four officers from the Ninth Infantry. Her lights also extinguished, she inched toward the *Star* and tied up alongside her. Within an hour the soldiers from Governor's Island had climbed aboard with their rifles and equipment. When they were safely below, the two ships untethered and sailed off in separate directions.

Around 9:00 p.m., the *Star* cleared the sandbar at Sandy Hook and bore south in the Atlantic's near-coastal waters.

Four days later, on January 9 at 1:30 a.m., she arrived at the entrance to Charleston Harbor. The channel lights were out, and the buoys removed.

Without navigational markers Captain McGowan and his pilot crept up the outer channel slowly for the next two and a half hours, sounding to measure the water's depth and steering through a thick haze that covered the horizon from east to west. Around 4:00 a.m., they saw a light through the mist and concluded it was issuing from Fort Sumter.

McGowan turned southwest, the light guiding him into the main channel. Then he dropped anchor, deciding to wait until morning. He'd cut his own lights at midnight and felt confident the *Star* had gone undetected.

At daybreak, McGowan resumed moving up the channel. The brilliant morning sun had cleared away the haze, and visibility was excellent.

Soon McGowan spotted a small boat about two miles ahead lying near the shore. She burned three lights at his ship, one blue and two red, asking the *Star* to identify herself.

McGowan gave no answer. He sent the soldiers from the Ninth below decks, leaving only his crew up top.

The steamer was the *General Clinch*, one of two guard boats that had been scouting the harbor against intruders. Charleston authorities had notified the patrol crews about the possibility of a resupply mission after receiving Alex Jones's telegraph

Running up the main channel, the *General Clinch* began shooting off rockets to alert rebel sentinels around the harbor. On Morris Island, The Citadel's cadets raced over to their field artillery.

McGowan trailed behind the *General Clinch* at a steady clip. With the troops aboard his ship secreted below, he was hoping she would be taken for an ordinary merchant vessel and allowed to continue to her destination. But that hope was shattered. The *Star* was about two miles from Fort Sumter when the Morris Island battery erupted with a startling roar, its twenty-four-pound long guns concealed by a screen of high-standing brush.

The first ball was a warning shot across the bow. Up until that point, McGowan had not caught a glimpse of the hidden gun position.

But when he looked in the direction of the cannon burst, he saw a palmetto flag fluttering atop the dune.

The *Star* had been displaying the stars and stripes at the stern as she entered the channel. Now McGowan had a crewman hoist an immense U.S. ensign at her fore. He wanted to leave no doubt they were firing at an American vessel.

It did nothing to deter the gunners. A second twenty-four-pounder fired as the *Star* came on, but the ball missed its target and splashed into the water just behind her rudder. Then the barrage grew heavier. One cannonball skimmed past the pilothouse, another flew between the engine's smokestack and walking beams, and yet another finally struck its target, smashing into the planks behind the fore-rigging.

As the shelling continued, Captain McGowan resolved to press on toward his destination. Then he saw two steam tugs up ahead near Fort Moultrie. They were moving quickly to cut him off, and one had an armed schooner in tow.

The captain faced a difficult choice. He did not want to abandon the garrison at Sumter. But he also did not see how his unarmed, defenseless ship could get past the schooner without being blown out of the water.

Soon he would have to choose. Minutes after the first shots were fired at the *Star*, a second group of artillerymen opened up on her from the walls of Fort Moultrie. McGowan knew he would have to pass within three-quarters of a mile of Moultrie to reach Fort Sumter—easily within range of the pounding guns.

He saw no alternative but to raise the white flag, turn his ship around, and take flight "to avoid certain capture, or destruction." The harassment continued as she headed back down the channel to the sea and did not stop until the cannonballs began falling harmlessly short of her stern.

On the ramparts of Fort Sumter, a crestfallen Abner Doubleday watched the ship's retreat through his spyglass. The previous evening, he had noticed one of the rebel patrol boats flashing a conspicuous signal, surmised "something must be coming," and climbed the wall again at first light to see if his hunch was correct. He was soon joined at the parapets by Major Anderson, his officers, and their men. Everyone's spirits soared, and there were cries of joy and relief throughout the fort. Eager to watch the ship's approach, many of the troopers' wives came to stand beside them, only to have their spirits sink as the *Star* turned away.

After she faded into the distance, Anderson descended to his quarters and penned an outraged letter to Governor Gist about the "hostile act" committed against the ship, calling it "without parallel in the history of our country, or any other civilized nation." He had chosen restraint over opening fire on the nearby Charleston batteries, certain the latter would start an all-out conflict between the states. He had not wanted to be the spark that ignited the powder keg.

Because the *Star* was a civilian ship, there is debate over whether the shots directed at her from Morris Island were the opening salvos of the Civil War. The facts support this reading of history; the steamer was assailed while flying the flag of the United States, and the Southern blockade of Fort Sumter was enforced with the booming discharge of cannons. As the standoff dragged on, American troops and their families were left to endure the depredations of a frigid, tempestuous winter.

Whether or not the nation was ready to acknowledge it, the aggression in Charleston Harbor was a thundering flashpoint between North and South. There would be no turning back.

·   ·   ·

Flashing over the telegraph wires, the hostilities in Charleston were reported by the country's newspapers often with journalistic bombast. The January 10 edition of Baltimore's *Daily Exchange* had a front-page article titled: "War Commenced! The *Star of the West* Fired into from Fort Moultrie and Morris Island."

Billing itself a newspaper of the "Republic of North Carolina," the *Yorkville Enquirer* trumpeted: "THE WAR HAS BEGUN! The *Star of the West* Fired Into!! REPORTED TO BE SINKING!!!"

Not all the nation's dailies equaled the *Exchange*'s surplus of exclamation marks and dearth of accuracy, but regardless of presentation, the flare-up in the Charleston harbor riveted the country.

Whatever the state of Will Cushing's health, he had undoubtedly heard about the incident during his absence from Annapolis. His patriotism and readiness to fight for Old Glory were unwavering, and with every midshipman needed to defend the Academy, it seemed uncharacteristic of him to fabricate an excuse to be off campus. But inconceivable as it seemed, that is exactly what he did.

On February 2, Will finally showed up at the Academy, nearly a month late and barely in time for midterms. On arrival, he was called at once to Blake's office.

The superintendent, it turned out, had bumped into Commodore Smith at an officer's function and sympathetically asked if his wife was feeling better. The question had drawn a perplexed look from Smith. Elizabeth was not unwell, he replied.

One can only imagine the stunned look on Blake's face at the time. What was he to make of Cushing's story? He knew the youngster was not academically inclined. The strictures of classes and study appeared boring to him, and he reveled in juvenile pranks. For each of the past three years, Cushing had accumulated a tall stack of demerits for misconduct. Still, Blake was reluctant to believe the young man had so blatantly lied to him or been away over three weeks under false pretenses.

When confronted by the superintendent, Will denied using his relative as an excuse, angrily pointed a finger at Blake, and accused him of dishonesty. A member of the "Ananias class," he charged, referring to the hypocritical biblical apostle accused of lying to man and God.

It was a reckless, impulsive tantrum—and a grave error in judgement. Blake was no civilian professor like Roget. He was a senior admiral, and the military equivalent of a college president. For Will to insult someone of his stature was foolish.

A man of sound, calm disposition, Blake kept his composure. He may even have excused Will's conduct for a while. Meekness and humility could be virtuous traits, but Cushing was an officer in training, and audacity was desirable in a future commander of men.

Blake held off taking disciplinary action. If Will had used his head when the dust settled, and offered the superintendent an apology, he might have dodged any punishment more serious than a token reprimand.

True to form, however, he made matters worse.

•   •   •

Midterms took place the second week of February, and Will managed to show up for all his tests. At best, his preparedness was woefully inadequate.

He had been letting his appearance slip since November—when the atmosphere on campus grew heavy with talk of war and student resignations—and it had not improved with his time away. His long hair was often messy, and his uniform disheveled. Also, he slept late and stayed clear of study halls.

Although Superintendent Blake dismissed Will's story about a bedridden relative, the youngster had told the truth about his own poor health. He was hacking, pale, and had clearly come down with some ailment during his absence. Blake sent him to see the school surgeon, James Palmer, for a physical before the start of exams, asking him "whether in your judgement, he is entitled to special consideration if found deficient in his studies."

The doctor's evaluation had no specific diagnosis for Will. But he did state in his favor that his extra week of leave was "not an unusual period of absence from class by reason of illness." On the question of special consideration, Palmer offered the example of another sick student, John McFarland of Pennsylvania, who had been in the hospital and "cut off from studies." The student insisted he would have no difficulties with his tests, since they were "only a review" of what he'd already learned in class. According to Palmer, this was "exactly the case with Mr. Cushing. He has not appealed to me to recommend him to special consideration, and I am unaware of any reason sufficient to justify me in volunteering to do so."

In ordering the physical, Blake appeared to be giving Will a gift; a ready out if he failed his tests after the midshipman's insulting eruption in his office. With a torrent of Southern students leaving the Academy, the superintendent needed Will and every other man on hand to safeguard the campus and the USS *Constitution*. From a practical standpoint, it made sense to keep Will at the Academy.

There was also a strong chance that as Blake reflected further on Will's outburst in his office, he lost patience, in his own quiet way, with his insubordination. Once Palmer said Will's illness would *not* affect his test preparations, any excuse for a poor midterm performance was lost, giving the superintendent a free hand to oust him for poor grades, while also taking away any grounds for official appeal.

Fortunately for Will, his mixed exam results were good enough to give him hope, even if the easy-going Blake had given him no insight into what he might do to him. He earned typically good marks in the fundamentals of seamanship, navigation, and naval tactics, and acceptable scores in chemistry and political science. His only failure was the Spanish exam.

Judging from a March 1 letter to his cousin, Will appeared unconcerned about his test scores and his future at the Academy. The warm, spring-like Friday found him in buoyant spirits, his window open to admit the fresh air. He playfully wrote:

Dear Cousin Mary,

That's a good beginning, isn't it? And "a good beginning makes a bad ending." Therefore, you must not expect a long or interesting letter. I can imagine you saying, "All the better for being short." Then, to be obstinate, suppose I make it a long one....

Will told his cousin of his "consumptive cold," punctuating his sentences with throat-clearing *"ahems."* He found reason to complain about the unseasonably mild weather, stating it was, "the warmest day that it has ever been my lot to suffer," He replied to an inquiry Mary had made about his plans to visit the Smiths in Washington, telling her, "I intend to go [to] the 'city of magnificent distances' next week."

Abraham Lincoln was taking the oath of office on March 4, and Will wanted to be there for the ceremonies, "but circumstances over which I had no control have detained me." Still, he planned to be there later in the week. "I will go Thursday, and I expect to see a good time," he wrote.

In Will's mind, failing Spanish should not have been an obstacle to his graduation. Annapolis graduated thoroughbred naval officers, and cadets left its halls with great seafaring acumen. Academic accomplishments carried less weight and were considered irrelevant by many naval officers.

So, he was feeling confident and saw himself on the verge of achieving his longtime dream of reporting to a ship of war with a full commission.

He was sadly mistaken.

•   •   •

A March 13 letter from Lieutenant C. R. P. Rodgers to Commodore George Blake, written in answer to a note Blake had sent him earlier that day, read in part:

> In answer to your last question, whether if Mr. Cushing should graduate or enter the service, he would, in my opinion, prove to be an efficient or subordinate officer…I would respectfully state that from what I have seen here, and from what I have heard of him from you, I do not think him likely to prove either efficient or subordinate. Mr. Cushing has not given that promise of usefulness and correct conduct which would entitle him to go forth into the Navy, stamped with the approval of his school, which is one of probation as well as of instruction.

Rodgers's note was one in a series of behind-the-scenes communications with Blake—and it sealed Will's fate at the Academy.

On that same day, Blake sent this terse report to the Navy Department:

> February semi-annual examination, 1861. Midshipman William B. Cushing. Deficient in Spanish. Aptitude for study: good. Habits of study: irregular. General conduct: bad. Aptitude for Naval Service: not good. Not recommended for continuance at the Academy.

The superintendent's report was Will's undoing.

One can only imagine his distress at his imminent expulsion. The prospect of returning to Fredonia unsettled him. He could not go back in disgrace.

Will's dream was to sail the world as a United States naval officer, a leader of men. His one way forward—the only acceptable way for him— was to seek reinstatement to the Academy. But to have any chance, Will decided he would need to appeal to his cousin, Commodore Smith. Smith's influence had secured him an invitation to Annapolis years ago. Now, he might supply some key advice or even persuade Blake to reexamine his decision.

Will must have felt great trepidation about approaching him. Word spread fast in Washington power circles, and Smith would view his expulsion as a family embarrassment. "Old Guts," as Will called him, would not conceal his anger or disappointment.

But Will was grasping at whatever slender hope he could and was willing to swallow his pride. Soon he was on board a train to the capital. As it left the station, its wheels clanking over the tracks, Will feared Annapolis and the Navy were behind him forever. Apart from asking Cousin Joe for help, he lacked anything close to a plan. The future looked bleak.

CHAPTER FIVE

I WILL GAIN A NAME IN THIS WAR

Trepidations aside, visiting Cousin Joe and asking him to intercede on his behalf opened an important door for Will. Nine days after he was sacked from Annapolis, on Friday, March 22, he reported to the Pennsylvania Avenue office of Gideon Welles, Secretary of the Navy. With an austere disposition and sprawling white beard that would gain him the nickname "Lincoln's Neptune," Welles was an imposing figure in the capital. The case of young William Cushing did nothing to brighten his austere countenance.

The resignations of two hundred Southern officers and midshipmen had left the Navy disorganized and depleted, with gaping holes through-out the service. The Academy had invested significant resources into training its midshipmen, and the loss of someone like Will, who was both passionately loyal to the Union and just a few months away from graduation, was a terrible waste.

Welles also knew the Confederacy had formed its own navy in late February, appointing as its secretary the former Florida senator Francis Mallory. With his keen mind and thorough knowledge of maritime warfare, Mallory was not a man to be taken lightly. Having chaired the

Senate Committee for Naval Affairs, he had studied the powerful fleets of England and France as they transitioned from wooden to ironclad warships and was determined follow their example. Welles's intelligence sources told him Mallory had dispatched emissaries to Europe to obtain vessels and shipbuilding supplies for a massive buildup of force.

As if that weren't sufficiently troublesome for Welles, the nightmarish situation at Fort Sumter was also bearing down on his thoughts. Days earlier, the Assistant Secretary of the Navy Gustavus V. Fox had traveled there on President Lincoln's directive and visited Major Anderson under the hawkeyed scrutiny of a Confederate escort. Fox was now returning to Washington with his status report; no one expected good news. Down to their last reserves of salt pork, flour, and rice, the blockaded garrison was in desperate need of aid, yet to send relief ships would inevitably mean war. With the time for decision at hand, Lincoln was weighing every move and its consequence.

Presumably because of the perilous naval situation and Will's family, Welles gave Will's petition for reinstatement serious attention. Will came fully prepared too, bringing a note written by another cousin, Commodore Smith's son, a respected attorney. Despite his unhappiness over Will's dismissal, the younger Smith felt Will merited greater leniency from the Academy, which was notorious for its high tolerance of student hijinks. Why was he not afforded such consideration? Most of his behavioral lapses—absence from roll call, absence from chapel, oversleeping—were, in Smith's view, decidedly inoffensive, and the note emphasized his virtues over his imperfections.

Along with this document, Will came armed with written appeals from twenty-one of his classmates, and New York Congressman Alfred Ely, a family friend.

Welles wanted to grant their requests. He had strong admiration for Commodore Smith, whose words of support were persuasive. And it did not hurt that Will seemed genuinely respectful and apologetic.

But George Blake had weighed in before the meeting and asked that his decision stand. He and Captain George Magruder, his ordinance chief (a Virginian who later resigned from the service with all his clerks) found

Will "wanting in certain elements which were requisite to the makeup of a good naval officer, and that to reinstate him would be detrimental."

Their observations struck a severe blow to Will's hopes. Welles had held his cabinet post for just over two weeks and was a politician with a background in law and journalism, not a career Navy man. Though the final decision belonged to him, he was uncomfortable overruling the objections of the Academy's veteran officers—men with whom he would have to cultivate vital working relationships in the coming days—and reluctantly upheld their objections to Will's reinstatement. He would not return to uniform.

Welles never forgot the "saddened disappointment and grief" that shadowed Will's features. But the secretary felt his hands were tied.

He did, however, offer Will one consolation. In recognition of his family background, he could leave Annapolis with the dignity of a voluntary resignation rather than have the stain of his expulsion entered into record.

Will was not about to argue. Unable to save his naval career, he could at least save his honor.

•   •   •

Lieutenant Charles W. Flusser had been a twenty-five-year-old assistant professor of gunnery and tactics in 1857 during Will Cushing's plebe year at the Naval Academy. Generally liked by the cadets, he was Will's favorite instructor. For Will, instructors fell into one of two groups: prim academics or rigid martinets who had never seen action. But he saw Flusser as the genuine article: a sea dog who had spent years sailing aboard naval warships and taught from experience rather than textbooks and field manuals.

Maryland born, Kentucky reared, Flusser was short and sinewy, with a ruddy complexion, light brown hair, a thin beard, large piercing eyes, and a long, straight mustache, "the ends of which he sometimes unconsciously pulled while talking." Vigorous and quick of movement, a bit restless, he was as skilled at riding a horse as helming a ship.

Flusser's usual naval dress was "a blue jacket given open to the breeze, without waistcoat" and a cap perched brashly to one side of his head. But he was more polished than his appearance suggested. His father Thomas, the immigrant son of a Czech merchant prince, had run a finishing school for young women in Annapolis—a "gentle-school," he called it—before being sworn into the Kentucky bar. His favorite pupil eventually became his wife, and she gave birth to seven children, Charles among them.

Ingrained in Flusser from an early age was dignified gallantry. In boyhood, he often stayed up all night reading to his mother. He could quote Shakespeare and the Bible and was fluent in Spanish, French, and German. His love of words and literature remained with him all his life, and his greatest pleasure as a young man had been reading stories of "wars, sea, and battles."

In the autumn of 1858, shortly before Will began his second year at Annapolis, Flusser took command of the brigantine *Dolphin* with the Paraguayan Expedition, a mission to extract an apology from the Latin American nation for an attack on a United States vessel. When the task force returned in December 1860, its gunboat diplomacy successful, Flusser traveled to visit his family in Tennessee, with a stop in New York. At one point in his travels, he ran into some Southern officer friends who offered him a high staff position in the budding Confederate Navy. He declined angrily; Flusser's bedrock loyalty to his country was unshakable.

At loose ends, Will headed back to Annapolis and called upon his old mentor for advice. Flusser welcomed the company, inviting him to stay at his place. They both had reasons to be despondent.

Flusser's visit home had been emotionally taxing. His father had passed away while he was at sea, and his mother and all but one of his brothers and sisters supported the South. When they prodded him to quit the Union Navy, Flusser lost patience with them. As the atmosphere became tense and quarrelsome, he even grew prickly with the family cook, a black slave who chided him that he was no better off than she was for having to do what his "master" Uncle Sam told him to do.

His rail trip back to Annapolis added insult to injury. When Flusser attempted to retrieve his baggage, the Navy trunks holding his uniform and sword had vanished, something he would blame on the baggage handler at the Louisville depot who overheard him urging his brother and childhood friends to be loyal to Lincoln and the Union.

Will's future at the time was painfully unclear. He was close to having nowhere to go, except back to Fredonia, and he could not return there and salvage any scrap of pride. He had informed none of his usual confidantes of his dismissal from the Academy—not

Lieutenant Charles W. Flusser, U.S. Navy. Will Cushing's friend and mentor, he earned the nickname "Flusser the Lionhearted" with his daring raids against Confederate shipping. *U.S. Naval History and Heritage Command*

Cousin Mary, not his mother, not Alonzo, though they would likely learn of it anyway, probably from Commodore Smith. He seemed to have dropped off the face of the earth.

At West Point, a worried Lon wrote their mother about Will's disappearance:

> I have been anxiously waiting for some news from home or from Washington for some time but none reaches me. Willie for all I know may be dead, maybe in Fredonia or at Annapolis or a member of some voluntary military organization.... it is a terrible misfortune that this thing should have happened now of all times—a first classman just about to get his diploma

and above all a war breaking out—many resignations in the Navy and a glorious chance for distinction and promotion.

By the second week of April, Will's state of mind verged on despair. In a deep fix, he saw no way out.

But the morning of Friday, April 12, 1861, changed everything for him and the country.

•   •   •

After meeting with Major Anderson at Fort Sumter in March, Gustavus Fox had returned to Washington with two conclusions. The garrison there needed food and other necessities quickly, and a surreptitious drop could occur right under Confederate noses.

The feasibility of a successful supply run—and troop delivery—occurred to Fox during his visit to the fort while he waited to be picked up by the same rowboat that had brought him there hours earlier. Standing high upon the ramparts after nightfall, he heard the rhythmic creaking and dipping of oars but saw no sign of the boat until it bumped against the granite island's little wharf.

Although Anderson, an army man, had abandoned the idea of provisioning his garrison after the repulse of the *Star of the West*, Fox was more optimistic. Fort Moultrie's guns were three-quarters of a mile to the east, and Charleston's newly constructed Cummings Point batteries were the same distance in the opposite direction. As he gazed out at their vague outlines in the darkness, Fox had posed a question to himself: If from his vantage directly above the pier, he hadn't been able to see an approaching small craft at night, wouldn't far-off insurgents also fail to discern it under similar conditions?

Charleston's shore batteries would be on the lookout for another heavy draft cargo vessel like the *Star*, one that would need to approach Sumter in high water. Thus, if under cover of darkness the stores sent to the fort were in small craft—at low tide, when the Confederates did not expect it—the operation had a greater chance of success.

He planned on sending the provisions and troops as far as the channel entrance on a "large, comfortable sea steamer" and then transferring them to powerful civilian tugs. The tugs would run the stores deep into the harbor, then put them into the water on launches with muffled oars and row up to the fort. Escorting the steamship and tugs would be the screw sloop USS *Pawnee* and the *Harriet Lane*, a swift, multi-gunned sidewheel revenue cutter out of New York.

Within days of sharing the plan with President Lincoln, Fox left Washington for New York, where he was to quickly prepare the merchant steamer SS *Baltic* for the mission. The *Baltic* was chartered like her predecessor the *Star of the West* at an outrageous cost and crammed with troops and supplies. Fox's convoy would soon grow to include the steam frigate USS *Powhatan*, one of the largest and best-armed ships in the Navy with its two Dahlgren howitzers and five twelve-pounder cannons.

On April 9, Fox set sail for Charleston Harbor. He expected to rendezvous with the *Powhatan* at the sandbar three days later, but complications dogged the operation from its outset. Unbeknownst to him, on April 6, the *Powhatan* diverted on another mission after a series of confusing miscommunications and conflicting orders. One of the tugs, the *Thomas Freeborn*, stayed at the New York dock, its owner developing cold feet about leasing out his vessel for the mission. The other two tugs, the *Uncle Ben* and *Yankee*, set out as planned but never reached their destination. A strong gale struck the convoy soon after it passed Sandy Hook, a barrier spit off the coast of New Jersey. High, billowing waves separated the tugs from the other ships and sent them toward shore. Both were seized by Confederate officials, the battered *Yankee* minus her smokestack, which had been clawed away by the wind and then blown into the sea. Severe weather would harry the remaining ships for the entire 637-mile expedition.

At 3:00 a.m. on April 12, Fox arrived at the meeting point ten miles east of the Charleston lighthouse to find the *Harriett Lane* there, ahead of him. Her able commanding officer, Captain John Faunce, had sailed out of New York a day before the *Baltic*, outstripped the storm, and reached the sandbar at dusk the previous night.

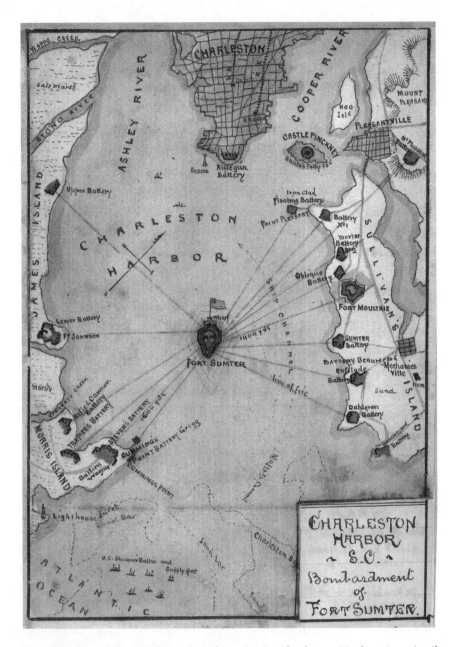

Fort Sumter and the Southern shore batteries in Charleston Harbor circa April 1861. *Library of Congress, Geography and Map Division*

Long before Fox showed up, the rebels had spotted the *Lane* in the channel. While awaiting the other vessels, lookouts on Charleston Harbor saw her, sending rocket flares to signal their patrolling tugs of her presence. For the next eight hours, the spy boats made repeated passes of Faunce's side-wheeler, inquisitively coming up close and then returning to shore. For the *Lane*'s crew, it was a night of raw nerves and sleeplessness between turns at the watch. They could feel the insurgents' eyes on them.

The *Baltic*'s arrival relieved some of their anxiety; they were no longer alone in hostile waters. When the *Pawnee* finally came in around six that morning, dropping anchor two miles to the east, Faunce and Gustavus Fox turned their ships around to confer with its captain, Stephen C. Rowan.

After both men joined him aboard the sloop, Rowan insisted that his orders were to await the *Powhatan* at the bar. But Fox had resolved to deliver the provisions without delay, asking that the *Pawnee* go with him.

Rowan refused. "I am not going in there to inaugurate civil war," he insisted. But he would offer Fox an alternative. His ship had a launch and cutter meant to support the absent tugboats during their supply runs. Bristling with armaments, they were at the assistant secretary's disposal.

Back on the *Pawnee*'s deck soon afterward, a determined Fox steamed toward the harbor entrance, the *Harriet Lane* following close behind. The channel was unmarked, its buoys removed as they had been when the *Star of the West* made her approach three months earlier. They would need to scout for a way in.

The two vessels were nearing the island when Fox heard the rhythmic pounding of cannons, and then saw "smoke and shells from the batteries which had just opened fire on Sumter." Moments before, at 4:30 a.m., a mortar man at Fort Johnson on the western shore had sent up a single red flare, the fiery shell sizzling through the fog-swept dimness as it arced into the water outside the fortress wall. An explosive mortar round had followed at once from the same battery.

Then the rest of the Confederate harbor batteries came alive. Cummings Point. Fort Morris to the east. Moultrie toward the channel mouth. Others. Johnson had waited only until the outlines of the fort were visible in the predawn light to signal the attack.

Aboard the *Lane*, off-duty crewmen poured up onto the deck from below, awakened from their strained, uneasy dozes by the crashing volleys. Joining the sailors on watch, they climbed atop the wheelhouse and other elevated vantages to observe the massive barrage of artillery shells and glowing hot shot. Shocked and horrified, they could see Sumter's guns belching orange flames in answer. But the outmatched federal garrison, encircled by hostile batteries, was pounded from all directions.

Inside the beleaguered fort, General Abner Doubleday huddled in an empty ammunition storeroom opposite Cummings Point. Weeks earlier, Fort Moultrie's batteries had been positioned to fire directly into its officers' windows—including his own. When the rebel commander of the Charleston defenses sent a dispatch warning his forces were about to attack, Doubleday moved his bed to the magazine, thinking it a safer place to bunker.

It hardly seemed that way to him now. The walls around him shivered from the impact of the cannonballs, thick choking smoke filling the room as projectiles from the battery drilled through the magazine's wall. As chunks of crumbled masonry spilled around his head, Doubleday grew almost certain that the wall would collapse, and the incoming shells detonate the powder—some loose, some bundled—on the floor of the room.

But the feared explosion did not occur. Doubleday survived the night and would soon evacuate the fort with Lieutenant Anderson and the rest of the federal garrison. The rebels had claimed Sumter for the Southern Confederacy.

There was no longer any hope of peace. America was at civil war.

•   •   •

On April 24, 1861, Lieutenant Charles Flusser and William Cushing stood amid a crowd of thousands as a military bugle and drum band sent its brassy serenade into the apple blossom–scented air between the Severn River and the long parallel line of campus buildings. Paraded out in their dress blues, the Academy's young acting midshipmen had joined the newly arrived troops of the Massachusetts Eighth and New York City Seventh Regiments on the lawn. With them were civilian members of the school staff—professors, mess cooks, groundskeepers, and others—along with a great many locals who had assembled to view the ceremonious proceedings with curiosity and unease.

Etched into every middie's face were similar emotions. Despite the sunshine, music, and fragrant spring breeze, it was an occasion of great sorrow, one they had hoped never to see.

Five miles away at the harbor entrance, the USS *Constitution*, her decks guarded by 1,300 infantrymen armed with muskets, pistols, and cutlasses, waited to be boarded by Lieutenant Rodgers and the one hundred seventy midshipmen embarking for distant Newport, Rhode Island, where the Naval Academy was about to move for a period of uncertain duration. Maryland was no longer a safe place for the education of its students; the attack on Fort Sumter marked the end of what brittle peace had prevailed between North and South. On April 13, Major Anderson had raised the white flag after two days of steady pounding by rebel guns. Worn down by months of living under siege, his tattered, half-starved garrison and their families were allowed to evacuate the fort's smoldering ruins and flee north aboard the *Baltic*.

Their surrender brought turmoil to the nation. On Friday, April 19, President Lincoln, after conferring with Gideon Welles and Secretary of State William Seward, proclaimed a blockade of all Southern ports. His order had the effect of declaring the Confederate states belligerents and gave federal Navy ships the legitimacy of international law to prevent foreign countries, and Union states, from trading freely with them. No cotton or tobacco was allowed out of the ports without special dispensation, and no essential goods or munitions were to reach their docks.

That same day in Baltimore, civil uprisings seethed over into uncontrollable riots as secessionists and antiwar protesters flung bricks, stones, and bottles at federal troops traveling from Massachusetts to the nation's capital. The mayhem in the city claimed the lives of over a dozen citizens and four soldiers, then quickly spilled over into Annapolis and its satellite villages where organized groups of Confederate sympathizers destroyed miles of railroad tracks, set fire to bridges, and tore down telegraph wires and poles along the roads. "Millions are watching with great anxiety to hear the fate of the capital of the United States," wrote one newspaperman.

The downing of the telegraph lines interrupted the Academy's communications with Washington, leaving it isolated and unprotected amid the spreading violence. Fearing his beloved campus would be overrun by agitated mobs, Superintendent Blake positioned howitzers at the gates and informed the Navy Department of his urgent predicament, adding that he had heard rumors that secessionists were planning to hijack *Old Ironsides*.

On April 20, Blake received orders from Secretary Welles either to defend the *Constitution* or destroy her. The proud avatar of the United States Navy wasn't to fall into enemy hands. Two hundred miles to the south in Virginia, the commander of the Gosport Naval Shipyard, facing a similar predicament, deliberately burned the facility to cinders, scuttling and torching the federal warships anchored at its docks.

Blake could no longer postpone his decision. He ordered the *Constitution*'s guns double-shotted, or loaded with two cannonball shots, reducing their long-range efficiency but giving them greater closeup firepower against marauders. Her boarding nets were raised, and students armed to the teeth.

Early the next morning, he sent a schooner downriver to reconnoiter for insurgents, having heard reports of an arriving ferryboat. It was to his great surprise and relief that he discovered the vessel carried not rebel attackers, but Brigadier General Benjamin Butler and the Massachusetts Eighth.

The regiment was en route to Washington on a mission to bolster the city's defenses. Having sailed to Baltimore from his home state, Butler and his troops had planned to disembark in the city and then take the railroad forty miles south to the capital. But he was stymied by Maryland's Governor Thomas Hicks, who feared the arrival of more federal soldiers—the detested New England *Yankees*, no less—would spark further outbreaks of violence.

The general did not react well to the governor's snub. A man of brusque, sullen demeanor, with one sagging eyelid and a vast, high forehead whose lines perpetually turned down in a humorless frown, Butler insisted his ferry pilot chug upriver to the Naval Academy. He could then bypass Baltimore altogether, land with his men, and quarter in the school's buildings.

By the time the 8th put ashore, the New York regiment had also arrived at the school. Both were welcomed by Superintendent Blake. Butler, in the meantime, was undeterred in his goal of reaching Washington by rail, intending to bring his troops down by train from Annapolis Junction.

He would find the line in shambles. Catching wind of his arrival, pro-Confederate officers of the Annapolis and Elk Ridge Railroad had waited till cover of darkness and then sent out a work train to pull up large sections of rail. They left only a single broken-down old locomotive at the station.

Butler at once assembled a team of volunteers to repair the tracks and guard them against further destruction. He also blockaded the line north of the station, closing it to enemy troop trains that might try using it to attack the Academy or Washington.

On April 22, Butler wrote Governor Hicks that he would "peaceably, quickly, and civilly, unless opposed by some mob, or other disorderly persons, march to Washington, in obedience to the requisition of the President of the United States. If opposed we shall march steadily forward."

With the general's infantry set to resume their advance, Blake knew he could no longer wait to ensure the safety of the *Constitution*. He ordered Lieutenant Rodgers to take command of the ship, which was to be boarded by the midshipmen, towed downriver to the open sea, and then temporarily brought into the New York Navy Yard, where she would drop anchor until a final destination was found.

Over the next twenty-four hours, Blake put his students to the task of packing away the trophies of war, flags, and other items kept in the Academy's lyceum and transferring them to *Old Ironsides*, where they were stowed away carefully for transport. Two companies of Butler's men had stayed on the frigate to defend her while she was loaded up.

As senior officer and ordnance instructor at the Academy, Lieutenant Flusser oversaw the ship's outfitting for the journey. With a detail of Butler's men at his disposal, he brought the *Constitution*'s twenty-four spar deck cannons onto the *Maryland* to lighten the frigate for hauling to open water. Will Cushing, who was still staying at his house, offered to help, marking his first return to the campus since his dismissal. But coming as a visitor, not a student, was awkward for Will. He felt hollow inside knowing his old friends and classmates were about to move on without him.

The *Constitution*'s departure hardly went off without a hitch. Even with her spar guns removed, the old ship's weight pulled her keel down to the muddy bottom not once but twice before she was finally afloat. As night fell, a "heavy rain squall threw her aground again." At one point the Eighth Regiment's volunteer crew spotted vessels sailing upriver and prepared for an armed showdown, thinking they carried Confederate attackers. But the newcomers were friendlies, who had come to aid in towing her to New York. The charter steamer *Baltic*, fresh from the fateful encounter at Fort Sumter, also arrived to transport officers, faculty members and their families, and what was left of Academy memorabilia not already loaded on the *Constitution*.

Now, three days after the arrival of Butler's Eighth, Will Cushing watched the middies board a ferry that would take them to the waiting *Constitution*. Only an onlooker, he felt empty and lost as his friends and former classmates made their final salutes, marched toward the wharf in procession, and left for New York.

The Naval Academy was now an Army encampment and school remnant. At Annapolis station, Butler's repairmen, many of them carpenters and tracklayers in civilian life, were able to get the rails relaid within hours. The line was needed for the impending influx of Union troops.

The same day the *Constitution* set off on its journey, a steamship flotilla carrying 8,000 added infantrymen arrived at Annapolis in transit to the capital. Within two days, the number swelled to 14,000 troops, either ashore or about to land with their supplies, munitions, and horses.

On April 29, Butler ordered four new engines and ten passenger cars from New York. But it was impossible to know when they would reach him, and he could not rely on the frowzy old locomotive at the depot to keep the lifeline between Annapolis and Washington open. Butler knew he would need better, newer engines to keep the men and supplies moving. At the same time, he had to find someone who could reliably direct traffic in the overcrowded harbor and ensure the safety of the ships.

There was an immediate solution to the last problem.

Impressed with Lieutenant Flusser's herculean efforts to meet the demands of readying the *Constitution* for departure, Butler asked that Superintendent Blake assign him to his command and put him in charge of the army transport service. As captain of the port, Flusser energetically oversaw the movements and protection of troops and cargo in the harbor and before long began organizing raids "which captured vessels and supplies."

Experience gave him an edge plotting those raids. Before his admission to the Naval Academy, a teenaged Flusser had been employed by the United States Office of Coast Survey, the nation's official nautical chart maker. He was intimately familiar with the network of rivers, inlets, bays, sounds, and streams in the Chesapeake Bay area and knew how and where those watercourses connected to enemy territory. It enabled him to plan missions that could succeed through speed and stealth, "cutting-out" expeditions in naval parlance.

Serving under General Butler, his first mission would be to bag a couple of desperately needed locomotives. By May 1, Butler's gangs of tracklayers and engineers had extended the rail from Annapolis Junction to the campus wharf, easing the transport of supplies and equipment from the waterfront. This became crucial to Flusser's scheme.

Bush River in Hartford County was a major tributary of the Chesapeake about fifteen miles northeast of Baltimore. The Philadelphia Wilmington & Baltimore railroad station was above the Union blockade near a rail bridge at the river crossing. Like much of the state, the area was a hotbed of Confederate support, and on the morning of April 20, a large group of Baltimore police and pro-slavery Maryland Guardsmen had joined forces to burn down the bridge, leaving a pair of engines stranded in the yard.

Flusser saw them as ripe for the taking. If he could bring a ferryboat upriver to the station, he was convinced he could haul the locomotives aboard, bypass General Butler's blockade over water, and float them down to the new rail spur at the Annapolis wharf.

It isn't clear why Will Cushing, now a civilian, tagged along on the caper, but he had been inseparable from his mentor for weeks and surely was up for it. In any event, during the first week of May, Flusser, Will, a handful of infantry regulars, and a number of mules or workhorses left the Annapolis wharf on a light-draft ferryboat, steamed by way of the Severn into the Chesapeake Bay, and with the Pooles Island light shining in the southern distance, rounded the cape at Gunpowder Neck and bore northeast into the lower Bush River.

The charred, impassible railroad bridge was about six miles above the inlet, and Flusser's party probably found both the bridge and depot unguarded, for there is no record of their meeting with opposition.

They would work swiftly under cover of darkness, uncoupling the locomotives from any passenger trains connected to them, hitching them to their draft animals, and dragging them up the ferry's lowered ramp to its deck. Then the group was off into the night.

A few hours later, Flusser returned to Annapolis with his captured engines, offloaded them at the wharf, and "ran them himself" over the new track spur to the railway station. The jubilant cheers and applause he received along the way would have contributed to his "great glee," as would General Butler's praise for his bravado.

Perhaps having learned his new port officer was a book lover, Butler gave him a small, colorfully illustrated volume of maritime adventure titled *Naval Enterprise: Illustrative of Adventure, Heroism and Endurance.* Printed in London by Frederick Warne and Company, it recounted the heroic escapades of men like Rear Admiral Horatio Nelson, the fisher boy Joe Cracker, and the Royal Navy's heroic Crimean War figure, Captain William Peel, who was said to have saved his comrades by calmly tossing a live shell over a parapet after it landed near his battery's powder keg.

In gaining the general's appreciation, Flusser also saw an excellent opportunity for his protégé, Will.

At the time Butler gave him the book of naval derring-do, he mentioned that he had received it from Assistant Secretary Gustavus Fox, his closest friend and college roommate at Maine's Bowdoin College. Flusser had the opening he needed. Might Butler be able to ask Fox a great favor on behalf of a member of his cutting-out party? William Cushing was one of his former students at the Academy, a relative of Commodore Joseph Smith, and an "acting" midshipman of tremendous promise, who had been dismissed from the Naval Academy because of his admittedly mischievous conduct but was eager to make amends. Seeking a chance at redemption, Cushing had already been to see Secretary Welles. Though Welles liked the boy, he had felt compelled to let his expulsion stand. Might it be possible for Fox to speak to Welles on Cushing's behalf?

A grateful Butler agreed to lobby his friend. It worked; Gideon Welles consented to a second meeting with Will. Within days, Will was on a train full of infantrymen shuttling down to the capital from Annapolis Junction. Packed among his luggage was the very book of sea stories Butler had given Flusser. He had passed it along to Will hoping its seagoing adventures would inspire him and occupy the time as he traveled.

But Will already felt upbeat. After weeks of hanging around Washington and Annapolis with little hope, he was now hurrying to a very important meeting to consider his future.

• • •

Washington, D.C., was on edge. Arriving at the brick, stucco, and brownstone railroad depot at New Jersey Avenue and C Street, Will thought the city looked nothing like the one he remembered from recent visits, and even further removed from the place he had stalked at all hours as a congressional page. Its bars and shops were almost vacant; many suspicious city inhabitants refused to leave their dwellings to move among the tents, horses, and supply lines of assembling federal troops.

As the soldiers mustered outside the station, they drew black glances from scattered onlookers and foul curses from behind open windows. The capital was a Southern city, and its people, mostly sympathetic to Dixie, saw them as an occupation force.

Tossing his luggage into a horse-drawn taxi, Will climbed inside and went bumping along the rutted dirt road that was Pennsylvania Avenue. He would not have been surprised by the resentful jeers he'd heard at the station; the citizens of Annapolis also held anti-Northern sentiments.

But the hostile atmosphere did nothing to dim the hope burning in his breast. He believed Secretary Welles had been persuaded to take a fresh look at his readmission to the Navy. Otherwise, why else would he have consented to see him again?

Soon Will was back at the Navy Department, facing the white-bearded Father Neptune across his desk. Why, Welles asked, do you want to rejoin the service?

Will had probably rehearsed his appeal many times in his own mind.

"My passion, and life, are in it," he said. "In some capacity, I am determined to live and die in the profession."

Impressed by Cushing's heartfelt response, Welles had instant sympathy for him. For all the youth's disciplinary problems, no one had ever questioned his courage or seamanship.

In fact, Welles had made his decision even before Will finished. His reasons had as much to do with pragmatism as with the youth's "perseverance, enthusiasm and zeal" and the support of his well-connected friends. The Navy had an extreme man-power shortage, and Welles was eager to fill its depleted ranks. Allowing Cushing to serve—with certain stipulations—seemed a winning proposition for the country.

The secretary told Will he would give him a second chance, but he would not be allowed to return to the Academy. Instead, Welles would appoint him an Acting Master's Mate—the equivalent of a modern petty officer—aboard an active gunship. If he acquitted himself well, and avoided disruptive incidents with his superiors, he could rise to full midshipman's status and be eligible for further promotions.

The eighteen-year-old accepted these terms with unreserved gratitude.

"I consider this a first step," he promised. "I will gain position, and you will never have cause to regret my reinstatement."

It was done. Welles instructed him to report at once to the USS *Minnesota*, a steam schooner readied to sail out of Boston as flagship of the Home Blockading Squadron. Backdating his paperwork to April 1, he sent Will on his way with dispatch, for there was not a moment to lose. Under command of Commodore Silas H. Stringham, the schooner was to make sail within days.

●   ●   ●

May 7, 1861
My Dear Cousin:

I can write but a few hasty lines. I am an officer on board of the splendid steam frigate *Minnesota*. We have just left our moorings, and as I write we are moving under steam and sail out of Boston harbor. I am going to fight under the old banner of freedom. I may never return, but if I die, it shall be under the folds of the flag that sheltered my infancy and while striking a blow for its honor and my own.

I cannot tell you exactly where to write me. This is the flagship of "Home and Blockading Squadron." Wherever there is fighting, there we will be, and wherever there is danger in the battle, there will I be, for I will gain a name in this war.

I must now say good-bye. God bless you, Mary. I will write you from homeward bound vessels as often as possible.

Your cousin,
William B. Cushing

The 265-foot-long, 51-foot-wide, square-rigged, sail and steam–powered wooden gunship was truly a splendid, majestic vessel. In an earlier time, she had spent two years carrying U.S. diplomatic envoys between the Far Eastern trading ports of China, Hong Kong, and Japan. On her return home, she was drydocked at the Charles River Navy Yard and given a thorough repair and refit—including installation of a pair of eleven-inch smoothbores at the stern, another two at the bow, and space for a crew of 600 officers and men. In all, she was a manned floating arsenal of between sixty and seventy heavy guns.

As she was prepared for recommissioning, the newspapers had it that the vessel was sailing directly to the mouth of the Mississippi River, in the Gulf of Mexico, to intercept vessels "expected at New Orleans with valuable arms and munitions of war, purchased by the rebels in Europe." But that may have been deliberate misinformation. Disinclined to trust the mail or telegraph wire, Gideon Welles had his instructions about the ship's actual destination delivered to Commodore Stringham under confidential seal on May 1:

> The President has found it necessary to issue proclamations closing the ports of those States which are resisting the laws of the Federal Government.... The moment the *Minnesota* is ready ... you will proceed with her with all dispatch to

Hampton Roads, at which point other steamers and vessels
will be directed to rendezvous as they shall be fitted and
equipped for service....

Once at "the Roads," moreover, Stringham was ordered "to protect
our commerce, suppress piratical or illegal demonstrations, and guard
the public interests *in that quarter.*"

Acknowledging receipt of the secretary's communique, Stringham
assured him repairs and improvements on the ship had been going on
around the clock for weeks, with the bulk of the yard's eight hundred
engineers, carpenters, caulkers, and other tradesmen even working Sun-
days to get her in perfect war trim.

Will Cushing arrived in Boston the first week of May, barely in time
to sail with the ship. By then the flag had been hoisted at the fore and the
officers were all aboard. The only thing left was for the *Minnesota*'s
captain, Gresham Von Brunt, to give Stringham official confirmation of
her readiness.

At 8:30 a.m. on May 8, the boatswain's whistle shrilled, and she
started underway, leaving amid a great fanfare from the crowded
wharves. Crewmen climbed her rigging and, perched high atop the
masts, waved farewell to their gathered friends and families. As she
passed Castle Island in the harbor, the guns of granite-walled Fort
Independence pounded out a salute.

Standing at quarters, Will's excitement could not have been any
greater. He was hot to prove his merit and justify Gideon Welles's show
of faith in him. Yet despite his sincere intentions, he would have trouble
getting out of his own way.

CHAPTER SIX

"STAND BY FOR BOARDING!"

On Friday, April 26, 1861, two days after Will Cushing watched the *Constitution*, a symbol of the U.S. Navy's proud past, sail from Annapolis to a safer haven, Stephen Mallory shared his vision of the Confederate Navy's future with President Jefferson Davis.

Mallory laid out his ideas in a comprehensive written report. He was exceedingly mindful of Europe's armor-plated, or ironclad, warships. France had launched its 5,600-ton, single-screw FS *Gloire* in 1859 after the Crimean War, and England followed suit soon after with the 9,200-ton, two-screw HMS *Warrior* and HMS *Black Prince*. By 1861, the Royal Navy required that all new generations of seagoing frigates have armored hulls, effectively lowering the curtain on the age of the wooden man-of-war.

The United States had lagged behind Europe in making the transition, but some American designers were pushing for iron over wood. Back in 1842, the civilian shipbuilders Robert and Edwin Stevens of Hoboken, New Jersey, won government approval for what they promised would be the first U.S. ironclad. Construction of *The Stevens Battery* was budgeted at $600,000, but twenty years, several redesigns, and a hundred-thousand-dollar cost overrun later, a belt-tightening Navy official quashed the deal. The ironclad was a "craft that would never float," he contended.

Secretary Mallory, however, remained convinced that armored gunboats were not only practical but necessary for a modern naval force—specifically to counter the Yankee blockade of Southern ports. Recognizing he had no way to match the size of the federal fleet, Mallory set his sights on constructing fewer but stronger ships than the northern blockaders. "I propose to adopt a class of vessels hitherto unknown to naval service," he wrote in his April report. "The perfection of a warship would doubtless be a combination of the greatest known ocean speed...with a battery of one or two accurate guns at long range...."

On May 10, as the USS *Minnesota* steamed toward Fort Monroe to join the growing Home Blockade Squadron, Mallory sent an urgent appeal for funds to the Confederate House Committee on Naval Affairs: "not only does economy but naval success dictate the wisdom and expediency of *fighting with iron against wood without regard to first cost*," he advised.

The committee found Mallory's words persuasive. The same day, Jefferson Davis authorized a million dollars to send agents overseas for the engine and armaments needed to convert existing civilian steamships into gunboats. More importantly, he supplied another *two* million dollars for the "purchase or construction of one or two war steamers in England or France, fully armed and equipped ..."

Mallory knew the fastest way to add ironclads to his navy was to buy them. On May 17, he instructed a representative, Lieutenant James F. North, to travel covertly to France and negotiate the purchase of a *Gloire*-class armored frigate. The French had commissioned three in total, and Mallory hoped to buy two, sweetening his offer with a diplomatic reminder of the economic benefits France could expect from a thriving, independent Southern republic.

But Mallory kept an open mind should the French not sell. Mr. John A. Stevenson of New Orleans, a wealthy entrepreneur with spectacular muttonchops and résumé, proffered an enticing project. The owner of three slaves and a committed secessionist, Stevenson had been a grocer, real estate owner, and riverboat commander, and was now a cotton grower and commission merchant with a brisk shipping trade. In addition to his diverse business portfolio, he served as secretary of the New Orleans Pilots Benevolent Association.

Around the middle of May, seeing a new commercial opportunity that dovetailed neatly with his Confederate passions—and his desire to prevent blockaders from starving his mercantile enterprises—Stevenson traveled to Mallory's headquarters in Montgomery, Alabama, carrying an armload of sketches and wooden models for adapting "some of our heavy and powerful towboats on the Mississippi as to make them comparatively safe against the heaviest guns afloat, and by preparing their bow in a peculiar manner...render them capable of sinking the heaviest vessels ever built."

Stevenson even had a boat in mind for his first conversion. Built in Massachusetts, the sturdy icebreaker *Enoch Train* was once part of a merchant fleet that ran between Boston and Liverpool England, and had made trips to Russia, South America, and San Francisco. For the past two years, she had served ably as a towboat on the Mississippi river.

Stevenson's planned modifications to the tow would extend her length from 128 to 143 feet, her width from 26 to 33 feet, and her depth 12 1/2 feet to 17 feet. An inch-and-a-quarter thick layer of riveted iron plates would cover her entire frame, curved like a cigar or ostrich egg so enemy fire could strike only glancing blows. Built up with massive seventeen-inch beams to reinforce her bow, she would glide low in the water, so just a small part of her exposed hull was above the surface. As an ingenious touch to prevent boarding by enemies, the boiler had pumps for ejecting steam and scalding water over the vessel's entire surface.

But the *Enoch Train*'s most significant refit was also her main weapon: the pointed, underwater ram at her bow. This, Stevenson stressed, would slash through the wooden hulls of the small blockade boats taking up positions at the mouth of the Mississippi River to harry Louisiana's merchant traffic. As added enticement, Stevenson assured Mallory he could achieve his conversion for two hundred thousand dollars, far less than the cost of building an entirely new ship from scratch.

Mallory appeared noncommittal as he pondered his options. Disappointed, Stevenson returned to his hotel, leaving his models and drawings on the secretary's desk. Before boarding the train to New Orleans on the evening of May 21, he wrote directly to President Jefferson Davis about his plan and included a mild jab at Mallory for failing to explain his low level of enthusiasm.

But he misread Mallory's silence. Rather than a lack of interest in Stevenson's design concept, the secretary was only giving careful thought to its practicability. Before Stevenson left town, the secretary had ordered his chief ordnance officer, Captain Duncan Ingraham, to investigate buying two-to-three-inch thick wrought iron plates and "the best means of forwarding them to New Orleans."

Ingraham spent the next week visiting ironworks owners from Nashville to Atlanta but did not find any that could produce the plates with urgency. Their mills turned out railroad tracks and needed months to adapt the machinery to a different purpose. Also, the Nashville company's mill was in Kentucky, perilously close to the Ohio border, and its proprietors had no stomach for drawing the attention of Union spies by taking on a Confederate military contract.

Mallory was slowed but not stopped. He had not forgotten Stevenson's ram or its possibilities.

Iron against wood.

The secretary remained hopeful his envoy in France would be able to purchase one of the *Glorie* gunboats. But one way or another, he would have an ironclad. Where he acquired it, and how soon, were the only questions.

FORTRESS MONROE, OLD POINT COMFORT AND HYGEIA HOTEL, V?

Fortress Monroe, shield of the Chesapeake Bay and headquarters of the Navy's North Atlantic Squadron. *Library of Congress, Geography and Map Division*

•   •   •

Built entirely of stone by military engineers, Fort Monroe occupied an isolated spit of land shaped like the claw of a predatory bird and was the lone Union sanctuary at the southeastern tip of the Virginia peninsula, rebel country. Surrounded by water on three sides and linked to acres of coastal salt marsh by a bridge of weathered, moss-stained wooden boards, it resembled nothing so much as a medieval redoubt, and was called the Gibraltar of the Chesapeake Bay.

Around 10:00 a.m. on May 13, 1861, the screw frigate *Minnesota* joined the blockade fleet assembled outside the fort's forbidding walls. A thirteen-gun black powder salute boomed to greet the flagship and was answered in kind by her cannons. Already at anchor were the full-rigged sloop-of-war *Cumberland*, her masts soaring above the water, the powerful steamer *Monticello*, the *Quaker City*, a brawny commercial side-wheeler fitted with a huge Parrott long rifle and eight broadside guns, and Captain John Faunce's revenue cutter *Harriet Lane*, which had taken part in the ill-fated Fort Sumter resupply attempt. Hovering nearby were a pair of stout little tugboats, the *Yankee* and *Young America,* the latter serving as tender to the flagship.

Will Cushing gazed off to starboard from the *Minnesota*'s gun deck, his eyes on the Union flag fluttering high atop Monroe's gray southeastern wall. Five miles away, the sun was shining down upon "a new banner raised in defiance—an emblem of treason. The rebels had possession of Norfolk and were forming an army in Richmond." Though angered by rebel actions, Will felt a swell of pride at the sight of the gathered blockade squadron and the resounding thunder of the cannon salute.

"My motto is: 'Death to the traitor!'" he wrote his mother, predicting he would see "hard fighting in a day or two."

Blockade duty would turn out to be anything *but hard fighting.* Much of it was monotonous, repetitive routine—waiting for a merchant vessel to leave port and drilling while one waited and waited some more. Whether Will was exaggerating to his mother or not, the *Minnesota* made some early interdictions. This may have influenced Will to think he was about to see the action he craved.

A day after she dropped anchor, the frigate seized three prize ships. The *Emily Ann, Mary Willis,* and *Delaware Farmer,* tobacco schooners out of Richmond, all surrendered to the speedy *Harriet Lane* without a fight. The cutter approached, intercepted, and strutted its firepower. A cry of "Stand by for boarding!" went out from the targeted merchant ships, and white flags went up.

At Commodore Stringham's command, the schooners were to be brought to a district court in Philadelphia, where the monetary value of their cargo would be adjudicated, and shares of the spoils divided among the *Minnesota's* officers and hands, Faunce and his men.

On May 14, the trio of merchant ships was towed out toward Philadelphia by the stalwart *Yankee.* Appointed prize master of the *Delaware Farmer* owing to a shortage of officers, Master's Mate Will Cushing thought her "lubberly" Southern crew unworthy of the slightest compassion. He saw their civilian status as meant to play upon Union chivalry so they could slip past the blockade with their cargo and "exchange the fragrant weed for powder and shot ... required for our slaughter."

Plagued with trouble from the outset, the convoy was barely past Cape Henry at the southern mouth of the Chesapeake, when the *Mary Willis* broke loose from her tow line. As the *Yankee* turned to recover the schooner, the *Emily Ann* lurched sideways in its backwash. Her mainmast thrown off balance, it sprung its stays, toppled into the foremast like a downed tree, and was cut away to save the ship.

Then, on the second night of the voyage, a storm came roaring over the ocean. On the *Delaware Farmer,* Will felt the repeated shock of waves pounding her sides in the heavy wind. Soon leaks were springing up everywhere. As seawater sloshed on the rocking, swaying deck, the pumps backed up, unable to drain the rain and seawater.

Will surely thought back to his transatlantic cruise on the *Plymouth* and the monstrous gale that overtook her near the Azores—only now he thought his Southern crew too unreliable to navigate the crisis.

There was a flash of lightning and then "a despairing cry" from the men. As they froze in horror, Will looked out into the darkness and saw a large vessel coming in the tempestuous night.

He could not stand by helplessly. Dashing to the wheel, he swung it hard to port. Her flooded deck tilting crazily, the schooner sheared away from the advancing vessel—but it was too late to prevent a collision. There was a hard thump, a sickening crunch of wood against wood, then another thump.

Will braced for the worst, convinced he would never see daylight again.

But instead of striking the *Delaware Farmer* bow-on to cut her in half, the big vessel's hull raked across her side, slamming into her forward and aft. As it pulled astern, Will spared a glance over his shoulder from his position behind the wheel and realized the ship had torn away the *Farmer*'s starboard bulwarks, one of her sails, and three or four backstays, dragging them with it into the rainswept darkness.

Relief filled him—along with an appreciable feeling of satisfaction. It had seemed impossible that he could save the ship. But he'd made the narrowest of escapes, passing the only kind of test that mattered to him. His business with the Navy was to face death, and he hadn't flinched.

On Saturday, May 18, the *Yankee* reached port with all three captured schooners trailing along behind it. Beaten, scarred, and soggy, the *Emily Ann* and *Delaware Farmer* were nevertheless still afloat.

Eager for a glimpse of the first Southern war prizes delivered to their city, Philadelphians flocked to the wharf to celebrate their arrival. Cheered for bringing in the battered *Delaware Farmer*, Will expected a whopping cash return on her...around $75,000.

But things did not turn out that way. The owner of the schooners argued in court that they had been subject to illegal seizure. They were bound for *Baltimore,* he insisted, a port not under embargo, conducting a private transaction that had nothing to do with the procurement of Confederate weapons. Persuaded by his denials, the judge ordered the ships released with their cargo.

The decision annoyed Will. He did not earn a single penny for his troubles. But his moment of glory at the docks made up for it, and he was also able to squeeze in a hurried visit with Alonzo. Ordered to return to his blockade squadron on a ship out of New York City, Will detoured to West Point by railroad and regaled his brother with an account of his heroics at sea.

Then he was off to rejoin the *Minnesota.*

Back at Fort Monroe, he discovered that his pluck in saving the *Delaware Farmer* had impressed Commodore Stringham. On May 24, Will was again made prize master of a captured merchantmen, the square-rigged bark *Pioneer.* In a fast turnaround, he was to bring it to New York at once. But with the *Minnesota* still shorthanded, he would have only a single Union man, Master's Mate John Harrington from the *Cumberland* to sail with him. The original Southern crew of sixteen was left onboard to see the bark to her destination.

Will was naturally leery of the Southerners, and he and Harrington took turns keeping watch over them. As he wrote his mother from the *Pioneer*'s cabin on his first night at sea, "I feel the weight of a brace of revolvers on my belt, and I know not at what moment the crew may try to retake her. But your boy's ready, and I trust no son of yours is a coward. Now I must go and have the pumps sounded in order to see that none of the crew have scuttled her."

But the prisoners had no such designs or may have prudently abandoned them after taking sharp notice of their captors' sidearms. By the final week of May, the *Pioneer* had reached New York without a hitch.

Will was sure his successful prize runs would convince Commodore Stringham to recommend him for a promotion. But that would have to wait until he returned to the squadron, and he first needed to find a way back. With the USS *Colorado* readied at the Charlestown yard in Boston, Will reported as ordered to the ship as soon as possible, then sailed out with her to meet up with the *Minnesota* at Charleston or Pensacola at the southern margin of the flagship's operational area.

Again, he took a quick side trip to see Lon, hopping a train out to West Point on May 27.

The two talked away the night in the cadets' barracks. Will told Lon he was glad finally to prove his merit. He also exaggerated and told Lon that he was promised reinstatement into the Naval Academy. Lon may have suspected his younger sibling of rashly getting ahead of himself, but after months of worrying about him, he put his doubts aside. It was a relief just to see Will in high spirits.

The next morning the brothers exchanged farewell hugs at the railroad station, and then Will was gone. On his return to the school, Alonzo received a disciplinary citation for letting an unauthorized person sleep over in the barracks, but he accepted it quietly, and later wrote his mother to tell her of Will's heartening visit.

Will would reach Boston to discover the *Colorado* delayed at the shipyard until June. With nothing to do but wait for completion of her outfitting, he decided to look up some local family members. There were maternal relatives in and around the city. Aunts and uncles he hadn't seen since his father's death, and cousins he had never met. He was eager to reconnect with his mother's family.

Will made the most of his stay in Massachusetts, and he was wise to enjoy it. The coming weeks and months would not be very generous with such respites.

•   •   •

Charles Flusser had been very busy. He was also bored to fits.

In late May 1861, the Department of Annapolis was created as a Union zone of military control stretching for twenty miles on each side of the railroad from Annapolis to Washington, and as far as Bladensburg to the east. As the department's operational hub, the one-time Naval Academy campus was crowded with thousands of federal troops that had disembarked at the harbor and filled its buildings to capacity—so much so that many were forced to bivouac in tents sprouting up like mushrooms across its grounds. The surrender of Fort Sumter in April had prompted President Lincoln to issue a call for 75,000 ninety-day enlistees, and men responded in great numbers, drawn by the prospect of steady military pay and a widespread assumption that the war would not last long. With these reinforcements came a constant stream of army supply transports. Offloaded at the Severn River wharves, their cargo was shuttled to the main rail depot on the new track spur and then put aboard trains bound for the capital.

Meanwhile, General Butler was transferred to Fort Monroe, with command of the department most recently falling to Nathanial P. Banks, the third in a succession of generals to hold the post.

As June approached, Lieutenant Flusser decided it was his turn to move on. He had superbly carried out his role as captain of the port, but was tired of the "tame and safe" and the tedious, bureaucratic grind of shore duty. In applying for a transfer to active naval duty aboard a warship, Flusser had his request granted as a reward for his consummate professionalism.

When the seventeen-year-old twenty-two-gun sloop-of-war USS *Jamestown* was recommissioned at the Philadelphia Navy Yard on June 5, 1861, Flusser went aboard as an executive officer. Three days later, he was off with the ship.

The *Jamestown*'s area of operations would be far to the south. As formulated by General Winfield Scott, President Lincoln's blockade of Confederate ports was tactically sound but hindered by logistical realities; it soon became clear that nature's work in shaping coastal geography and the work of the federal blockaders were at vexing odds. Strung along a tangle of waterways that traced meandering lines across 3,500 miles of shoreline, the rebel harbors could have multiple inlets, and were often tucked away in recessed coves, deltas, and bays, or found in winding tributaries too narrow and shallow for large, heavy warships to easily navigate. Southern forces, meanwhile, exploited their intimate knowledge of the local coast by sending patrol boats into the harbor channels and installing gun batteries at critical points along the shore.

Faced with the colossal task of choking off one hundred fifty known Southern ports, the Coast Blockading Squadron split into two geographically distinct fleets around the middle of May. Admiral Stringham would command the Atlantic Blockading Squadron, which remained based in Hampton Roads and covered the Virginia Capes to the Florida Keys. The Gulf Blockading Squadron was responsible for the area of the Gulf of Mexico stretching from Pensacola, Florida, to Brownsville, Texas. The *Jamestown* and Flusser were dispatched on picket duty along the one-hundred-thirty-mile stretch of coastline between Savanna, Georgia, and Fernandina, Florida, where it remained for two long, blisteringly hot months.

Charles Flusser's legendary career as a blockader was underway. It would eventually lead him to cross paths again with his friend and occasional reclamation project, Will Cushing. But in the summer of 1861, neither of them foresaw how closely intertwined were their destinies.

•   •   •

William and Alonzo Cushing were, in many respects, polar opposites. Will was impulsive by nature, Alonzo steady as a rock. Will was hot-tempered, rebellious, and confrontational, Alonzo easygoing and affable. Will was an indifferent student (even when he attended class), while Lon was conscientious and reliable, spending long nights at his books before final exams, studying by candlelight.

Nor did the brothers look much alike. Will could be lax, even sloppy, in his appearance, notably in the months before his ouster from Annapolis. But Alonzo was always clean-shaven and crisply uniformed, an exemplary West Point cadet. Will wore his hair long around his pale, slender face and had a whipcord-thin frame and bouts of poor health like their father. By contrast, Lon kept his hair clipped short and spent many long, hard hours weightlifting in the school gymnasium, building up a bulky, muscular 170-pound physique. He accurately described himself as "a sizable lad."

While both stood about five feet, nine inches, the best physical clue that Will and Alonzo were related was their startlingly bright, forceful blue eyes. There was a certain look about them, too, springing from an inner confidence, which had a way of igniting confidence in those around them.

The brothers also shared a zealous patriotism that may have owed much to the influence of cousin John "Old Guts" Smith, the commodore. But wherever their powerful love of country originated, they embraced it fully and without question, showing little or no tolerance for Southern classmates who had turned their backs on "the Stars and Stripes, American Eagle and Yankee Doodle."

From Lon's perspective, Will's back-to-back trips to West Point in the spring of 1861 could not have come at a better time. The outbreak of hostilities had divided the student body, cutting it in half with waves of resignations. Lon got a lift from seeing his younger brother alive and well and was relieved to know he was back in the Navy, even if it was on a probationary basis. Still, he was mostly downhearted. It was hard to see friends leave to become the enemy. His country was at war with itself, and there was a grim, helpless feeling about it all.

Every student on campus felt the conflict's tangible repercussions. In May, the War Department had promoted the first class ahead of schedule, bumped the second class up a grade, and reduced its five-year curriculum to four in an effort fill the Army's ranks with qualified officers. For the thirty-four cadets in Lon's class, this order crammed almost an entire year's studies into six weeks.

Frazzled and sleep-deprived, Lon hunched over his books from 5:00 a.m. to 11:00 p.m. daily, breaking only for meals and drills, with the upperclassmen's recreational period slashed from half an hour to five minutes in length.

"We would all be grey-headed in six months if it was to continue this way," he wrote his mother in June. But with only a short while left until graduation, the cadets were philosophical about accepting the academic rigors. Then, as Lon penned, it would be "hurrah for a brush with the rebels."

His test results proved commendable. He scored ninth in military engineering, seventh in ethics, eleventh in ordnance and gunnery, and twelfth in his class overall. The one area in which he would have trailed well behind Will—had they attended the same school—was in compiling demerits. Lon received just fifty-three to the almost two hundred racked up by his younger brother, making "Bill Coon" the family's crown-wearer in misconduct.

The next few weeks barreled in fast. At the end of June, Lon graduated from the United States Military Academy and was commissioned a first lieutenant with the 4th United States Artillery, Battery A. His orders were to report to the adjutant general of the Army in Washington, D.C., with other new lieutenants from his class. On July 3, he reached Washington by B&O passenger train and took a horse-drawn bus toward the War Department, following the same bumpy, pitted route Will had traveled when he came to meet with Gideon Welles. By month's end, Lon was back aboard a troop train, going off to fight in the first major battle of the war on the fields of Manassas, Virginia, just twenty-five miles outside the capital.

What quickly came to be known as the Battle at Bull's Run claimed the lives of 5,000 men. And left a horrified nation with the growing realization that the nightmare of civil war would not end soon.

For Lon and other Union soldiers it was a bloody education.

•   •   •

Readers looking for variety in the Thursday, June 27, 1861, edition of the *Nashville Union and American* would have found it aplenty. Loudly anti-abolitionist and staunchly pro-Confederacy, the daily paper was a busy amalgam of news, advertisements, and notices.

Page one alone featured nearly an entire column of ads for Dr. J. H. McLean's medicinal product line, including his Strengthening Cordial and Blood Purifier, a concoction to "infallibly" make men strong and vigorous, and mount the bloom of health on ladies' cheeks; his Universal Pills for liver complaints, biliousness, headache, et cetera; and his Volcanic Liniment, an "indispensable" remedy for paralysis, neck stiffness, gout, sore throat, earache, and a wide-ranging gamut of other ailments. Also on the page were advertisements for Dr. Wright's Celebrated Rejuvenating Elixir for mental and physical depression; and Old Sachem Bitters and Wigwam Tonic, recommended for constipation and related digestive disorders. Meanwhile, P. Harse, M.D., was offering families of the Nashville Rifle Company free medical services, and Dr. William Wambaugh of 146 South Summer Street was touting his scientific discovery: Electric Water "in which patients are bathed in currents of electricity."

Thompson and Company heralded its second seasonal importation of English embroideries and lace. Stretch and Forbes boasted its large stock of trusses and supporters, and Ward's clothier its $18-a-dozen made-to-measure shirts. The wholesaler A. Land was selling military caps available for "lowest cash rates," W. B. Whiteman was offering three cents per pound for rags; the 290-acre Rogers farm on Yellow Creek was for sale at a bargain, and a valuable house servant was for hire, enquiries to be made at his office.

Among its many advertisements, the paper also managed to find room for some news and a list of United States soldiers who had left the Union army to join the Confederacy. One man named for North Carolina was Brevet Major James G. Martin, Quartermaster, Sixth Infantry. On resigning his commission, Martin traveled to Raleigh from his post on the Kansas frontier and, by unanimous vote of the state legislature, was named adjutant general in the North Carolina State Troops and commander of all its military forces and defenses, with the consolidated duties of quartermaster and chief commissary, pay, and ordnance officer.

He spared no effort carrying out those responsibilities. "Horses were bought in Kentucky and hurried in droves through the mountains," a local historian would recall. "Saddles and harness material were secured by special agents in New Orleans and rushed to Raleigh by rail. Powder works and arsenals for the manufacture and remodeling of arms were created. Camps of instruction were established, and skilled armorers secured to make sabers, bayonets, and swords by the thousands. Shoe and clothing factories for the troops were located at several points in the state.... Cannon were provided for the artillery and the forts were erected and strengthened on the coast."

It was natural that Martin would turn toward building up his coastal defenses. There was only so much fabric available for uniforms, so much metal to be melted down for guns, or so many crops to go toward feeding the troops. Eventually, he would have to deplete his resources in the South and buy them from foreign merchants. That made it essential to find a way around Lincoln's blockade and keep the ports open to commerce.

But that was only half the reason for his focus on the coast. Just as the Confederacy needed to hold it, Martin knew the federals would look to occupy it. By wresting control of North Carolina's ports, the enemy would be able to land supplies for delivery to their forces in the state's interior—and in nearby Virginia—over the course of a long military campaign.

From the first, Martin's eye fell on Roanoke Island. Lying between the mainland and the Outer Banks, it had the large, brackish Pamlico Sound to its south, Albemarle Sound running north of it nearly to Virginia's southern border, and narrow Croatan Sound stretching along the island's ten-mile western shore to separate it from the mainland. Albemarle Sound also gave entry to the shallow, serpentine Dismal Swamp Canal, an essential backdoor route to blockaded Norfolk harbor.

New Berne, Beaufort, Edonton, Elizabeth City…all perched on the sounds, making them natural targets of the Union. Roanoke was key, Martin knew. The Union would inevitably look to gain a foothold on the island and use it as a marine base of operations.

With no time to lose, Martin made it an early priority to contact the Confederate Navy Department about obtaining small, light draft gunboats to guard the shallow coastal waterways against attack. He also expressed interest in floating batteries—mammoth self-propelled, flat-bottomed offshore artillery barges, the first of which was tested in Charleston Harbor during the bombardment of Fort Sumter.

Secretary Mallory had reached similar conclusions. In the coming months, he would authorize a host of naval contracts to shipbuilders from Norfolk to Memphis, even reaching out across the Atlantic to companies in Liverpool, England. Meanwhile, Richmond's Tredegar Iron Works was engaged to build at least one armored floating battery to protect the Sounds and Roanoke Island.

Martin had brought the secretary onboard, knowing a naval fleet was logistically essential for his state—and if the shipbuilder was closer, even better. It was also reasonable for him to see the strategic benefits—and financial rewards—of handing some work over to his Elizabeth City family business.

At that point, the shipyard needed all the contracts it could get. Martin's younger brother, William, still ran it in name. But in June 1861, the militia he helped found became integrated into the Seventh North Carolina Volunteer Regiment. With William appointed its commanding officer and his energies suddenly consumed by war preparations, he had placed his law clerk, Gilbert Elliott, in charge of the yard.

General Martin knew Elliott too. Along with his brother, he was a friend of the young man's family and had been instrumental in securing his invitation to the Naval Academy. While Elliott had declined to attend, his choice worked to the Martins' benefit. They would have had a tough time finding another person with his rare combination of intelligence, enterprise, and trustworthiness.

In the summer of 1861, General Martin made Elliott his agent and began introducing him to Confederate officials involved in the acquisition of military vessels. Suddenly, Elliott was busy hiring workers, negotiating the purchase of timber, engines, and equipment, and trying to balance the yard's books to turn a profit. The venture offered the Martins potentially great financial gains, but there were many risks. Building government ships required large outlays of funds and resources before a single payment came in. And if enemy intelligence caught notice of the facility's entry into military shipbuilding, they might raid it and confiscate the vessels...or burn the yard to smoldering ashes as they had done at Gosport.

Martin oversaw what he could from his Raleigh headquarters. He directed projects toward the yard, connected Elliott with the right parties for buying materials, and offered advice and instruction on legal and contractual matters. But the business would succeed or fail on Elliott's management. Suddenly he was a full-time contractor. He could not have imagined that shipbuilding would become the center of his life.

•   •   •

The largest, most powerful of the eleven vessels scuttled and burned at the Gosport Navy Yard, the 275-foot long, forty-gun steam frigate USS *Merrimack* had suffered extensive fire damage to her hull, sinking beneath the Elizabeth River so only her smokestack and timbers were seen at low tide.

Less than a month after the Yankees abandoned the yard, Stephen Mallory had authorized the frigate's salvage. For a Confederacy that had "nothing in the shape of a navy...not a single ship-of-war," the total loss of such a valuable prize would have been an insupportable waste. Mallory's agents in England and Europe had met reluctant sellers in his bid for an ironclad, but if a warship were reclaimed from local waters, even in part, he felt it might just allow him to hedge his bet.

The yard's new commandant, Flag Officer French Forrest, had huffed and puffed in skeptical disagreement, thinking the effort an expensive waste of manpower and resources. But there was only one secretary of the Navy, and orders were orders. On May 18, Forrest had contracted the B&J Wrecking Company out of Norfolk to undertake the recovery operation.

On June 18, French wrote General Robert E. Lee a terse, one sentence letter: "We have the Merrimack up and just pulling her in the dry-dock."

Specifically, he meant Dry Dock #1. The fleeing Union troops had done what they could to blow up the large granite pier, planting gunpowder charges underneath it before they evacuated. But Virginia militiamen had rushed in at once, pulling fuses to prevent the explosions.

Towed to the dock, the *Merrimack* was burned to her copper line—the topmost edge of the hull's underwater copper sheathing—and down through to the interior of her berth deck. Flames had ravaged her gundecks too.

Forrest took one look at her and grumbled skeptically to anyone in earshot, believing the ship's condition confirmed his doubts. He did not see the practical use of a charred, blackened hulk.

Mallory took a very different view. He had already invested $6,000 of his navy's money on the effort to dredge the *Merrimack* to the surface. His engineers at Gosport estimated an added $450,000 was needed to restore the ship to her former condition. But Mallory feared that the moment she entered the river, she would be outnumbered and outgunned by the enemy's blockade fleet—and at extreme risk of being sunk again.

Unless…

He had by no means forgotten John Stephenson, the New Orleans commission merchant, and his plans for the *Enoch Train*.

On June 22, Mallory called a hush-hush conference in Richmond with Lieutenant John Mercer Brooke, naval constructor John Luke Porter, and chief engineer Lieutenant William Price Williamson. A universally recognized astronomer and hydrographer, Brooke had an impressive list of scientific accomplishments under his belt. Among them inventing the fathometer, being part of a team that charted the eastern Atlantic, and designing an experimental rifled naval cannon that—if it passed trials—would be far more lethal than a conventional smoothbore.

It was Brooke who had recommended the other two for Mallory's committee. Earlier that month, the secretary had informed him of his ambitious plan to ironclad the salvaged *Merrimack*'s hull and machinery. Brooke then gave some preliminary sketches with written explanations for each drawing.

"Mallory wants me to make some calculations with regard to floating batteries," he told his wife Lizzie, shading the truth for secrecy's sake. "It is impossible for me to tell whether I shall remain in Richmond or be stationed at Norfolk."

By Norfolk, he meant the Gosport yard, five miles south of the city. After reviewing Brooke's penciled roughs, Mallory had assigned a "practical engineer"—one of the yard's master carpenters—to work with him on finished sketches. But Brooke found the draftsman "lacking in confidence and energy...and averse to performing unusual duty." Commandant Forrest seemed to have encouraged naysaying among his men.

Arriving in Richmond on June 23, Brooke insisted the apathetic carpenter return to the yard. He then met up with Porter in Lieutenant Williamson's office at the Confederate Navy Department. Williamson held a distinguished reputation as a mechanical engineer, while Porter, a specialist in hull construction, had designed an innovative, flat-bottomed floating battery back in 1846. Porter called his armored platform the Floating Battery Bomb Proof for Harbor Defense—a name as unwieldy as the platform itself—and, like Stephenson the previous month, brought a scale model into the huddle.

The men left their conference with a design that incorporated many features of Porter's floating battery, but with the hull extending underwater, and a curved extension of its shield—a submerged ram—upfront at the bow. The vessel would bristle with ordnance that included two Dahlgren smoothbores, two howitzers, and four Brooke rifles. Surely not by coincidence, its design resembled the plans Stephenson left behind with the secretary, borrowing his idea to shave costs by repurposing the hull. This made him an unseen presence in the room and an uncredited fourth member of the group.

In his office with the three who were at the conference, Mallory reviewed the sketch, gave it his nod of approval, and then dispatched Brooke and Williams to the Tredegar works to try and obtain suitable engines for the vessel. Meanwhile, Porter volunteered to make a clean ink drawing that the secretary could forward through to the proper bureaucratic channels.

Within a few weeks, Mallory got approval for his pet project from the Confederate Congress. He requested $175,000 above the cost of repairing the *Merrimack* and was told the appropriations were forthcoming.

It was a lucky thing, too. At Gosport, on Mallory's express orders the *Merrimack*'s transformation into an ironclad was already in progress. He had not waited on a formal go-ahead to start the project.

•   •   •

Assigned to the Gulf Blockading Squadron, the giant screw frigate USS *Colorado* sailed out of Boston Harbor shortly before daybreak on June 18, 1861. Standing at quarters in the predawn light, Will Cushing felt a strong tug at his heart; his grand time in the city had ended, and he was off to war again.

Will would miss Boston. The New England branch of his family had won his lasting respect and affection, his uncles and aunts hosting him with open arms, his pretty female cousins showing him around Chelsea, across the Mystic River, and then taking him up north to see the town of Salem. While he had known his uncles were bankers and assumed they would be worldly and sophisticated, he was surprised by how splendidly everyone treated him. There was even a reception at one of their homes, with introductions to their circle of refined friends.

Will enjoyed the party, bubbling with good-humored laughter. There was only one sticky moment, when he felt obliged to correct a young man.

"We should whip the rebels in three months!" the man crowed, clearly meaning to impress the guest of honor.

Will stopped mingling with the guests. He had listened to a fair amount of boasting about Yankee superiority—it was early in the war, and the North was overtaken by a mix of patriotic fervor and overconfidence. Will already knew that his ship, the *Minnesota*, had been ordered to direct the attack on the Southern coastal batteries in Pensacola. He was told the rebels were ten thousand strong there and certain the fleet would have a hard, bloody fight before it could "whip" them. To diminish the enemy's strength was to belittle the courage of all those risking their lives to defeat them.

"I have spent four years with Southern officers and midshipmen at Annapolis," he said. "They are a brave and valiant people, and not only shall we not be able to whip them in three months, but it is probable that it may be three years before they are conquered."

Will's rebuke brought conversation to a halt. Civilians around him had not expected to hear a man in uniform singing the enemy's praises. But his hosts quickly smoothed over the moment's rough edges, and the laughter resumed.

Will later heard a rumor that one gentleman in attendance reported him to the shipyard's commandant for seditious talk. Whatever the truth, it didn't lessen his affection for Boston.

Now he was bound for Southern waters. By June 25, after a week at sea, the *Colorado* reached the bar outside Charleston Harbor, where Will expected to rejoin the *Minnesota* as it made for the Gulf. As his ship took blockade position at the channel mouth, he could see in the middle distance Fort Sumter and Fort Moultrie, fallen to the rebels, the Southern Stars and Bars floating above their ramparts.

At the beginning of the afternoon watch, Will gained a stark, closeup awareness of human fragility that would haunt him for many years. He was in the berth deck writing to Mary when he heard the watch bell, set aside pen and paper, and went up to the forecastle for his shift. His friend Harry Blake was also on duty, and they had paused for a brief conversation when the man straddling the fore topsail yard cried out, "Sail ho!"

Harry cast a glance across the water. Every passing vessel warranted scrutiny.

He hurried to get his sea glasses from below, wanting a closer look. But as he swung down onto the ladder it broke free of its fastenings, and he plunged into the hold, a drop of forty feet. "Down, down he went until his head struck with a dull crash on the edge of a cask."

Will scrambled down another ladder into the hold, calling out for help. Harry was "senseless" and in terrible pain, the "whole top of his skull" split open. Also, his spine seemed injured in the fall.

The men got him up off the boards and carried him to the sick bay, where the bloody gash in his head was cleaned and dressed. Will remained at his bedside, keeping a vigil over him, just as he'd stayed with the ailing Hartnell Dickerson as a boy. When he noticed Harry was sweating from pain and fever, he fanned him to make him more comfortable. It did not look good for his friend.

"A tall, dark-eyed, noble boy," he'd been Will's schoolmate at Annapolis, his shipmate, his frequent companion in the mess for three years. How often had they sat together griping about the food, their endless drills, their instructors, and in their final semester, as war loomed, wondering what the future held for them and their schoolmates?

Poor Harry, he thought sorrowfully. It will kill his father and mother to lose him.

Will stood over him for the next two hours, doing what little he could to ease his pain. Around 7:00 p.m., he briefly left the sick bay for his pen and paper, then returned to his side.

As he resumed his vigil, Will picked up where he'd left off writing to his cousin Mary Edwards. His mind going back to his own recent brush with mortality aboard the *Delaware Farmer*, he described the lightning flash, the vessel coming on through the darkness, and then the Southern crew's terrified screams.

He had seen death in that hard storm. As he wrote Mary, it was his "business to face it, and he "would try to do it bravely." But it had never felt so close before. Seeing Harry "cut off in such a manner" had left an indelible impression on him and brought an unbidden thought to his mind.

For the first time in his nineteen years on earth, he realized he might never see home again.

CHAPTER SEVEN

"I SHOULD BECOME A FIEND"

A few days after Will got back aboard the *Minnesota*, Lieutenant Pierce Crosby and Commodore Stringham put out a call for volunteers for an expedition into the Back River, which the *Wheeling Virginia Daily Intelligencer* described on July 26, 1861, as "properly an arm of the sea, about midway between Old Point and York River." The expedition itself "consist[ed] of 300 men and 7 field pieces, upon the propeller Fanny, with 6 launches belonging to the ships of war in the harbor and to the Naval Brigade."

Will, craving action, volunteered.

It seemed ages since his reluctant goodbye to Boston. When he'd reached Charleston Harbor in late June, the *Minnesota* had already sailed, Commodore Stringham having returned to Fort Monroe with a load of prisoners from captured merchant vessels. With the *Colorado* continuing south to the Gulf of Mexico, Will hauled himself and his sea trunk onto her sister ship, the USS *Wabash*. Also on blockade duty off Charleston, she had received new orders to join Stringham's squadron.

Will transferred aboard knowing Harry Blake had miraculously survived his fall. The frigate had brought two skilled New York surgeons to the fleet, and they operated on him with apparent success. There was a good chance he could make a full recovery, and that heartened Will.

Though eager to rejoin his ship, he spent close to a month on the *Wabash* before she left the Charleston blockade. He was bored; his berth was comfortable enough, and the summer heat was not yet at its peak. But with Fort Sumter and its Confederate flag in plain sight, he'd longed to do something more than chafing unarmed rebel merchantmen with displays of the ship's guns, like a lion "showing them a good row of teeth."

He got his wish, somewhat, when he returned to the *Minnesota* on July 21 and heard about Lieutenant Crosby's expedition. General Butler ordered it, concerned about Southern troops massing at Sewell's point to the south and at Back River on his isolated garrison's northern flank. A company out of Monroe had destroyed several supply ships there in June, but Butler's intelligence from scouting parties and Crosby's own follow-up reconnaissance showed more nearby.

On the morning of Thursday, July 25, Lieutenant Crosby and his raiding party forayed out on their mission behind enemy lines. The newspapers had the number of launches wrong; there were eight, not six—besides the *Fanny*, four manned by Navy men from the *Minnesota*, the other four by Marines out of Fort Monroe. Quartermaster on the first launch, Will steamed nine miles up the Back River and met no resistance from rebel scouts along the shore. The party burned ten small oyster boats and towed an eleventh back to Hampton Roads with its load of corn, bacon, furniture, and other provisions. The raiders believed the boats they destroyed had been in the reeds since the blockade's imposition, the one in tow running supplies to Confederate forces a handful of times. A woman found aboard insisted it belonged to a local judge, who had planned to seek refuge further upriver.

Before quitting the scene, Will took "supreme pleasure" in setting fire to a vessel with his "own hands," and in bringing the "rich" furniture back to the Roads for auction. He also recovered a long-barreled musket, powder, plume, cap, and red shirt shed by a fleeing Confederate—the shirt being a dead giveaway that he was a Zouave. Will's glee when he wrote Cousin Mary about this find shows that he had lost none of his Naval Academy scorn for the crimson-clad militiamen.

The mission gave Will barely a taste of the action he craved, but it was a welcome change from sitting at anchor on blockade duty and a chance to take his mind off the gnawing anxiety he'd felt about Alonzo since his return to the flagship. By then every man aboard had heard about the catastrophic Battle at Bull's Run, some two-hundred fifty miles northwest in Virginia. There had been reports that thousands were killed, some two-thirds of them Union soldiers.

Will was aware his brother Lon had been in the thick of the fighting. But he did not know whether to count him among the living or the dead.

•   •   •

Swollen with hydrogen, a huge balloon rose up and up into the early evening sky. It had been launched from a clearing on the Hampton River, out beyond the walls of Fort Monroe. The breeze was strong, whipping the basket slightly about on its ropes, making it difficult for the aeronaut to ascend to his desired height.

"Professor" John LaMountain was not a university professor strictly speaking but earned the honorary title as an innovator in the science of flight and wizard in the production of lighter-than-air gases. Now, he hoped to climb high enough to see as far as the James River and Sewall's point, where General Butler feared the Confederates were massing for a strike on his garrison. Butler's concerns had not been put to rest by the failure of the Back River expedition to locate a rebel encampment. Based on other intelligence, and the enemy's success at Bull's Run, he was convinced they were out there, somewhere.

But LaMountain discerned no sign of Confederate troop movements through his spyglass. There was a lone sloop on the Back River, near the spot Lieutenant Crosby's party had raided that morning; that was all.

William Barker Cushing, U.S. Navy. *U.S. Naval History and Heritage Command*

His closeness to the earth was a frustration, however, enabling him to see no more than five miles around. He needed calm air and altitude to do his rarefied work.

Two thousand feet below, and a little to the south, where the great ships of the Home Blockade Squadron bobbed on the blue Chesapeake water, Will Cushing gazed up at the professor's improbable floating sphere from the deck of the USS *Minnesota*. Like the rest of the hands, he was amazed by the sight. But his thoughts kept wandering even further off, toward the western part of the state and his brother Alonzo.

By now the broad details of the calamity at Bull's Run were common knowledge. The Southern general, Beauregard, had been gathering his forces near the rail station at Manassas Junction for over a month, spreading them out along the creek by which the battle gained its name. Over twenty-thousand strong, they were dangerously close to Washington…within twenty-five miles, and in full control of the station, where they could easily receive supplies and reinforcements. On July 18, Brigadier General McDowell, the Union army commander in the capital, led his men out of the city to drive them back toward Richmond, planning to cross Bull's Run and strike at the Confederates' left flank, while sending a single column out to his far-right flank as a diversion. Three days later, he attacked.

Union General Robert Patterson was supposed to have cut off Southern reinforcements at Piedmont Station to the west. But he was too slow to prevent some nine thousand Confederates under General Johnstone from boarding a train there. At Manassas, they poured from their railroad cars and attacked federal troops exhausted from hours of fighting in the oppressive heat. The charging rebels howled and yelled like demons.

It was a disaster for the North. Some editorialists angrily called Patterson a traitor. Charitable voices insisted that at the advanced age of seventy, he should not have led the mission. But he had "played the Grouchy" in the terrible affair, as the newspapers put it. His troops had not arrived on time, and Southern forces rallied. The Union ranks broke and fled across the plain, leaving thousands of men dead, their bodies unburied in the fiery summer sun.

Many influential voices in the press directly blamed President Lincoln for the failure at Bull's Run, asserting that he had badly underestimated the enemy's strength and rushed his army into battle with inadequate training and preparation. Published appeals called for an immediate armistice with the Confederates, or even to disband the military in hopes of a quick political compromise. This editorial criticism resonated with a Northern public suddenly and rudely awakened to the gruesome realities of civil war.

The debacle left Lincoln knowing the conflict would be longer and costlier in human life than expected. He also began to understand the importance of making his voice heard above those of his critics. As the nation's elected leader, he would have to encourage and inspire its citizens through the coming ordeal. But it would be a while before he learned to use fully the power of presidential communication.

For Will, the battle's chaotic aftermath had brought personal anxiety over Alonzo's fate. He knew his older brother was with McDowell's Grand Army, commanding a gun battery section. Confusion and disarray characterized the Union retreat, and information from the front was piecemeal. Will had not heard from Lon and was concerned for his safety. The spectacle of LaMountain's balloon continued to be a distraction from his real thoughts.

As he awaited word over the next several days, Will considered resigning from naval service to join the volunteer army. No doubt the relative idleness of blockade duty was particularly frustrating during this time. He ached for more than skirmishes and sporadic interdictions and wanted to be closer to his brother.

"It seems as if I might be some protection to him in the hour of action," he wrote Cousin Mary on July 31. "If the rebels should kill him, I don't think that I would be a man any longer. I should become a fiend."

From the time they were children, he had been the precocious one. The one who convinced Alonzo to jump the schoolyard fence and follow along on truant escapades. It was never anything Lon would do on his own. He'd always applied himself to his education and before leaving for West Point had told Will to do the same. In many ways, Lon was more father to him than Milton Cushing ever was, and Will loved him more than his own life.

"For myself, I care nothing," he wrote. "I am drifting about the world with every wind and tide. I take my fate with me, and whatever it may be I hope to meet it like a man."

As he waited two weeks aboard the *Minnesota* for news about Lon, Will came to think his fate might be to stew eternally at anchor in the oppressive August heat. He had recurring headaches and grew annoyed with his superiors. Boredom and inaction were a poisonous combination for him.

There was a lieutenant that in his eyes had "lorded it over his junior officers" with his words and attitude. One night when the man took his turn as officer of the deck, Will found him fast asleep. He could have chosen to wake him and reported him for neglect of duty. Instead, he decided to embarrass him. Bringing over several men to watch, he swung a lighted lantern in front of the officer's face to show how deep in slumber he was, gaining a few cheap chuckles from other eyewitnesses. But he'd made a ranking officer the latest target of his hostility, which rarely ended well for any subordinate.

Feeling lonely and isolated, Will didn't reserve his irritation only for his higher ups in the Navy. In a letter to his cousin, he charged that no one seemed to care enough to answer his mail, a complaint that went back to his days at the Academy. Will was governed by his heart, and Mary was one person he opened up to, but she was a great distance away. That she was also a young woman living her life and that naval mail deliveries were notoriously slow, did nothing to calm his sense of neglect.

Hardly satisfied with slinging accusations at his cousin, Will wrote that the townspeople of Fredonia—quite a few of whom were relations—were cowards for not forming their own volunteer company in the army. "I would come home and raise a company myself if I thought it could be done," he told Mary.

In early August, Will finally heard from Alonzo. His brother had not only survived Bull's Run but conducted himself with bravery and distinction. During the battle, Lon wrote, he was attached temporarily to the 2nd U.S. Artillery, Battery G, under the command of Lieutenant Oliver Greene. Installed near a railroad crossing between Manassas and Centreville, his section engaged enemy troops from the outset, relentlessly pounding Confederate infantrymen as they tried to march across the Long Bridge over the Potomac to the capital. After the rebels broke through Union lines, Lon's gunners covered the federal retreat along the wagon trail from Centreville to Washington, taking various positions on the road from July 21 into the next day. When the clouds burst open on the morning of July 22, the torrential downpour transformed the roadsides to muddy washes and left them "strewn with knapsacks, blankets and other impediments of the returning soldiers who plodded along towards Washington from the battle of the day before."

For the next several weeks, the eight-mile stretch of road from Bailey's Crossroads to the Long Bridge on the Potomac River in Alexandria County became tent headquarters for remnants of the Grand Army. From the encampment, Lon's regiment sent out occasional scouting parties and "picket outposts in what appeared to our uneducated eyes to be appropriate points of vantage."

Will was tremendously relieved to hear from his brother. By all rights, it should have settled him down. But he fumed over the haughty lieutenant and still hadn't dropped the idea of resigning from the Navy to become Lon's battlefield guardian angel.

Unable to let either matter go, he hatched a plan.

•   •   •

After the lieutenant insulted Will in the wake of the lantern incident, he decided to challenge the officer to a duel. The Navy had prohibited dueling for some years, but there were certain unofficial conditions where a duel was recognized a "necessary safeguard of personal honor." Tradition, however, provided that an officer could turn down someone of lower rank without losing face—the rationale being that the older, experienced man would have the wisdom and maturity to avoid such an extreme resolution of a dispute.

Will had concluded the lieutenant would use his position as a cowardly excuse. Hence, he would resign from the Navy and *then* issue his challenge. This would deprive the officer of any face-saving way to wriggle clear of it.

"As long as I live, no man of any rank shall insult me with impunity," he seethed to Cousin Mary. He went on to explain his plan to resign, telling her he could follow his duel with the offending lieutenant with a reapplication to the Navy as a midshipman. Or, he added, join Lon in the land service. He could even follow in his brother's footsteps and attend West Point. "It seems foolish, but I have got to like the army better than the navy," he wrote. "I intend to make as broad a path through the world as I can for myself. And if I come to the conclusion that I prefer [being] a lieutenant in the army, at twenty-two, [to becoming a lieutenant in the navy] at thirty—I shall act on that conclusion."

Will hadn't paused to consider that West Point might not want him or asked himself what would make him more suited to its academic rigors than he had been at Annapolis. Moreover, the hypothetical three years he would spend earning a commission was completely at odds with his notion of joining Alonzo in the battlefield. But he was not thinking with the coolest of heads. He dashed off a letter of resignation to Flag Officer Stringham.

Stringham was far too preoccupied with his *own* plans to give any serious consideration to the letter. Along with Secretary Welles, General Butler, and others, he had begun organizing a major expedition, the first of the war to employ a large, joint land-naval attack force. With the *Minnesota* leading a flotilla of warships, the strike was to begin toward the end of the month at Hatteras Inlet.

Its aim, Will would learn to his excitement, was taking two important Southern forts.

CHAPTER EIGHT

THE FIRST WHIZ OF REBEL IRON

Forts Hatteras and Clark, on the southern tip of Hatteras Island, were barely forts at all in fact, but two makeshift Confederate earthworks of compacted sand, brush, and turf, with outlying log stockades to house the troops. Built hastily by slave laborers, they were meant to guard the watery divide known as Hatteras Inlet, which cut between Hatteras Island and Ocracoke Island to the south. This supplied a gateway through the Outer Banks to Pamlico Sound, a vast salt lagoon stretching along eighty miles of North Carolina and Virginia shoreline.

In May 1861, Elizabeth City's Colonel William F. Martin, at the direction of his brother James, placed his businesses in the competent hands of young Gilbert Elliott and landed on Hatteras Island with about seven hundred infantrymen from his 7th Carolina Volunteers. Their assignment was to defend the two makeshift forts and protect Southern smugglers and privateers using it to slip between the sound and the open sea.

The principal battery, Fort Hatteras, activated in June. Octagonal in shape with five-foot-high embankments, its armaments consisted of twelve pivot-mounted thirty-two-pound smoothbore cannons, complemented by several eight-inch guns. Additional thirty-two-pounders not yet mounted sat on the sand within the embankments. In the center of the fortification was a hundred-yard-long bombproof shelter from artillery attacks. It had ten-foot-thick sand and sod walls and a covered entrance built of timber and plank.

About five weeks after Hatteras went up, construction began on Fort Clark a half mile to the southeast. According to the same layout, its swivel-mounted thirty-two-pounders were positioned to cover the inlet's entrance.

By the end of July, Gideon Welles was under extreme pressure to stop the rebel vessels from entering and exiting the inlet at will. Their harrying of Northern commerce had grown brazen; late in the month, a three-gun privateer called the *Gordon* had seized a brig laden with three hundred sixty barrels of molasses, and just two days afterward a "saucy looking little pilot schooner," the *Florida*, took a second merchant vessel in the same area. Although a United States steamer gave chase, forcing the schooner to beach her prize, Welles knew he could not let the attacks go on.

Advancing a plan to block the inlet with sunken hulks, Welles sent an emissary, Lieutenant Henry Stellwagen, to buy decrepit old tugs and merchant vessels from ship owners in the Chesapeake vicinity. But Flag Officer Stringham disagreed with his idea, arguing for more decisive action. He believed the obstructions could never altogether close the waterway and felt that tidal currents and shifting sands would only form new waterways over time. The right move was to capture the forts and take control of the inlet, giving Union forces unfettered access to Pamlico Sound and the Southern coast.

Stringham found an ally in Major General John E. Wool, who arrived at Fort Monroe in August to relieve Benjamin Butler as Commander of the Department of Virginia and North Carolina. The change of leadership was immediately welcomed by the squadron.

"Butler is a citizen-officer and the troops do not feel the confidence in him that they do in General Wool...a regular army officer [who] has served his country long and well," Will Cushing wrote his cousin on

August 17, three days after Wool's arrival. "You may expect to hear of stirring work, as soon as reinforcements reach the fort."

Stirring work. Word, then, was already out. Determined to seize Hatteras Inlet, Silas Stringham expected the sea dog commander would back him up.

The two at once began discussing a simultaneous Army-Navy operation, and within a matter of days settled on a plan...although Butler, still at Monroe prior to his reassignment, later took full credit for it, claiming it leaped shiny and whole from his brain.

Butler was, in fact, ordered by Wool to lead the landing force, a contingent of about nine hundred fighting men cobbled together from the Army's Union Coast Guard, the New York 20th Volunteers, the New York 9th Volunteers, and the 2nd United States Artillery.

But it was Stringham's naval element that would provide the real show of federal power. Led by his flagship the *Minnesota*, his squadron would include the frigates *Susquehanna* and *Wabash*, the converted merchant steamer *Monticello*, the screw sloop *Pawnee*, and the Revenue Service cutter *Harriet Lane* with staunch Captain Julius Faunce at the helm. The rust bucket tows *Adelaide* and *George Peabody*, originally bought by Lieutenant Stellwagen to be ballasted with stones and sunk, would be fitted out as troop transports.

Stringham disapproved of the timing. August was the middle of hurricane season in the Outer Banks, and the winds had been tempestuous. "I cannot hesitate in pronouncing them unsafe in that stormy neighborhood," he appealed to Secretary Welles. But Welles insisted they were seaworthy...or at least fit enough to serve their purpose. In superior condition and bringing additional troops under the command of Lieutenant Pierce Crosby was the steam tug *Fanny*, which Crosby had taken up Back River in July and had lately served as a marine launch platform for Professor LaMountain and his surveillance balloon.

The "rough and boistrous" seas referenced by Stringham delayed the expedition until late in the month, sending vessels ashore and preventing him from bringing out rowboats to coal his ships. But by Friday,

August 23, the waters at Hampton Roads began to calm, and the mission was tentatively set for the following Monday.

That morning "[t]he weather was beautiful, and the sea smooth." Outside Fort Monroe, on the wharves of Old Point Comfort, Butler's troops, their colors held high, marched aboard the transports to the rousing music of a brass band. By 1:00 p.m., the warships assembled in line. The *Minnesota* steamed out of the Chesapeake in the lead and was soon rounding Cape Henry, bearing south toward Hatteras Inlet.

For Will it was a "great moment." Although the flotilla left under sealed orders, there had been no shortage of scuttlebutt about the nature of its mission. Given command of an eight-inch gun division on the quarterdeck, Will was "excited and eager" about the prospect of battle. He'd never been in charge of a gun crew, "never been fairly under fire" other than to take some scattered misses during the Back River expedition, and never seen himself in a role of true consequence like his brother Alonzo. Now that was at last about to change.

Around 4:00 p.m. the squadron came in sight of the rebel forts and dropped anchor to wait out the night.

The next morning, August 27, the federal squadron moved just southeast of Hatteras Island. On the *Minnesota*, Commodore Stringham began reconnoitering, hoisting out surfboats for his marines, and conducting other preparations.

At Fort Hatteras, meanwhile, Colonel Martin could see the federal warships massing off the inlet. A spyglass raised to his eye, he watched them for an hour or more, counting the number of vessels crowded with men.

Martin had between 250 and 300 troops garrisoned at the two forts. It would take at least 225 to work the guns properly, and he could not resist an enemy landing with the handful left over. His only hope was to send for reinforcements.

After a long search, Martin got hold of a small pilot boat, dispatching it with orders to Lieutenant Colonel George Johnson on Beacon Island, south of Ocracoke. Johnson had four volunteer companies under him and was to bring all the men he could spare to Hatteras's aid.

Martin expected the boat to reach the island in a few hours, hopefully before nightfall. He might then have his relief by morning.

On August 28, Silas Stringham woke his men before daybreak for an early breakfast. The wind had picked up and there was a heavy, foaming surf tossing up on the beach. But the sky was clear with no threat of rain. The troop landings would begin as planned.

Will got a clear view of the preparations from the *Minnesota*'s quarterdeck. He watched the ship's pair of twelve-inch guns get loaded aboard one of the surfboats and sent over to the *Adelaide*. He also watched General Butler, who had come aboard the day before, accompanying the marines onto the *Harriet Lane*. Shortly before 7:00a.m., the troops were signaled to disembark. With a bright sun overhead and the sea a glassy blue, Will saw the *Pawnee*, *Monticello*, and *Harriet Lane* move into position about two miles east of the enemy. Their task was to aid and give cover to the landings.

Less than two hours later, the squadron lined up in battle array, the *Wabash* taking the lead with the aged *Cumberland* in tow and the *Minnesota* following closely behind. Around the same time, the *Monticello*, *Pawnee*, *Harriet*, and troop transports pulled within two miles east of the enemy batteries. "The most perfect silence prevaile[d]" over the water as they advanced. The landings would only begin after the beaches, fortifications "and all the little skirts of woods where troops might...be concealed" were softened up with cannon fire.

At 10:00 a.m. the *Waubash* and *Cumberland* started the shelling of the island. Fort Clark's guns quickly answered—so quickly that Will initially thought their roar was the warships' fire echoing back at them. He would "never forget, or again experience," his "wild pleasure and excitement" as "the stern challenge and response passed over the blue water."

He was hardly alone in feeling such heady exhilaration. "I remember well our gallant old captain's look as the first whiz of rebel iron came to our ears," he later wrote of Commodore Stringham. "With flushed face and sparkling eye, he straightened his tall form, and with grey hair bared to the sun, stamped his foot upon the bridge and impulsively exclaimed, '*Glorious! Glorious—closer! Closer!*'"

Ten minutes after the *Wabash* and *Cumberland* opened fire on the beach, Stringham ordered the *Minnesota* to pass inside the other two vessels and join the bombardment. Will was fully "in the action," his guns pouring out hellfire.

The ships kept pounding the island, each vessel "a sheet of flame from bow to stern." A clever tactician, Stringham had them move in a continuous elliptical loop, "passing and repassing" as they took turns firing their cannons. They became moving targets, preventing rebel artillerymen from adjusting for range. It was an innovative maneuver in an era of stationary marine battles.

In the meantime, the *Harriet Lane* had led in toward shore, her drummer beating to quarters as the men primed and readied their guns. Close by were the transport *Adelaide* and Lieutenant Crosby's canal boat *Fanny* with a group of army regulars on deck. The squadron's "firing ha[d] now become rapid...the thunder and boom of cannon, and the bursting of the shells in the air over the forts presenting a startling scene." High plumes of sand rose up from the beaches where the cannonballs hit.

At 10:30 a.m., General Butler appeared in the *Harriet Lane*'s wheelhouse.

"*Land the troops!*" he shouted over the crash of the guns, pointing a thick finger at their debarkation spot.

The transports swung toward the island. As they drew near, the marines saw a stunning sight: the sound of the cannon fire had panicked the cattle in the woods and sent them "rushing down to and along the beach in large droves."

Onboard the *Harriet Lane*, Butler hoisted his signal to continue the landings. Flatboats lowered, the men rowed in. But the surf became rougher. High, roaring breakers flung the boats against the shoals. Swamped with water, tossing in the swells, few of them gained the beach.

Lieutenant Crosby, in part, saved the day for the landings. Back at Hampton Roads, he'd chained down the *Fanny*'s boilers against rough waters, volunteering to accompany the squadron so as to "have a light draft vessel to operate in landing troops." His foresight paid off.

Steaming close to Hatteras Island—closer than the larger *Harriet Lane* could approach in safety—Crosby guided some of the damaged flatboats past the rocks. When they would no longer float, he "took the *Pawnee*'s heavy launch and landed two more boatloads of troops, until the sea became so heavy [it] threw the launch upon the beach, dashing all the crew out of her onto the shore."

Altogether, only 315 regulars and marines—fewer than half the total force— reached the island, attributing their success to Crosby's brave resolve. The *Minnesota*'s two twelve-pound guns landed with them, though one was damaged while being brought ashore.

Around 11:00 a.m., as the landing boats struggled through the shoals, the *Susquehanna* took her turn firing on the island. "The cannonading on our part was incessant," wrote a *New York Herald* correspondent with the fleet, "and the air was alive with the hum and explosion of flying shell. [B]ut the enemy did not return the fire with any regularity, the [Union] battery being too hot for them, from the explosion of shells that dropped in at the rate of above a half-dozen a minute."

Rounds from Confederate guns either fell short of reaching the warships or passed harmlessly overhead. Stringham's tactics were perfect.

The pounding of the island continued without letup. Then, at 12:30 p.m., Will saw both forts lower their flags as Southern troops poured from the smaller earthwork in desperate flight. They went "rushing madly along the beach, while [the fleet's] shell[s] tore through and through them—and bursting, sent mangled bodies high in air, or buried them by dozens in sand graves upon the shore." Through his glass, Stringham observed that some went running toward Fort Hatteras while others tried fleeing the island in small boats.

Soon afterward, Butler's troops raised the American flag above the blasted ruins of Fort Clark, a reassuring sight aboard the Union ships.

It was now about 2:00 p.m. Stringham gave a cease-fire signal to the squadron and then ordered the *Monticello*'s captain, John P. Gillis, to "feel his way into the inlet and take possession" of Fort Hatteras. While the lowering of its Confederate banner was ordinarily a sign of surrender, he urged Gillis to be cautious.

His instincts were right. An hour earlier, with the landings underway and bombardment of the island in full force, Confederate General Martin had met with his officers at Fort Clark. They agreed the battery had been lost. Martin then sent word to his pickets in Clark's wooded outskirts. They were to spike the guns at the fort, take whatever they could carry, and fall back to Hatteras "under most terrible fire of shell." Once all the troops pulled together at the larger emplacement, Martin ordered them to resume the fight and make "as good a resistance as possible."

On the *Monticello*, Captain Gillis advanced only a short distance before she ran aground in the shallow water, hitting bottom hard enough to rock the entire vessel. That was when Martin's troops opened fire, their fourteen mounted guns "playing upon her at close range." While not exactly an ambush, Gillis would remember that the fort's colors remained down and called it an act of treachery.

Martin offered another explanation. In his report, he admitted that "no flag was raised upon Fort Hatteras," but maintained it was something that had merely slipped his attention, suggesting that the flag that normally flew over the fort was "torn to pieces by the winds and no new ones procured."

Whatever the story, Gillis returned fire at once from his starboard battery, the ship repeatedly striking the sandbar as the pilot struggled to turn her around. After an hour of retreating in fits and starts, the *Monticello* finally maneuvered out of the inlet and ran back to the flagship, Stringham covering with fire from his entire squadron. Although hit several times while making her retreat, the damage to her hull was minor, and her carpenters were soon pounding wooden patches over the holes.

Meanwhile, "a tug-steamer, towing a schooner filled with troops, was seen coming from the southward" to supply relief to the fort. The arriving vessels carried Colonel Johnson and the reinforcements Martin had summoned from Beacon Island—a total of about three hundred officers and regulars. Commodore Samuel Barron, the flag officer in command of North Carolina and Virginia's coastal defenses, would answer the call for aid sometime later that night.

It was now 6:00 p.m. As dusk approached the weather became squally. A sheet of thick charcoal-grey clouds lowered over the water. With a storm brewing over the Capes, Stringham had most of the squadron haul off for the night, leaving the *Harriet Lane*, *Pawnee*, and *Monticello* inshore to guard the troops on the island.

Will later recalled "a spirit of gloom and doubt" infiltrating the fleet. They feared a gale would scatter their vessels, "in which case the enemy might not only save their fort, but find our troops at their mercy." A tense, oppressive feeling grew almost palpable as darkness settled in.

About 9:00 p.m., however, the winds grew calmer. The clouds parted, and the moon appeared between them, painting a silver band across the water's surface. On the ships, everyone's mood began to lift. The men were astonished by how quickly the sky had cleared.

By sunrise, with the breeze pleasant and the sea moderate, Stringham was confident that he could resume his offensive. Signaling the squadron to weigh anchor, he ordered it back in toward the island, where he saw the main body of troops still near the point where they landed. After having the *Monticello* and *Pawnee* send out boats to provision them, he called for the entire fleet to prepare for action.

This time they found the fort's Southern banner raised. It bore out Lieutenant Martin's contention that he'd initially failed to notice it was down, and hoisted one brought over from Fort Clark that morning.

At 8:00 a.m., Stringham gave the command to re-engage the enemy, his ships no longer circling, but staying in stationary positions outside the range of Confederate guns, pounding the island with an overwhelming cannonball barrage. Will Cushing would recall that the concentrated fire on the fort was terrific, with sixty shells exploding inside its parapets in a single minute. Inside the fort, rebel officers had a slightly different count, estimating the rain of shells as between twenty and twenty-eight a minute—but whatever the number, the outpouring of fire was relentless.

The *Herald* reporter with the fleet gave his own details: "The shells continued exploding over, around and directly in [both] forts, with a fearful havoc," he wrote. "The whole squadron [was] now firing at once. The *Monticello*, with great courage, advanced far beyond any other ship, and poured her fire directly into the battery...the *Harriet Lane* approached still nearer, and discharged one of her large guns, with destructive results."

The squadron struck an ultimate blow at 11:00 a.m., when the *Susquehanna* fired an eleven-inch shell directly into the bombproof. The round plowed through to the adjoining magazine, setting it ablaze and destroying what remained of the fort's powder reserve.

Inside its flattened walls, the Southern officers took hurried council. There was no shelter left. The federal squadron had one hundred thirty guns to their twelve. Four men were dead and dozens gravely wounded. They could endure no further punishment. Ten minutes after the magazine went up in flames, Commodore Barron—who had relieved an exhausted Lieutenant Martin of command—displayed a white flag over Fort Hatteras, and Stringham ordered a cease fire.

That afternoon on the *Minnesota*'s quarterdeck, Will got a close-up view of the Southerners' unconditional surrender when Barron, Martin, and a third senior officer boarded the transport *George Peabody*. "Barron soon came over our side and surrendered his sword...and we took possession of captured men and property, bringing the prisoners...on board."

The North had scored a major victory that went beyond just capturing the forts. In General Butler's words:

> As long as we kept control of the sea, we could hold that post for all time with a small force...By doing so, we controlled the whole coast of North and South Carolina in the sounds, and held the water communication from Norfolk to Beaufort, South Carolina.

The Atlantic Blockading Squadron could now take a more active approach toward stopping blockade runners in the area. With direct access to Pamlico Sound, it no longer needed to have its ships drop anchor on the sea side of the barrier islands and wait for the smugglers to appear. Instead it could aggressively patrol the inland waters where they berthed and loaded up with cargo.

These tactics suited Will Cushing's thirst for action far more than the static, repetitive, and monotonous blockading duties he'd grown to despise... *except* that his future with the United States Navy was once again in doubt.

Forgot perhaps in battle, but waiting on Commodore Stringham's desk, was the letter of resignation Will had penned in preparation for challenging a superior officer to a duel.

Now, with the Battle of Hatteras Inlet behind him, Stringham would find time to read it.

●   ●   ●

On Saturday, August 30, 1861, the *Minnesota* detached from the squadron and sailed for New York with 678 Confederate prisoners from Forts Hatteras and Clark, as well as the companies that had arrived to strengthen their ranks.

The men "presented a curious and interesting appearance," Will wrote years later. "They were not, in that early stage of the war, content with the ordinary weapons of a soldier, but were loaded down with bowie knives and revolvers, each man a walking armory, evidently endeavoring to justify in dress the awe-inspiring titles they assumed, such as the 'Lenoir Braves,' the 'Tar River Boys,' 'Hamilton Guards,' and 'Jonesboro Tigers.' These are a few of the ferocious company organizations that I remember."

Stringham brought the flagship into New York Harbor on Monday, September 2, and with the aid of the volunteer Army regiment on Bedloe's Island, delivered his captives to old Fort Wood three days later.

That same day, the *Minnesota* turned back to Hampton Roads, albeit without the commodore, who took the railroad to Washington, sharing a private car with First Lady Mary Todd Lincoln and her children as they returned from a month-long vacation at the New Jersey seashore. He would arrive in the capital that afternoon and give his personal account of the Hatteras Inlet expedition to Gideon Welles.

By no accident, General Butler beat him to it. Immediately after the Confederate surrender, he'd hurried to Annapolis on the *Adelaide* and scrambled aboard a series of rail connections—including a midnight ride on a speeding locomotive—to reach Washington in the predawn hours of Sunday, September 1, four full days ahead of Stringham.

In his memoir, Butler took full credit for the decision not to block the inlet with sunken hulks, attributing it to his "usual hazardous bravado," while leaving out that it was Stringham and Wool's idea all along.

"I had positive orders from Washington to sink the sand vessels," he wrote, adding that he chose to disobey those orders feeling he could "do that with some safety...provided I got to Washington and carried news of the capture myself."

On his arrival in the capital—it was still before daybreak Sunday—Butler took a carriage directly to Postmaster General Montgomery Blair's residence, saw through Blair's study window that he was in conversation with Butler's old college roommate Gustavus Fox, and went in to share the news of his victory with them. According to Butler, Fox elatedly suggested they go across Pennsylvania Avenue to the White House and inform President Lincoln.

"We ought not to do that, and get him up at this time of night," Butler said. "Let him sleep."

"He will sleep enough better for it; so let us go and wake him up," Fox replied

Butler was out the door without further prodding. At the White House, he and Fox roused a bleary-eyed watchman, brought him to the Cabinet room, and then waited briefly for the president, who entered in his nightshirt.

"Everybody knows how tall Lincoln was, and he seemed very much taller in that garment; and Fox was about five feet nothing," Butler wrote, describing a merry scene. "In a few hurried words, without waiting for any forms or ceremonies, Fox communicated the news, and then he and Lincoln fell into each other's arms. That is, Fox put his arms around Lincoln about as high as his hips, and Lincoln reached down over him so that his arms were pretty near the floor, holding each other as they flew around the room once or twice, Lincoln's night shirt considerably agitated.

"'You have done all right, you have done all right,'" Lincoln exclaimed, grabbing Butler's hand. "Come tomorrow at ten o'clock and we will have a Cabinet meeting over it.'"

At the meeting, Butler gave Lincoln and his top aides his slanted version of "the reasons why he had not obeyed orders and stopped up Hatteras Inlet." When the *New York Times* and other newspapers published headline stories calling the strike *General Butler's Expedition*, Butler's narrative lodged in the public consciousness. In the telling, if not in truth, he became the operation's main planner.

His one-upmanship over Stringham and the Navy angered Will. As he bitterly wrote, "Our victory at Hatteras gave General Butler his first public opportunity of showing that *modesty* for which he afterwards became so conspicuous by making speeches that implied that to him the credit of our action was due…and accepting numerous serenades and dinners in the North for which common decency should have forced him to disclaim."

Admiral Stringham was not Will's idea of a great leader. He was rigid, aloof, and testy. But he was a lifetime Navy man, who had served in the War of 1812, Second Barbary War, and Mexican-American War. Despite questioning his leadership, Will did not question him as a warrior.

Back at Hampton Roads, Will took to calling him "Old Sting 'em." He intended no harm by the sobriquet, but meant it as a wry compliment, referring to the commander's relentless ferocity against the Confederates at Hatteras Inlet. It tickled his shipmates aboard the *Minnesota* and was one of many small remedies for the tedium of renewed blockade duty.

In New York, meanwhile, the Southerners taken prisoner with the surrender of the forts had nothing to alleviate their difficult circumstances. Shortly after disembarking from the *Minnesota* at Bedloe's Island, they were transferred to Governor's Island, where the commissioned officers were sent to Fort Columbus and the enlisted men to Castle William, a circular red sandstone fortification on the island's west point. All were without clean clothes, and many had arrived sick or nursing battle injuries.

The castle was a particularly inhospitable place of confinement. As the U.S. Army surgeon assigned to the island, Dr. William J. Sloan, wrote his commanding officer in a plea for improvements, "[The prisoners] are crowded into an ill-ventilated building which has always been an unhealthy one when occupied by large bodies of men. There are no conveniences for cooking except in the open air, no means of heating the lower tier of gun rooms and no privies within the area. As the winter approaches I cannot see how these 630 men can be taken care of under the above circumstances.... There are now upwards of eighty cases of measles amongst them, a number of cases of typhoid fever, pneumonia, intermittent fever, etc. I have taken the worst cases into my hospital and am preparing it with beds to full capacity...."

The situation would only deteriorate in the coming weeks. There were seven deaths in September, and men were soon passing away daily. Horrified by their unhealthy living conditions, William F. Martin tried to arrange for his brother James—who wore the hat of quartermaster, among many others, for North Carolina's army—to send the prisoners fresh uniforms, offering to defray most of their cost. Progress would be frustratingly slow as he wrote request after request to his Union captors, only to have them caught in bureaucratic snarls.

He also had escalating personal concerns. His mother was now alone in her Elizabeth City home, with no one to care for her except Gilbert Elliott, and the young man was already up to his ears in running the Martin family businesses. Hustling up new contracts for the shipyard had been difficult, leaving him short of cash for its bills and operating expenses. Therefore, he was forced to put at least one major project on hold.

In early September, Elliott, still reeling from his employer's capture at Hatteras, had a new headache arrive in the mail. The note was dated the 8th and addressed to William Martin from James Perry, a nearby sawmill operator and supplier of timber for the yard.

"The bill of ship timber ordered by you is ready and has been for several days," he wrote, adding a request for "10 or 15 bushels of salt." Perry may have been ordering the salt from a general store owned by a Williams relative, but for Elliott that was hardly the problem. His problem was paying for timber intended for a vessel "on the stocks," or under construction at the yard. Most likely "built on speculation," its completion demanded a sizeable financial outlay.

Perry's request left Elliott with a dilemma. If he wrote a check for the timber, sinking yet more funds into the unfinished vessel, it would put the Martin shipyard under greater financial stress. But Perry had cut and milled the wood to Martin's specifications. Failure to pay up would violate a good faith agreement, alienate a vital supplier, and seriously damage his firm's reputation.

Unsure of what to do, he turned to General James Martin for guidance—and Martin readily obliged. With his brother a prisoner of war, the general felt responsible for keeping the business solvent. At some point, he knew, it would fall on Gil's shoulders to generate profits. But he was just starting as manager of the yard, a difficult job under the best of circumstances. William's capture had made it even harder on him.

On September 14, General Martin wrote Elliott a letter of advice. His first suggestion was that Elliott collect on one of its own outstanding bills—something he could facilitate with his military rank and title.

Cobb's Point, on the Pasquotank River, was an outthrust finger of land just southeast of Elizabeth City. In July, General Martin had ordered a floating battery of four thirty-two-pound shore guns built there for the city's defense, pulling strings to have Colonel Lucien Douglas Starke put in charge of construction. His recommendation of Colonel Starke showed a shrewd, circular sense of reciprocity. A former newspaper editor, Starke had gained a license to practice law under the tutelage of his friend, William Martin; when Starke gained command of the offshore battery, he hired Martin's shipyard to build it. On completion of the work, payment was to be made through the state's military quartermaster—General Martin himself.

"When you get through working on the battery at Cobb's Point, make out your bill, get it certified (in duplicate) by the person who has charge of the battery and send it to me," Martin told Elliott. Which was to say that he and Starke would speed up the paperwork, so the shipyard was swiftly paid and reimbursed for its expenses. But he was already thinking past that contract. Without segue, he added, "Send me at once the dimensions of the vessel you have on the stocks, and when she could be launched, and how much she is worth the day you launch her. The Confederate States want some gunboats built. Could you build one or more, how soon, and at what price per ton or other measure?"

Martin was leaving Elliott with no doubt about his goals. An infusion of funds would help cover the shipyard's expenses, but its growth hinged on generating new deals. Over the next week or so, he would begin exploring Secretary Mallory's wish list for armed vessels and write a personal inquiry to Commodore William F. Lynch, who commanded the naval defenses at Roanoke Island, Virginia. The Confederate Navy was rapidly mobilizing, and Martin saw no conflict of interest in his family shipyard's reaping some financial dividends.

In Elizabeth City, Gilbert Elliott was on the cusp of becoming a bona fide shipbuilder.

•   •   •

After returning to the *Minnesota* from Washington, Commodore Silas Stringham waded into his backlog of paperwork. Over the next week or two, he would spend many hours writing reports and engaging in official correspondence.

Stringham took the time to pen letters of special recognition for several officers and seamen who had taken part in the Hatteras expedition, in some instances suggesting brevetting or promotion for meritorious conduct. "I am sure the [Department of the Navy] will pardon me for relating these incidents," he wrote after complimenting two seamen to Gustavus Fox. "I can only offer as an excuse the pride which I take in officers and men under my command who are thus ready to risk life in the service of their country."

Although Master's Mate Will Cushing had acquitted himself ably as a gun division commander, often within a few feet of Stringham, the flag officer seemed oblivious to his performance. He did, however, take notice of the letter of resignation on his desk that Will had given before the battle.

Will's request irritated the notoriously irritable Stringham. He and his captain ran a tight ship, and they knew about the ongoing friction between Cushing and one of his superiors. So, too, the lantern incident, and Cushing's challenging the officer to a duel.

But the nickname Cushing had given him—Old Sting 'em—must have topped the list of annoyances for the sixty-three-year-old flag officer, especially after it caught on with the *Minnesota*'s crew. Silas Stringham was a man of his era, and his strait-laced dignity came at the expense of any discernible sense of humor. Whether Cushing intended the nickname as praise or insult was of little or no consequence to him. To his eyes it was disrespectful, in keeping with the reputation for habitual impertinence pinned on Cushing at Annapolis. In the insular world of the naval officer, Stringham would know something of his checkered history, quite possibly from Gideon Welles himself, when he'd assigned Cushing to the *Minnesota* at the last minute.

On September 11, Stringham sent Welles and Fox a curiously worded letter about him:

Sirs,

I have the honor to enclose herewith the resignation of M. Mate W. B. Cushing, and to recommend that it be accepted.

His original and speculative turn of mind makes him unfit for naval service.

Your obt. Servant,
S. H. Stringham

And that was all Old Sting 'em wrote. Will was apparently out of the Navy yet again.

•   •   •

Alonzo Cushing was miserably sick. His symptoms had started in early September: high fever, weakness, nausea, and a terrible stomach grip. As the month wore on, Lon had been wearing down, and he was not alone. In the mud-caked tents of the crowded Alexandria County army encampment, men had fallen ill in near-epidemic numbers. It was the spoiled food and contaminated water; the stinking mounds of refuse and filthy latrines; the worms, maggots, and swarms of buzzing mosquitos; the heat, rain, and humidity; and the neglect of basic hygiene by the troops.

On September 18, Lon was diagnosed with an ailment of a "typhoid character" by J. J. Woodward, an Army physician who would play a sad, significant role in the nation's history, conducting autopsies of Abraham Lincoln and John Wilkes Booth. But that day among the tents, Dr. Woodward was only a battlefield physician who was prescribing a leave of absence to Lon, who balked, insisting he had too much work to do.

There was certainly no shortage of work. Just one day after the defeat at Bull's Run, President Lincoln had tasked the charismatic General George B. McClellan with putting together an expansive military force to defend the capital. McClellan swiftly assembled the Army of the Potomac, which would consist of ten divisions, twenty-five to thirty brigades, and some 90,000 troops largely from immigrant communities in cities like Philadelphia, Boston, and New York. A majority of the fighting men were Irish, with thousands of non–English speaking recruits from German and Italian city neighborhoods.

Hailed as an organizational genius, McClellan had risen quickly to general-in-chief of all federal troops. He owed a substantial part of his reputation for organization to the latest crop of West Point graduates—like Lon—whose leadership skills proved invaluable to his success in implementing Lincoln's directive.

Still attached to the 2nd Artillery, Lon was temporarily promoted to the rank of captain and made one of the young officers responsible for shaping a hodgepodge of culturally, ethnically, and linguistically distinct volunteer units into a cohesive fighting force. With vital duties that ranged from drilling to uniforming to getting horses, he felt like a shirker leaving camp for any reason. But his deteriorating health had robbed him of strength and stamina. He could not go on.

Reluctantly acquiescing to Dr. Woodward, Lon filed for a medical leave. He'd decided to recuperate with his oldest brother Milton, who had trained to be a pharmacist in Fredonia, tried his hand at it in Massachusetts, and recently moved to Washington to serve with the Department of the Navy. Milt had visited Lon at camp throughout the summer and now would bring him to where he lived, a small, two-story rooming house owned by a pair of elderly women located off Pennsylvania Avenue at 458 Twelfth Street West.

Both were in for a surprise. Alonzo had no sooner settled into a spare bed when younger brother Will showed up at the door to help with his convalescence. It was something that normally would have made for a happy reunion of the three Cushing boys, but Will had brought along some very unhappy—and unexpected—news from Hampton Roads.

The Navy had tossed him out again. Cruelly and unjustifiably, he asserted. And this time he was not prepared to stand for it.

•   •   •

It was Wednesday, September 25, 1861. Will had been at the Twelfth
Street rooming house with his brothers about a week, caring for Lon and
devising a plan for his reinstatement into the Navy. A letter from Mary
brought news of her imminent marriage to one C. W. Smith, a leading
merchant and occasional cow breeder from East Troy, Wisconsin, and
with the announcement came an invitation. Set for mid-November, the
wedding would take place in Will's hometown of Fredonia.

Will remained angry over Commodore Stringham's deeming him
"unfit" for service and had written to request that he clarify his asser-
tion. In his letter—which he wrote and probably hand-delivered to one
of Stringham's staff officers on September 29, accounting for his trip
back to the *Minnesota*—he requested that Stringham "state in writing
whether I did my duty" under his command, reminding him of his trips
"north with [the] prize vessels," and his "command of the quarter-deck
division of guns directly under your eye."

In his curt response nine days later, Stringham tried passing the
whole matter off onto the flagship's captain, "as you were more immediately under his command." But he did throw Will a crumb. "As
regards the times you refer to," he added, "I am happy to say your
conduct was meritorious."

It was the written equivalent of a reluctant grunt. But Will took
what he could get, raced back to Washington, and offered it to Welles
for his consideration.

The secretary agreed to think things over. To say he had a soft spot
for Will might be overly simplistic. Fairer to say, he'd seen something
special in him from the beginning, a unique spark. Welles's instincts
guided him. "[Stringham] thought Cushing too full of levity, too fond of
fun and frolic, to make a valuable officer," he later recalled. "The truth
was with his exuberant spirit he had too little to do; his restless, active
mind was filled with adventure and zeal to accomplish something that
would do himself credit and the country service."

Unlike Stringham, Welles valued cleverness and a bit of cheek as positive leadership qualities. But as in his earlier go 'rounds with Will, he was mindful of proper decorum and cautious not to disaffect the career Navy men serving his department. Before deciding, he turned to an officer of high standing and unimpeachable reputation for his opinion. Someone who not only knew Cushing's history, but already had been influential in pulling his hide out of the fire: Superintendent George S. Blake.

On October 15, Blake wrote Welles of Will:

> In my opinion the abilities of that young gentleman are very good. [While] at the Naval Academy, he was at times very idle and insubordinate and his failure in his studies was due to the former course alone. I am certain, however, that he can become a good officer, and as his services aboard the *Minnesota* have been satisfactory to the Department, I respectfully suggest that he be restored.

That was all the support Welles required. Four days later, on October 19, he restored Will to the Navy—but not as an acting master's mate. The secretary believed Will's service aboard the *Minnesota* more than qualified him for midshipman's status. He had shown courage and resourcefulness as a prize master and a cool head under fire. It was time to credit his best attributes rather than punish him for his worst.

Backdating his order to June 1—the date Will would have graduated from Annapolis—Welles warranted him a passed midshipman with his rating set at twenty-first out of twenty-six in the class of 1861. Like any other member of the class, he was now eligible for promotion to higher rank.

Though reassigned to the North Blockading Squadron, Will would not be returning to the *Minnesota*. Instead, Welles had the young man report to the USS *Cambridge,* a far smaller single-screw, thousand-ton gunship being sent temporarily to replace another vessel in the mouth of the Rappahannock River. The *Rescue,* an armed steam tug like the

Fanny, was ordered to go with her on patrol, forming a tandem suited to action in inland waters—the shallow creeks and tributaries where blockade runners would slip in and out of Confederate ports.

Welles believed that Cushing would thrive amid the action.

CHAPTER NINE

THE BETTER PART OF VALOR

A cold fog swirled around the USS *Cambridge* as morning filtered down the Rappahannock River on Thursday, October 31, 1861. Wrapped in his pea jacket, the ship's lookout peered through the smoky fog and spotted a small boat coming from shore. Its sail lowered to avoid drawing attention, the brown-skinned men at its gunwales rowed quietly closer, stopping a short distance off across the water.

Informed of its presence, Captain William A. Parker sent out a small party in a dinghy to investigate. It was hardly a surprise when they found the boat packed with fugitive slaves. Since coming on blockade a few days before, the *Cambridge* had picked up seventy slaves fleeing their Southern masters. This group would bring the number up to a hundred.

The escapees soon boarded the ship. Like many blockade ships captains, Parker had complained to his superiors about "contraband"—the federal Navy's term for runaways—overcrowding his vessel and exhausting its scarce provisions. But Parker felt the able-bodied men among them might help the Union labor force and would not deny them his protection. One slave would credit Parker's officers and crew with receiving his group kindly.

The runaways picked up that morning had brought some valuable information about a large schooner "loaded with wheat and [fire]wood [and] anchored some six miles from the mouth of the [Corrotoman Creek] branch of the river, or about twenty-six miles from the mouth of the Rappahannock."

Parker concluded it was a blockade runner and hurried to organize a cutting-out expedition. Because the creek was too shallow for the *Cambridge* to traverse, he would send the *Rescue* to capture or destroy the vessel.

Shortly after noon on November 7, the *Rescue,* its sides covered with frost, left the larger ship anchored at the confluence of the Rappahannock and Corrotoman and set out with its two, twelve-inch guns and a detachment of thirty men. In charge was First Lieutenant William Gwin, aided by two master's mates and a young midshipman, William Barker Cushing, who'd joined the crew of the larger ship in late October. Gwin had approached Will just before setting out and asked if he wanted to join the expedition.

Will's reply was an emphatic "Yes!" He had spent his first few days aboard the *Cambridge* on humdrum blockade duty, shooting ducks and gathering oysters with the men. Eager to go, he "at once made preparations for the work—put on my sword, loaded my revolver, took a Sharps rifle, and off we went."

The outset of the raid was uneventful; Will found it reminiscent of the Back River mission. His party saw rebel pickets in the brush along the way but did not take a single round of fire from shore.

They found the hundred-twenty-ton vessel—hull name *Ada*—about five miles up from the mouth of the creek. Driven aground by recent stormy weather, she lay high on a mudbank. On the shore nearby were seventy-five piles of corded wood, probably intended to go aboard as cargo.

Will was second to board the vessel, his pistol at the ready. But she was abandoned by her guards. A search turned up papers revealing she belonged to one Captain Pritchard, a notorious blockade runner whose name was known as far south as Charleston. It made the *Ada* a plum catch.

However Gwin and the men soon realized it would be impossible to claim her as a prize. Despite several tries at the cost of two broken hawsers, she would not budge. Their orders from Parker, then, were clear. They would take what they could off the schooner before burning her to the water's edge

Working quickly, they stripped the vessel of her running rigging and sails, all of which were reusable, and brought them onto the *Rescue* along with the firewood and some other items. Then they doused both the *Ada* and the woodpiles with turpentine and set them ablaze.

For two hours, they remained ashore to watch the ship burn, "making sure every part of her was in flames." Finally, the men went back to their gunboat and started downriver.

They were running straight into an ambush. The rebels had not fled but rallied at a narrow, tortuous section of the river called Mary's Point, around a hundred of them taking positions in the underbrush on both sides of the creek, with a company of two dozen riflemen waiting in a small house on the bank.

As the *Rescue* steamed past the point, a loud boom startled everyone on deck. Then a ball from a thirty-two-pound rifled artillery gun slammed into the canoe hanging on her port beam, blasting it to pieces and tearing it off the boat davits.

"*Struck once!*" Will shouted. His job was to man the ship's thirty-two-pounder smoothbore, and he went leaping over to it. No more than five feet away on either riverbank, the Confederate riflemen opened fire on the steamer from the concealing shrubbery. "*Now my lads, throw yourselves down behind the bulwarks and fire over them. Aim just where the smoke came from and let fly!*"

The shots from the hidden artillery piece coming "thick and fast," Will took his own instruction and trained his gun on the spot where he saw smoke rising from the bank.

Launched at close range, his first round of canister—a tin cylinder filled with iron pellets that dispersed on impact—exploded just in front of the rebel cannon and sent most of the artillerymen scampering for cover. But within an instant the cannon erupted again. Will continued throwing canister at the position until the great gun was finally silent, and then turned his attention to the house on the riverbank. Perched behind its windows, enemy riflemen directed a steady hail of fire at the tug.

Will fed a thirty-pound shell into his gun. He knew canisters would be ineffective; their payload was meant to rip through soft flesh and blood, not pierce wooden walls. But the fused, thirty-pound projectile, filled with black powder and shrapnel, would go off with devastating force.

The shell scored a direct hit, tearing the house "in pieces" and as Will would learn, killing or wounding every man inside. That took the fight out of the Southerners. Bloody and decimated, they triggered only a few more scattered rounds before the *Rescue*'s "gun and rifle finished the work, and [it] quietly steamed down the river" to the *Cambridge*.

The little gunship and crew had largely escaped serious harm despite losing the canoe and a spar. It had six shot holes through its hull and "any number of rifle balls lodged in [its] sides." Fortunately, none of the crew was killed, and only two wounded. When the shooting was over, Will discovered that one wooden splinter "torn off by a round shot" had pierced the fabric of his coat and lodged in his vest. He kept it as souvenir.

As the *Rescue* left the channel, it was greeted with cheers of elation from the sailors on the larger vessel's deck. They had heard sounds of the battle and been helpless to do anything but nervously await its outcome.

Captain Parker reported the mission as "perfectly successful" and conducted in a "spirited and brilliant manner." But there was more work to do over the next several days, and no one could rest.

At 8:00 a.m. November 8, the two Union vessels steamed a short distance north toward the town of Urbanna. The fugitive slaves had described a house on the riverbank used to store ammunition, as well as a Southern army encampment just to the rear of town.

Before reaching the storehouse, Parker saw an enemy battery, obliterated it with a barrage of cannon fire, and then continued upriver to

Urbanna. When the ships got there at 1:00 p.m., the town was "deserted by women and children. None but the soldiers remained."

Once again, the *Cambridge* relentlessly pounded her targets. After a full ninety minutes, Parker called a cease fire, dropped anchor, and had Lieutenant Gwin bring the *Rescue* closer inshore to resume the bombardment. By the time its guns fell silent, Urbanna was a deserted, smoking ruin. "We shelled them out of town in about two hours and cut out the mail boat from under their guns," Will recalled.

Parker kept steady pressure on the enemy over the course of the next two weeks. The day after their attack on Urbanna, the *Cambridge* and *Rescue* shelled more shore batteries. "They had not yet got their guns in position, but we demolished everything that was there." On November 12, the *Cambridge* returned to what remained of Urbanna for a cleanup operation and threw three shells at an abandoned magazine, incinerating its powder reserves. "After that," Will recollected, "we used to steam up the river thirty or forty miles every day to draw [Confederate] fire, but we had no more trouble."

The heavy action took its toll on the ship. Unfortunately, so did collisions with friendly merchantmen in bad weather. In the final weeks of November, the *Cambridge* "ran into a schooner, which we sunk, not without losing our bowsprit." Then an ocean gale blew in and caused more damage. The vessel was "strained" and began springing leaks.

Will heard she was going north for repairs, and longing to see his friends and family in Boston, crossed his fingers that the yard stay was more than speculation. Meanwhile, he found time to write letters. To Cousin Mary, he happily reported that Lon was back with Milton in Washington and "in perfect health," his weight up to a solid hundred-seventy pounds. In fact, Mary had seen him even more recently than Will; he'd felt well enough to attend her wedding before returning to active duty in mid-November.

Happiness over Lon's recovery aside, Will was effusive in praising his favorite brother's military accomplishments. "[He] has been promoted and is now chief of ordnance on General Sumner's staff," he wrote. "I don't know where he is going to stop in promotion. He ranks far above every man in his class. I am proud of his success, for I think such rapid advancement for a boy of twenty is entirely without precedent in the regular army." Turning to his own affairs, Will half-joked about the *Cambridge*'s poor condition, remarking that if she remained on duty in Southern waters much longer, "I might as well bid all my friends goodbye at once."

Will also found time to write his mother, giving her a graphic account the firefight on the Rappahannock. Unconcerned with the grey hairs he must have put on her head over the years, he exaggerated the size of the splinter that pierced his coat, mentioning it had been as large as his fist.

Will felt a need to prove his worth even to those who knew him best. Never content to be ordinary, he could hardly resist the urge to dress things up—like the toddler who'd once donned the stovepipe hat of a father who falsely claimed to be a doctor.

•   •   •

Shortly after her exploits behind enemy lines, the *Cambridge* received orders to leave the Rappahannock and take up duty on the Virginia Capes. Over the next three to four months, Will served primarily as her boarding officer. His routine was unvarying: he would bring suspected blockade runners to a halt with a warning shot from his pistol, inspect their papers for irregularities, and decide whether to search the vessel.

It was an arduous grind that taxed his physical endurance. The winter of 1861–62 was unusually severe over the mid-Atlantic states, with frigid temperatures, blowing winds, and frequent snow, sleet, and freezing rain. Will often found himself "out in open boats for five and six hours at a time, with the icy seas and sleet dashing over me continually. Several times I was too stiff upon return to step over the ship's side, and had to be hoisted on deck." His susceptibility to chronic bronchitis also led to a nagging, worsening cough.

Through all the rigors of the winter blockade, Will remained in a good humor. "I have thus far found my head in right place every night," he wrote Cousin Mary, directing most of his complaints at the shortcomings of his battered, creaky gunship. "The fighting days of the *Cambridge* are gone by, she is so much out of repair that she must go out of commission." The trip to Boston had failed to come about, but Will focused on the scuttlebutt about an ironclad being readied for sea by the Navy—one designed to counter an armored warship the rebels were said to be building out of the raised bones of the *Merrimack*. In one letter, he unequivocally told his cousin that he would transfer to her crew. How he knew this is unclear; he may have been dreaming, though he could have put in a request to Captain Parker or someone higher up the ladder. He'd clearly taken strong interest in speculation about her design and fighting capabilities. "She is two hundred feet long, [p]ierced for eighteen guns, and is heavily plated with iron. She is so constructed as to make any projectile that may strike her glance off," he wrote, adding, "When I get on her I shall be content."

But a newfound calm, if not contentment, had already settled over Will. He was grateful for the opportunity to be of service to the Navy and his country.

On February 24, he composed a letter to his mother that showed his growing maturity and newfound religious beliefs.

My Dear Mother,

It is blowing as if all the Nor'westers in the world had been tied up for the last twenty years, and had just broken loose. The waves have been rolling twenty feet high all the afternoon, dashing against us, and making the old ship shiver like a freezing giant...

The lower and top sail yards have been sent down and the top-masts housed. The wind howls through the rigging and the waves beat madly against us, waves that would almost dash right over our house at home. Madly they strive to rend this stout oaken frame, timber from timber.

Yet, how calm I feel, just the same as in the most beautiful calm that ever fell upon the bosom of old ocean.

A huge, roaring foam-crested mass of water comes dashing over the bows and sweeps the deck, fore and aft. Yet here am I with only six inches of plank between myself and the wild, deadly, sublime wrath of Nature's moving throne.

If there is one time more than another when one realizes God's greatness and His mercy, it is at such a moment as this. A man who has a heart, must think of the time when Christ said to such a sea "Peace! Be still."

He is *now* with those who are their country's defenders as He was with the apostles of old. His shield guards us and His arm is between us and death.

I am not, as yet, what the world calls a Christian, but I do believe implicitly in God's power and goodness, and that not even a sparrow can fall to the ground without His knowledge.

Often, I feel as held in the hand of God.

"They that go down to the sea in ships, that do business in great waters; these see the works of the Lord and his wonders in the deep."

As usual it is very late and I must turn in.

Give love to all dear ones.

Your affectionate son,
Wm. B. Cushing

•   •   •

The woman's first name was Mary; her surname may have been Louvestre or Louveste—spelled without the "r" by Secretary of the

Navy Gideon Welles—or even Touvestre. She was black, in her middle fifties, and wore the simple homespun clothing of the poor. Likely, she was an escaped slave; though some said she had bought her freedom with money earned through domestic skills.

What is indisputable is that on February 20, 1862, she arrived at the Department of the Navy requesting a private interview with Welles. "Not a word would she communicate in the presence of anyone," he recalled. There was a grave resolve in her demeanor.

Intrigued, Welles agreed to hear her out. When they were alone in his office, the woman revealed she was from Norfolk, Virginia, and brought news from the Gosport shipyard. Somehow, she had made the two-hundred-mile trip to the capital in the frightful cold, snow, and rain, passing through Confederate territory at "great risk to herself." By some accounts, she had received a written pass from her owner, or earlier owner, to visit a sick relative in the Shenandoah Valley. The pass, however, was used to go the other direction, past the Fredericksburg line into Union-held Alexandria, possibly with Underground Railroad assistance, which would have offered her food and shelter at safehouses along the way.

From Gosport, the woman brought information concerning the conversion of the frigate USS *Merrimack* into an ironclad warship. As she spoke, she pulled from the bosom of her dress a letter from an engineer at the yard. It is highly likely the engineer was William H. Lyons, who was Gosport's master mechanic and a Union spy, employed there since before the Southern takeover.

Welles had known about the work done on the frigate for some time. In the summer of 1861, he'd received intelligence—again likely from Lyons—that she had been raised from the Elizabeth River and was under rebuilding as a floating battery. But Welles soon grew suspicious that the rebels had more ambitious plans for the *Merrimack*. Plans in line with Stephen Mallory's goal of creating a fleet of steam-powered, fully mobile, armored gunships.

Still, Welles had a fuzzy picture of what was going on at the yard. The Confederates took "pains to keep their labors and purposes" secret and had even planted an intentionally deceptive newspaper editorial calling the vessel a failed "abortion" that would never float. Lyons, meanwhile, needed to be circumspect for his own safety. As Welles recalled, it was "with great difficulty" that the Navy Department could obtain reliable information from him and "others escaping through the lines," who were often fugitive slaves.

On Tuesday, January 28, 1862, a boat with fifteen escaped slaves had arrived at Fort Monroe with unsettling information. The *Merrimack* had been taken out of drydock the previous Saturday and made a trial run downriver the next day, mounting a ten-inch rifled cannon. Based on the slaves' account, shipyard workers and troops at Gosport were "jubilant in the belief that she could sink the whole federal fleet in Hampton Roads."

Early February had brought another report, this one from a Russian laborer who had been employed at the Norfolk yard. Showing up at the Roads as an informant, he reported the *Merrimack* was loaded with provisions and would soon be underway. At Fort Monroe, an anxious General Wool sent the report to Gideon Welles.

The secretary was only partly surprised. Though Welles had not thought the vessel so far along toward completion, he'd spent months preparing for the threat. In August 1861 he had appointed a special board of advisors to receive and examine proposals for a Union ironclad, sensing both sides of the conflict were racing toward a revolution in naval warfare. Chaired by his old friend Commodore Joseph Smith—whose "counsel and judgement" were of foremost value to him—the board included Gustavus Fox and two other admirals. On October 4, 1861, Welles signed off on a model they had favorably reviewed, imposing the condition that the shipbuilder deliver a seaworthy armored "turret vessel with guns of immense calibre" within a hundred days. At the builder's request, its name would be the *Monitor*, for it was meant to watch over the fleet.

But to Welles's disappointment, the contractor missed his January deadline, and February too had almost passed without delivery, taking with it a plan the secretary had kept secret from all but his closest advisors. For he had intended that "immediately after reaching Hampton Roads, the [ironclad] would "proceed up [the] Elizabeth River to the navy yard at Norfolk, place herself opposite the drydock, and with her heavy guns destroy both the dock and the *Merrimack*."

Welles knew that was moot now. The intelligence Mary Louveste (as he would remember her name) carried in her letter from Gosport corroborated everything else she told him. The *Merrimack* had left drydock and was ready to move on the attack. Moreover, the letter's detailed description of its armaments revealed the vessel had a fearsome cast iron ram at the bow.

Welles, no longer able to wait for the *Monitor* to be buffed and fully ready, sent an urgent, enciphered telegram to her captain at the Brooklyn Navy Yard:

> SIR: Proceed with the USS *Monitor*, under your command, to Hampton Roads, Virginia, and on your arrival there report by letter to the Department... Transmit to the Department a muster roll of the crew and a separate list of the officers of the *Monitor* before sailing from New York.

Unfortunately, a string of further delays would keep the ship in New York Harbor until March 7, by which time the *Merrimack* was poised to strike with devastating results.

●   ●   ●

Around 1:30 p.m. on Saturday, March 8, 1862, the officers and crew of the USS *Cambridge* were in a fine mood as they lay off Cape Henry on blockade duty. It was a beautiful sunny day over the Chesapeake, a light breeze coming from the northwest, the temperature having warmed almost to fifty degrees after a weeklong stretch of dampness and cold. There had been a chilly overnight fog, but it was gone by 8:00

a.m., giving the ship's lookout a clear field of visibility to Sewell's Point at the mouth of Hampton Roads.

Like his shipmates, Will was in good spirits, and not only because of the rare pleasant conditions up on the mast. Today was mail day, and Captain Parker had sent a boat to Fort Monroe for the delivery. When it had come rowing back to the ship minutes ago, loaded with mailbags, the men had greeted it with anticipation, eager to see what letters had arrived from home.

They had just taken in the boat when the lookout spotted a small fleet of vessels steaming down from Norfolk behind Sewell's Point, then rounding sharply west toward Hampton Roads. Three or four appeared to be a consort of gunboats and support ships. The leading ship, he thought with dismay, was surely the *Merrimack*—transformed, as had been long rumored, into an iron-plated monster. Mostly submerged, it slid low through the water, black smoke pouring from its stack, "like a sunken house with nothing but the roof above the tide."

Within moments, a signal gun cracked on the *Cambridge*'s deck, and her crew went rushing to quarters, mail delivery abruptly pushed to the back of their minds. Even as Captain Parker shouted out commands to the men, he realized his converted merchantman, with her handful of guns, could do little on her own to aid the squadron. But he also knew the old sailing frigate USS *St. Lawren*ce, boasting no fewer than fifty guns and a crew of five hundred, was some five miles to the south in the Chesapeake. If he could tow her to the Roads, her powerful broadside batteries might inflict substantial punishment on the rebels.

Parker bore over to the frigate at top speed, pulled alongside, and apprised her captain, Hugh Purviance, of the dire situation. The frigates *Cumberland* and *Congress* were under threat of attack off Newport News and needed to muster support.

The *St. Lawrence* slipped her lines at once. At 2:30 pm, Purviance called out *"All hands up anchor!"* and she was in tow for the Roads. But it would be three long hours before the *Cambridge* pulled the heavy old warship as far as Sewell's Point, where the crews of both vessels saw the USS *Roanoke* stalled in the water, her lines attached to three straining tugboats.

Will would discover that she and the *Minnesota*, his former ship, had been on patrol near Fort Monroe when the rebel attackers went steaming through the harbor mouth. Calling for tugs to help them negotiate the shallow harbor waters, the two deep draft frigates immediately started in pursuit—the *Minnesota* steaming after the rebels at a fair seven or eight knots. But *Roanoke*'s screw shaft broke, and the tugs, for all their muscle, could not get her to stem the current.

The *St. Lawrence* and *Cambridge* had no sooner passed her than they began taking fire from the Confederate batteries—some thirty-one guns—at Sewell's Point. One of the shells exploded low on the *St. Lawrence*'s bow but she was only slightly damaged. The *Cambridge* attempted to reply, the rounds from her eight-inch guns falling short of the enemy batteries, as did two full broadsides from the *St. Lawrence*. The *Cambridge*'s pivoted rifles, with their greater range, were effective. Manning one of them, Will took adrenaline-fueled joy in shooting away the rebel flagstaff, silently vowing to repeat his feat of gunnery if the banner reappeared.

At 5:25 p.m., the two vessels cleared Sewell's Point and entered the harbor. It was near dusk. Will never forgot the carnage before his eyes. Flames painted the water orange in the dying light. "The *Cumberland* had gone down hiding her crushed sides and bloody decks beneath the waters of the James," he later remembered. "[A] white flag at the masthead of the *Congress* told us that her fate was sealed, and that her brave commander, Joe Smith, was no more." Joe Smith was his cousin, the thirty-year-old son of Commodore Joseph Smith. Will had known the younger Smith his entire life.

He found out later that the *Merrimack*, escorted by her tugs, had made directly for the *Cumberland* after entering the harbor. She glided past the *Congress* to starboard, three hundred yards away, hitting the ship with broadsides, her bow gun firing grapeshot at the targeted frigate ahead. Keeping a steady course for the *Cumberland*, she continued to fire away as the two vessels struck back with volley after volley. But their fire had no effect, "the balls glancing upwards, and flying off, having only the effect of checking her progress for a moment."

There were heavy spars at the *Cumberland*'s bow, a defense from underwater mines. As the *Merrimack* closed in, she tore through them as if they were piles of sticks, then plowed into the doomed frigate's hull amidships with a "noise of crashing timbers [that] was distinctly heard above the din of the battle."

"Take to the boats!" shouted her captain. His ship was lost.

The men hardly had a chance before she went down with her colors flying, the ram buried inside her like an iron tusk. As she listed onto her side, water lapping over her deck, she nearly pulled her attacker down with her. But the *Merrimack* drew free, fired another broadside at the frigate, "again dashed against her with her ironclad prow, and knock[ed] in her side." Her rigging mangled, her topmasts poking up above the waterline, the crippled frigate sank helplessly to the bottom, men leaping overboard to save themselves.

A quarter mile to the east, the *Congress* had hoisted her jib and topsails, desperately making for shore after a brief but ferocious engagement with two of the Southern escorts. Seeing the *Cumberland*'s swift destruction, Captain Smith wanted to avoid a similar fate for his ship and hoped the Union land batteries could protect her.

He was too late. *Merrimack* had swung back around on the offensive. Even with a tug helping her along, the *Congress* ran aground as the ironclad approached, sealing her fate.

Merrimack had not escaped her collision with the *Cumberland* unscathed. As she wrenched free of the mortally wounded vessel, most of her ram had broken away, but there was nothing wrong with her broadsides. They raked the *Congress* with grape and hot shot and alternately pounded the Union shore batteries that had opened fire from Newport News. Three of the rebel escorts soon joined the barrage on the frigate, "firing with precision and doing great damage."

Stranded, under attack from several directions at once, the *Congress* was an easy target. Her guns knocked out by direct hits, men were "swept away from them with great rapidity and slaughter," some falling to balls fired from the friendly batteries. Soon the decks were awash with blood. Struck in the chest by a shell fragment, Will's cousin, Captain Smith, had died instantly. Over a hundred members of the crew perished in the vicious encounter.

Informed of Smith's death, the ship's executive officer had made a grim decision. With his commander lost, his men killed "without any hope of relief," and not a single functional gun left to bear against the enemy, he reluctantly hoisted the white flag, manning the boats and sending the wounded ashore.

Surrender did not spare the *Congress* from destruction. Fires had broken out in her main hold, sickbay, and wardroom, and they were rapidly spreading throughout the ship. As dusk fell on Hampton Roads, the sky turned red with the glow of her burning.

On the *Cambridge*, Will Cushing no sooner saw this terrible scene than he realized the rebels were not finished. Just inside the harbor mouth, the *Minnesota* lay grounded on a sandbank. Will could see the *Merrimack* bearing down on her from Newport News, supported by three Confederate gunboats. As the *Cambridge* and *St. Lawrence* sailed into the channel, *Merrimack* took position off the flagship's starboard bow and opened fire.

It was now ten minutes to six, nightfall, and the harbor was still illuminated by flames. The *Minnesota*'s batteries, erupting in her defense, could do nothing to penetrate her attacker's armor—and the flagship's plight was about to worsen. As the *Cambridge* moved up the channel in aid, the *St. Lawrence* rumbled to a sudden, jolting halt close behind on her tow line. Incredibly, she had also run hard aground in the harbor's shallow water and shifting currents.

With the tug *Young America*, Captain Parker tried to pull the frigate back afloat, knowing her batteries were desperately needed against the *Merrimack*.

But then the *Cambridge* herself came under fire. The *Merrimack* and her consorts had no intention of letting her get any closer.

The *Cambridge* responded with what little firepower she could bring to bear. At his pivot gun, Will heard a loud boom overhead, felt a sudden burst of heat, and then a stinging pain low in his forearm. A 104-pound shell had detonated above the deck, gauging out an inch of flesh above his wrist and leaving his jacket sleeve torn and bloodied. Also wounded were several other seamen, among them a fellow officer and member of the gun crew. But they remained at quarters exchanging fire with the ironclad terror.

The engagement continued for close to an hour. And then, as dusk turned to darkness, an abrupt lull fell over the harbor. Without warning, the *Merrimack* and her escorts hauled off from the *Minnesota*, skirting past the *Cambridge* and *St. Lawrence*, as they rumbled back toward Sewell's Point.

But flames and wreckage remained. After dark, the *Cambridge* returned to the *St. Lawrence*, made fast, and towed her to Fort Monroe. Parker asked permission to go to the *Minnesota*'s aid but was ordered to remain in the anchorage. Assistant Secretary Fox had arrived at the fortress ahead of the battle, watched the *Merrimack* retreat under fair headway and concluded she was not seriously damaged. Believing she would return under the morning light to try and finish what she'd started, he wanted the *Cambridge* to, in Will's words, prepare "for a desperate and hopeless fight."

Will was in a bleak mood—and understandably so, after his cousin Joe's death and his own injury. But later that night, his wound cleaned and bandaged, he penned a letter to his mother that showed courage and resilience had not deserted him:

> I am all right for tomorrow's fight. I was highly complimented by the Captain and Commodore. The Captain said, "You are highly honored in being the only officer wounded." I do feel so.

My hand is very stiff and I can't write more. The rebels took us by surprise.... Some of the frigates must have lost a great deal of life. Two were destroyed. You can imagine how hot the fire was. I shot the rebel flagstaff away on the Sewell's Point battery with my rifle gun, and I will try to do as well tomorrow.

While it would be a long, restless night at the Roads, the fleet received some encouragement around 9:00 p.m. The men aboard the *Cambridge* were in position for a close look. One member of the crew, a Mainer named Williston Jennings, was on watch when he saw "a funny looking little craft [come] in and lay-to off our starboard bow." Its deck awash, no more than two feet above the water, she looked like a raft with a big tank on her deck."

After the wholesale destruction caused by the *Merrimack,* the vessel's approach had put the men on edge...until the officers informed them it was the Union ironclad USS *Monitor.* "She reported to the flagship and then steamed up to where the *Minnesota* lay aground," Jennings recalled.

Will felt hope spread among the crewmen. The *Monitor*'s "providential arrival changed the aspect of affairs, and we waited the morrow with an eagerness amounting to impatience."

But as the *Monitor* guarded the vulnerable *Minnesota* through the night, the *Congress* burned at the far end of the harbor. The rampant fire extended from her hull to the top of her main mast, her standing rigging ablaze against the silhouetted buildings of Newport News. Between midnight and 1:00 a.m., the flames reached into the ship's magazine, and she blew up with a terrific roar that echoed across the water and brought the entire crew of the *Cambridge* on deck. The men could only watch in horror as whatever was left of the *Congress* went down into the cold, dark water.

She was gone.

•   •   •

A little before noon on Sunday, March 9, a pensive Gideon Welles left the White House after an emergency meeting of the cabinet, walked across Lafayette Square, and decided to stop briefly at St. John's Church on his way home. A large accumulation of dispatches from Hampton Roads had told him everything he needed to know about the horror visited on the fleet by the *Merrimack*. What he did not know was whether his answer to the ironclad, the *Monitor,* had arrived from New York in time to fight off a second attack. The uncertainty was like a cat clawing at his mind.

Welles's fellow cabinet members were thrown into a downcast mood by the news, with Secretary of War Edwin Stanton predictably the most agitated. Welles disliked the impulsive Stanton, thinking him a sensationalist, quick to disparage any opinions not his own. And that morning he'd been at his emphatic worst, Welles thought, barely letting others in the cabinet speak.

"The *Merrimack* will change the whole character of the war...she will destroy [one after another] every naval vessel...lay all the cities on the seaboard under contribution," he'd rattled off without a breath. "I will notify the Governors and municipal authorities in the North to take instant measures to protect their harbors!" Known for courtroom theatrics, Stanton turned toward a window and nodded toward the wide Potomac outside. "I have no doubt the monster is at this moment on her way to Washington," he exclaimed. "Not unlikely, we shall have a shell or cannonball from one of her guns in the White House before we leave this room!"

Secretary of State Seward's grizzled brows had sunk at that fantastic prediction; his sensitive nature made him prone to depression. But offer him a bit of hope, and he would take it.

"It is doubtful whether the vessel, so loaded with armor, would venture outside of the Capes...certainly she cannot, with her draft of water, get into the sounds of North Carolina," Welles assured him.

Then he'd glanced pointedly at Stanton. "Nor is she omnipresent, to make general destruction at New York, Boston, Port Royal, and so on, at the same time."

The Secretary of War frowned. "What is the size and strength of this *Monitor*?" he challenged skeptically. "How many guns does she carry?"

Welles stayed calm. "Two," he said. "But of large calibre."

Stanton turned away from him with a mixture of contempt, amazement, and distress. But Seward's despair lifted visibly.

"We have, perhaps, given away too much to our apprehensions," Welles went on. "I see no alternative but to wait and hear what our new battery might accomplish."

With that, Stanton huffed out a disgusted breath and left the room. Moments later President Lincoln ordered his carriage and followed him out, heading over to the Navy Yard to poll his naval officers for their opinions on the situation. Welles, exhausted, decided to head home to freshen up for what was sure to be a long, nervous day ahead.

He now exhaled wearily and stepped under the porticoed entrance to St. John's Church. Some peaceful moments of worship could do no harm, he thought.

But he gained no reprieve inside the church. As he walked up the aisle, he saw his dear friend Commodore John Smith there for the service. Knowing the *Congress*, commanded by his son, had gone down, he felt it his responsibility to break the news to him.

Smith pulled him aside by the arm, spoke to him quietly. The Commodore's face went white.

"The *Congress*, sunk!" he exclaimed. He began hastily buttoning his coat. "Then Joe is dead!"

Welles shook his head, thinking the conclusion premature. "That does not follow. The officers and crew doubtless escaped, for the shore was not distant."

But Smith just stared at him with chilling calmness. "You don't know Joe as well as I do," he said, his eyes never deviating from the secretary's face. "He would not survive his ship."

Welles never forgot Smith's cold, steady gaze as he finished buttoning up and then hurried outside. He would see it clearly in his mind not long after their chance encounter, when he learned that Joe had indeed perished at Hampton Roads. There in the church, it had not mattered that John Smith was one of the most powerful men in the United States Navy. To Welles, he was simply a father among many anguished fathers who had suffered the loss of a beloved son in battle.

Now he would have to find the words to tell the boy's mother.

•   •   •

At 6:00 a.m. Sunday, a bright, clear dawn broke over Hampton Roads. Although the water was calm and eerily quiet, there was hurried activity aboard the federal squadron's surviving vessels.

On the *Cambridge*, Will Cushing and his shipmates piled their folded hammocks and seabags around the engine and boiler before going up to the deck. Captain Porter had ordered all hands to stow them there in anticipation of battle, hoping to cushion the impact of enemy fire.

Once at his station, Will saw the rebel fleet "pressing boldly out [from Sewell's Point] . . . to finish the awful havoc that she had inaugurated" the night before. The sun glistened off the ironclad's side as she steamed toward the *Minnesota*, preceded by the Confederate sidewheel gunship *Yorktown* with her varied armaments. Despite the concentrated efforts to pull her off the shoal overnight, Will's old ship was still close to where she had grounded.

Meaning to offer her aid, Captain Porter dropped anchor and waited for the frigate, but a signal from the *Roanoke* brought him to an abrupt standstill. The flag officer wanted none of his vessels blocking the channel.

Will quickly learned the reason, noticing "a black speck that moved out from behind [the *Minnesota*], something far from prepossessing in appearance and calculated to excite laughter, were it not that it bore the grand old flag, that would never have risked disgrace."

The *Monitor* had hovered protectively near the frigate overnight and was making straight for the oncoming *Merrimack*.

There were several loud percussive bursts as the rebels' opening volleys struck the *Minnesota*. Watching from a distance, Will could not have known whether they issued from the ironclad or her consorts, though he was certain they caused severe damage—indeed the fire killed and wounded many aboard the frigate. The *Minnesota* issued an immediate retort, but she had settled into a pocket of soft mud that left her broadsides tilted upward and made her shells go astray. Still, the single heavy gun she could bring accurately to bear scored a direct hit against one of the tugs, sending her back to Sewell's Point in a crippled condition, a large shell buried in her ribs.

Then the *Monitor* closed with the Confederate ironclad. Will saw "a puff of smoke [roll] lazily from [her] turret" with her first shot—and the battle was on. "The two now went to work in earnest fighting at close quarters, exchanging iron blows that cracked sharp and distinct against adamantine sides," he later wrote.

Guns roaring, they dueled for a time without either sustaining major harm. Along with thousands of others on the shore and in the anchorage, the *Cambridge*'s men were no more than anxious spectators to the clash, Will recalled, "riveting us with intense interest to the scene."

To the astonishment of the *Minnesota*'s Captain von Brunt, the *Merrimack* dwarfed the *Monitor* in size, the federal ironclad's shallow draft being half that of the Confederate warship's. Still, he thought them evenly matched. "Gun after gun was fired by the *Monitor*, [their fire] returned with whole broadsides from the rebels, with no more effect than so many pebblestones thrown by a child," he reported. "After a while they commenced maneuvering and we could see the little battery point her bow for the rebels, with the intention, as I thought, of sending a shot through her bow porthole; then she would shoot by her and rake her through her stern. In the meantime, the rebel was pouring [repeated broadsides], but almost all her shot flew over the [submerged propellor], and when they struck the bomb-proof tower the shot glanced off without producing any effect."

On the *Cambridge*, Seaman Jennings saw the *Merrimack* make several attempts to ram the federal ironclad, "as she did the *Cumberland*, but she was so slow that before she could get at her the [smaller] craft was somewhere else."

The morning's battle had raged for forty minutes when, at 9:30 a.m., the *Cambridge* received orders to move toward the Confederate-occupied Fort Macon in Beaufort, North Carolina. The flag officer had received intelligence that the captain of the rebel steamer *Nashville*, in the company of two experienced Southern blockade-running pilots, had arrived in Bermuda on February 28 aboard a fully loaded cargo steamer from London. Now, the *Nashville* had anchored at a railroad wharf outside Fort Macon just two months after she was caught transporting a heavy shipment of British rifles to a Confederate port. The logical deduction was that her captain was again about to transport foreign arms to the rebels, to be loaded by rail under the fort's protective guns.

Captain Porter immediately weighed anchor and made down the bay. The *Merrimack* had, at that point, retreated toward the mouth of the Elizabeth River and fallen out of sight behind Sewell's Point. At the same time, the *Monitor* had steamed closer to the *Minnesota*. Everyone aboard the *Cambridge* hoped that meant victory for the little Union ironclad some were calling a "cheesebox on a raft." But it would be a while before they were certain.

As for Will Cushing, he knew one thing without question as his ship made off: it had been "a day big with the fate of future navies." The *Cambridge* was heading toward an enemy harbor, where it—and he—could be of far greater use than at Hampton Roads. Perhaps some action on behalf of Old Glory lay ahead.

In the meantime, he ignored the dull throb in his wounded hand, unaware of the infection spreading through it.

●   ●   ●

Beaufort Harbor, between Cape Henry and the Cape Fear River at the southern boundary of the Outer Banks, was North Carolina's only deep water ocean port and a vital commercial shipping center for the Confederacy. On Tuesday, March 11, the *Cambridge* reached the choppy waters off Fort Macon, a pentagonal, stone-and-brick-walled citadel built to guard the harbor after the War of 1812. Already on station was the heavily armed steam gunboat USS *State of Georgia,* with the bark *Gemsbok* in support

The blockaders' plan was simple: They would anchor outside the range of the fortress's guns, ready to intercept the *Nashville* whenever she tried to make away with her cargo of rifles. But the *Nashville*'s skipper had several distinct advantages. He could push his lightweight cruiser to thirteen knots, two or three knots beyond what the *State of Georgia's* commander James Armstrong had been able to coax out of his lumbering ship on her best days. Also, the harbor had three channels by which the speedy *Nashville* could slip into the sea, leading Armstrong to conclude it would take a force of five steamers to bottle her up.

The *Cambridge*'s arrival made for just three federal vessels on station—and the *Gemsbok's* power was by sails alone. Meanwhile, the fort's rebel garrison was keeping a close eye on the flotilla, signaling its attention on March 12 by firing two warning shots from the ramparts, one of which splashed into the water just thirty yards from the *State of Georgia.* The next day, at 9:00 a.m., and then at 1:00 p.m., heavy cannonades could be heard rumbling from the fort.

Will was riled by the enemy's bold defiance. All the waiting frustrated him. With the weather deteriorating, he felt the time had come to end it, and he wanted an active role in doing so. It did not matter that after months on the ship's frigid deck as boarding officer, he'd fallen into a poor state of health or that his hand was looking worse—over the past two or three days it had gotten increasingly red and swollen.

His patience wore even thinner on March 15, when the *Cambridge*'s lookout saw the *Nashville* move closer to the harbor mouth, getting up steam for her departure. Then on the next day, the *State of Georgia* returned to the Roads to replenish her depleted coal supply, leaving the *Cambridge* and *Gemsbock* at anchor off the port.

Tired of Captain Parker's inaction, Will approached him with the idea of leading a cutting-out party into the harbor to capture the blockade-runner. Parker refused; he was not about to deviate from his plan on the suggestion of a young subordinate and felt he had the *Nashville*'s channel of escape covered.

Will took the captain's turndown personally.

The night of March 17 was pitch dark, with the moon not yet risen, and the water's surface black and featureless. The *Cambridge* lay a mile outside the harbor's southeastern channel, the *Gemsbok* about a half a mile away off the shorter, shallower south channel. At twenty minutes to eight, the little bark's lookout saw, in near silhouette, the *Nashville* pulling out to sea from Fort Macon without a light on. As the men beat to quarters, she signaled the *Cambridge* with a rocket flare and report from her bow gun, then turned her twenty starboard broadsides toward the channel. A sailing ship could not outrace a steamer, but she might cut her off in flight.

The moment the *Nashville* came under the bark's guns, her crews fired as quickly as they could load. The enemy's lights twice flashed fore and aft, a coded signal for assistance. That convinced the *Gemsbok*'s skipper Edward Cavendy that she was struck, but her fireman stoked her blast higher and away she sped.

About the same time that the *Nashville* moved out of range of the bark's guns, the *Cambridge* appeared to the southeast. No one aboard had seen the *Nashville*, but they had seen the *Gemsbok*'s shells explode to the north and fired their port guns into the night. But the blockade-runner had already escaped with her cargo of arms.

In the days and weeks that followed, Parker would offer the Navy its pick of explanations for the botched mission. It was the intense darkness, the absence of any other steamships on blockade, and bad information from the *Gemsbok*'s pilot that there was "not sufficient water in the channel through which [the *Nashville*] escaped for her to pass out." Leaving no excuse untried, he also pointed out that the *Nashville* was a "much faster steamer than the *Cambridge*."

Cavendy frowned at those claims in his own report. "I feel confident in saying that had I been in charge of a steamer instead of a sailing vessel, with my present officers and crew, the course of the *Nashville* would have been finished," he said unambiguously. Will would never let go of his disdain for Parker afterward. "[The captain] should have worn petticoats instead of the blue and gold of a dashing service," he wrote scathingly.

The episode was a disappointing blow to the prestige of the blockade squadron after its impressive victory at Hampton Roads. An embarrassed and angry Gustavus Fox called it a "Bull Run for the Navy." Gideon Welles approved of a Court of Inquiry that led to recriminations flying in all directions and eventually delivered a mild wrist slap for Parker.

But long before the inquiry got underway, the *Nashville* successfully delivered her rifle shipment, loaded more Confederate freight at Wilmington, and stole past blockaders again, masquerading as a British vessel named the *William L. Wragg*.

By that time, Will had detached from the *Cambridge*, granted a month's sick leave by a panel of naval medical personnel. Weakened by exposure and his wound seriously infected, the nineteen-year-old left for Fredonia on March 27 and placed himself under his mother's care.

•   •   •

Will arrived at Mary Cushing's doorstep in terrible shape. Emaciated and feverish, his hand a source of constant pain, he was suffering a severe recurrence of the hacking coughs that would plague him throughout his life.

His worried mother put him to bed at once and spent the next several weeks nursing him. For the first two weeks, there was no improvement.

Confined to his old upstairs room, he soaked his sheets with sweat and could hardly sleep at night because of the aching discomfort in his hand.

As mid-April sunshine bathed the mountains of western New York, Will's health finally took a major turn for the better. He had already grown impatient with his convalescence; most of the young men he'd known growing up were off to war, and Lon was far away with the Army of the Potomac. Gone, too, was Cousin Mary, who had settled into married life with her new husband in Wisconsin. Without those closest to him, Fredonia was a lonely place.

Shortly before May, Will's childhood friend Ella Kingsbury told him of a social at the old First Baptist Church of Fredonia. Ella still lived in the house where she'd grown up across the street; it was her father, the pastor, whose cow a ten-year-old Will had taken out to graze for pennies a day.

The night of the get-together, a bored and restless Will slipped out his window, shimmied down the porch column, and hastened over to the church near the town common. His mother, who had restricted her patient's activities to his bedroom, only learned of his escape, to some amusement, once he returned hours later. His time away at war had changed him, she noted; he now carried himself with his head high and his shoulders thrown back like a true military man. But underneath it, she still the saw a mischievous boy who was "impatient of restraint... quick to feel, and prompt to act."

"You must be feeling well," she said in a stern tone meant to camouflage her affection.

"I suppose," he said, hardly fooled.

Both knew he would soon be leaving her tender care.

Just days later, in fact, Will received orders to report to his former ship the USS *Minnesota*. Having undergone extensive repairs after the *Merrimack*'s attack, she was now back on duty at Hampton Roads. He was to leave Fredonia at the earliest opportunity.

First, though, he took the time to stop by the offices of the *Censor*, where his brother Howard had worked as a printer's devil. Thinking

Will's exploits with the Navy would be of local interest, the editor had asked him to recount them for a feature story. He happily obliged, adding some obligatory flourishes.

Mary Barker Smith Cushing wasn't pleased. Very much a Puritan at heart, she believed his naval service a matter of duty, not glory-seeking; nor did she approve of her son's knack for peppering his stories with detailed recollections of violence and bloodshed. But Will, who always brought a gleam to her eye, talked her into giving the editor his letters home for publication.

He was back on the *Minnesota* by the end of the month, no longer a master's mate but a seasoned midshipman. After six weeks of inactivity, he was feeling healthy and rested and was eager to rejoin the war.

He did not have long to wait.

CHAPTER TEN

WARLIKE ANTICIPATIONS

On March 11, 1862, two days after the *Monitor* fended off the *Mer-rimack* at Hampton Roads, President Lincoln removed George McClellan from his role as the general-in-chief of the Union Army, leaving him to continue as top officer of the Army of the Potomac.

Months earlier, McClellan had devised a plan to transport a hundred thousand troops over the Rappahannock River to the tidewater town of Urbanna, Virginia—thereby outflanking the rebel forces encamped near Washington—and then march them fifty miles to Richmond, where they would seize the Confederate capital. Naval support was to arrive via the James River, with the ships embarking from Fort Monroe. But for a variety of reasons, McClellan's operation had stalled for weeks, convincing some in Washington that his willingness to do battle did not match his organizational skills. When the general suffered a bout of typhoid fever in early January, he delayed the attack until spring, angering Lincoln's top congressional supporters and advisors. Believing the combined pressures were too much for McClellan, they suggested dividing the positions of supreme commander and leader of the Army of the Potomac.

Lincoln's support for McClellan may have weakened, but it held up until early March. However, the destruction brought to the fleet by the rebel ironclad on March 8, mixed with concerns that enemy troops were about to launch a long-feared offensive against Fort Monroe, strained his patience. Convinced it was necessary to strike a blow upon the Confederacy, Lincoln acted. In the future, McClellan was to serve as head of the Army of the Potomac only and concentrate his energies on the taking of Richmond. An angry McClellan complied.

By this time, McClellan had also abandoned his original plan. The *Merrimack* was repulsed but not destroyed. She was still a fearsome presence looming over the James River, a threat to the entire wooden fleet. Lincoln's closest aides panicked, worrying that she would attack and sink their ships even as they tried their amphibious troop deliveries. McClellan concurred. He proposed to move the Army of the Potomac to the Virginia Peninsula between the James and York Rivers and lead them northwest in an overland march to Richmond.

Lincoln approved the idea despite his private reservations that fighting would be prolonged and bloody. He did not see how the army could avoid going head-to-head with a deeply entrenched enemy in its push through Southern territory and prayed they would not find themselves surrounded and cut off from aid and resupply.

His misgivings were justified. The advance was slow, fitful, and marked with a series of costly engagements. The worst bloodshed came in early June when Southern forces under General Robert E. Lee retreated toward their capital to form resolute defensive lines. Casualties mounted on both sides, leaving the fields strewn with corpses.

As a member of General Sumner's staff, Alonzo Cushing experienced some of the campaign's fiercest fighting. In the closing days of May, the Confederates ambushed the Army of the Potomac at a rail terminus called Fair Oaks Station outside Richmond. On a muddy road littered with bodies, Lon was bringing dispatches to the front when his mount collapsed underneath him. As Lon toppled to the ground, a bullet struck him in the chest. He survived, unlike his horse, by a stroke of luck: a small dispatch book and pistol he'd tucked away in a breast pocket stopped the round. With only the wind knocked out of him, he fought on for hours until the enemy finally retreated into the woods. "We slept with the dead and wounded all around us that night," he remembered, "but the groans did not disturb me much as I was tired…the Confederate dead were heaped three deep on the field in some places, and we were three days in burying them, and then had to burn a great many which had become exceedingly offensive."

The next few weeks brought a lull in the conflict. With the Confederates withdrawn toward Richmond, and Union troops marshaling at the city's outskirts in substantial numbers, Lon grew convinced the enemy's fall was near. Nothing blunted his optimism—not the incessant rainfall, steamy temperatures, long, wet days in the saddle, constant shelling from rebel batteries, or outbreaks of highly infectious typhoid and malaria in camp. "If their whole army was unable to whip half of ours as it stood ten days ago, how beautifully we will be able to sweep over their whole force, entrenchments and all, when our reinforcements come," he wrote Will on June 10. "Hoping you may get a few days leave and come up to see me in Richmond when I get my quarters established there."

But Lon's confidence in a swift victory proved chimerical. General Lee and his forces had regrouped around the Southern capital, bolstering their strength with Stonewall Jackson's grizzled infantry command—the same howling foot brigade that had routed the federals at Bull's Run. Fought around Richmond from June 25–July 1, a series of vicious engagements known as the Seven Days Battle rocked McClellan's confidence and led him to retreat to Harrison's Landing, a deepwater site along the James River that was part of the sprawling, Union-occupied Berkeley Plantation.

Staggered by the loss of 16,000 men, McClellan's army spent a month recovering on the banks of the James as Union gunboats hung offshore on picket duty and a steady stream of transports brought arms and supplies from Fort Monroe, returning loaded with the sick, wounded, and Confederate prisoners of war.

On July 4, a disheartened Lon was temporarily reattached to Battery A of the 4th Artillery at the request of General Sumner, who had selected him to fill the vacant post of chief ordnance officer, a promotion that came with two brevets acknowledging his steady courage and dependability under fire. Lon stayed in camp while readying himself for his new assignment—and it was there that he got his wish to see Will, if under different circumstances than he'd envisioned back in June.

What would bring the brothers together was a major summit about to take place at Harrison's Landing. Convened by the president, it had in attendance General McClellan and the North Atlantic Blockading Squadron's new flag officer, Commodore Louis M. Goldsborough. The president was unhappy with the way things had gone on the peninsula and wanted an explanation from McClellan, as well as a plan for moving forward with the campaign.

It was early evening on Tuesday, July 8, when Lincoln and his aides sailed up to Harrison's Landing aboard the schooner USS *Ariel*. On their approach, they received a ceremonial cannonade from the *Minnesota*, aboard which the red-bearded, 300-pound Commodore Goldsborough had already arrived for the conference. In an extraordinary bit of serendipity for the Cushing boys, Will was chosen for Goldborough's staff and accompanied him ashore.

Without wasting any time, Will managed to duck out of the flag officer's sight and hurriedly found his brother amid the multitude of tents along the riverbank. Lon, ecstatic, introduced him to General Sumner, who in turn introduced him to the "most noted generals"— namely Couch, Hooker, Sedgewick, and Peck, the corps commanders of the Army of the Potomac—and then brought him out for Lincoln's twilight review of the regiments. Thousands of muskets fired into the darkening sky in salute, their reports followed by hearty applause, as the president rode up and down the lines on horse. His presence gave a needed boost to their devastated morale.

At Sumner's invitation, the Cushing brothers joined Lincoln's mounted entourage, trotting along behind the generals. Honored, Will rode proud and upright, noting how tall the president was in the saddle, and how he looked even taller in his black stovepipe hat. He was roused by the way men stared at Lincoln as he passed their excited ranks, occasionally making eye contact with one of them or pausing to lift his hat off his head and wave it around to acknowledge their cheers. Most, if not all, of the soldiers at the inspection shared Will's awe. "What a depth of devotion, sympathy, and reassurance were conveyed through his smile," wrote one in his journal. "We knew that 'Old Abe'—as he was called by the people that loved him, trusted him—was true."

The review lasted three hours, finally ending at nine o'clock that night when Lincoln, McClellan, and Goldborough hustled off to conduct their talks. Will did not, however, go back to the tent reserved for the flag officer's aides... or even to the *Minnesota* the next day. Instead, he stayed out of sight, secretly bunking in his brother's tent. Listening raptly to Lon's stories of the Seven Days Battle, he became "so fired up" that he "could not resist the temptation, in defiance of discipline" to fulfill his old vision of fighting alongside Lon with the artillery corps.

Rumor had it that the rebels were preparing for a major push to drive the Union forces out of Harrison's Landing. By then, Will had commanded cannon crews and worked big naval guns in the heat of action. He knew he could do the same thing on the ground and dreaded having to endure another dull stretch of blockade duty. Why not be of use in the camp's defense?

Will might have volunteered for the land service, but no attack occurred, possibly because the Confederates had intelligence that McCellan was planning to withdraw later that summer. Will, "disappointed in my warlike aspirations," decided to make haste back to Norfolk and avoid reprimand.

Irritated by his disappearance, Commodore Goldsborough instead put him under suspension, but his punishment would soon end.

A former superintendent of the Naval Academy, Goldsborough was "a typical seaman of the old school; imposing in person, loud in voice, genial in temperament, and very much inclined to let the youngsters have their way up to a certain limit. [C]omplaints of the midshipman's misbehavior, so long as he knew it was of the sort which had always been peculiar to midshipmen since they first began, rather nettled him."

"As a midshipman is hardly considered a responsible being, I was soon released [from suspension]," Will wrote later, alluding to Commodore Goldsborough's general level of tolerance. But his old family friend Secretary Welles was likely pulling strings behind the scenes.

The timing was also right for Will. On July 16, Abraham Lincoln signed the Navy Grade Pay and Regulation Act of 1862, which advanced sweeping changes in the Navy's organization and pay scale. In large part enacted to address a shortage of line officers, the decree ordered Secretary of the Navy Gideon Welles to promote and commission hundreds of new officers from the grade of master's mate and up.

Back at Norfolk, Will could not help but foster hopes of a jump in rank. Yes, he'd had some unpleasant brushes with naval discipline. But he had always conducted himself well in the heat of action. He felt deserving of promotion under the president's act and waited optimistically for notification from the Department.

In the meantime, he returned to blockade duty aboard the *Minnesota*, occasionally volunteering to assist with mail runs to relieve boredom. These pickups and deliveries had their own distinct hazards; the Union held hostile possession of the Virginia and North Carolina waters, and rebel snipers along the shore were a constant concern. During one run, Will was in the mail steamer's pilothouse when five bullets pecked through its side, one bullet taking off three of the pilot's fingers.

Will mentioned this matter-of-factly in a letter to Cousin Mary just before signing off with a simple goodbye. The newlywed must have been thrilled to read such cheerful parting words.

•   •   •

In August 1862, after the new legislation passed Congress, Welles's handpicked advisory board signed off on a document backdated to July 16. It read:

> We hereby certify that William Barker Cushing has the moral, mental, physical and professional qualifications to perform efficiently all his duties, both at sea and on shore, of the grade to which he is to be promoted, and recommend him for promotion.

Will had achieved nearly everything he'd wanted since his first year at Annapolis, despite his many problems. He jumped two full ranks to lieutenant and received a large hike in pay. To his mother, he was exuberant, "Perhaps it will interest you to know that I can glory in being the only man who has ever reached my rank at anywheres my age. Just think! A lieutenant in the most exclusive branch of the regular service. I rank with a captain in the regular army, and get nearly two thousand dollars a year, and I am not yet twenty. Aren't you glad for me, mother dear?" What was more, Will could at last repay his mother for her lifetime of difficult sacrifice. "I can, as regularly as clockwork, send home $50 monthly," he wrote. "No more work for you, dear Mother. No more toil and sorrow for your children!"

Making the moment even sweeter, Will could request an officer to serve under. For him there was truly only one choice.

"The fighting man of the North Carolina Sounds," was what he called his close friend and mentor, Lieutenant Charles Flusser. "Daring to the death and chuck full of fight." Back in January, Flusser was given command of the light gunboat *Commodore Perry*, aboard which he'd patrolled the sounds since the capture of Roanoke Island, organizing one trademark cutting-out expedition after another...and wreaking bloody havoc on Southern shipping.

All Will needed was Flusser's recommendation, along with approval from the commander of the blockading force in the sounds, Captain Henry K. Davenport. He now headed to New Bern, North Carolina, the home base for Davenport's flagship the USS *Hetzel*.

•   •   •

Will reached New Bern in late July only to find Davenport away on Navy business. Flusser, however, was in town and very pleased to see his former student. As Will had hoped, he appointed him his first officer once Davenport arrived to rubber-stamp the paperwork.

Flusser acquainted him with the *Perry*, a 150-foot sidewheel steamer armed with two nine-inch guns, two thirty-two pounders, and a howitzer. Although its full crew complement was over a hundred men, a typhoid outbreak ravaging the fleet had left it shorthanded. Nevertheless, Will met many of his future shipmates, and on Davenport's return, was officially assigned to the boat.

He spent the next few weeks on duty aboard the *Perry*, patrolling waters off Plymouth under Flusser's leadership. Flusser had earned autonomy in choosing his operations, unique in the Navy. As was written of his leadership abilities in a naval biography:

> The fight for possession of the sounds was serious business, and [he] was the most active man in it. He enjoyed the confidence of his eminent superiors...and was given a rather free hand by them. Plymouth was his usual headquarters and depot. From there he controlled his little squadron. When there was nothing doing in aid of the army his vessels roamed the rivers, breaking up contraband trade. The total value of captured property, including cotton, was enormous. There were many expeditions, generally cooperative [with land forces], and the soldiers seemed to enjoy the dashing hazardous adventures in narrow winding rivers, fighting guerrillas

and masked batteries on the banks, making marches and attacks where least expected by the enemy.

Will shared Flusser's bold, fiery nature, and throughout August and September, he eagerly soaked in his style of command, gaining invaluable experience from his penchant for unpredictable lightning raids. He was learning fast.

•   •   •

The typhoid epidemic worsened in September.

When one of Will's crewmates aboard the *Perry* came down with the fever and was transferred to a large hospital ship in the harbor, Will paid him a few visits to pick up his spirits.

On one of his visits, the man's condition seemed much improved. "You look better today!" Will said with a smile.

"Oh no, I am not," the man replied dolefully. "I'll bet twenty dollars I will die before tomorrow morning."

Will thought him depressed from his illness. "Done!" he said, reaching into his pocket for a bill. Then he noticed his friend was empty-handed. "Well, where's your money, man?"

The man gestured to his knapsack. "I'll leave the sum with my doctor," he said.

Will left his friend's bedside thinking he'd made his bet in jest. But when he returned the next morning to collect his winnings, he found to his sorrow and dismay that he'd won. The sailor had died.

Shortly afterwards, Will himself came down with fever—most likely contracting it from his unfortunate shipmate. But his case was mild and with proper medical attention his health improved within ten days.

He was sitting up in his bunk when Flusser arrived to see him in late September. "You had better get well," the commander said. "There's fighting in the offing."

Will felt a stirring. "Aye, aye, sir!" he replied in a thin voice.

Two days later he was back on his feet. Four days later he was aboard the *Perry* preparing for their mission, and five days after Flusser's visit, October 2, Will steamed off with the gunboat to the fiercest action of his young career.

CHAPTER 11

IRONCLAD OF THE ROANOKE

The year 1862 had started promisingly for Gilbert Elliott. Commissioned to build three wooden gunboats at ten thousand dollars each for the Southern Navy, the industrious eighteen-year-old was optimistic that he might soon turn a profit for the struggling Martin & Elliott shipyard. Though Colonel Martin was no longer in Union captivity, having been released in a prisoner exchange late in 1861, reorganizing his command consumed his attention, leaving him disengaged from his business affairs. Thus, while Martin and his brother undoubtedly lobbied for the gunboat contract behind the scenes, it fell on Elliott to negotiate its terms and keep everything on schedule.

That schedule would have been a formidable challenge even under the best of circumstances. In his haste to bolster the Confederate naval force, Secretary Stephen Mallory had insisted that Elliott supply firm delivery dates in advance, "time being more important than money" to him.

Elliott, eager to close the deal, offered to build three boats in the highly compressed period of four months.

On January 6, Mallory extended a multi-hull contract for three wooden gunboats; Elliott was to deliver them from his shipyard in early

May. Incremental payments were to be made and bonuses given, contingent on the work's progress.

Elated and energized, the young shipbuilder would soon find himself under growing stress. The project needed a significant outlay of funds for timber and other materials, and he was still wrestling with cash flow problems tied to the incomplete—and still unsold—hull on the stocks, which remained a huge financial drain on the yard. Meanwhile, the Navy Department was seriously overdue with a $5,000 partial payment on the Cobb's Point offshore battery. Apologetic, Mallory wrote to inform him the delay was due to "want of the Treasury notes, which cannot be printed and signed fast enough to meet the demands upon the Treasury."

Elliott may have accepted his explanation, but it did nothing to alleviate his debt. He'd hoped to use some of the Cobb's Point payment to buy materials for the three gunboats and had in fact asked the secretary for an early advance on that contract to help cover initial expenses. Mallory politely refused, writing that "the Department cannot advance the first payments…as you request, as no progress has been made with [the boats], but will take care in making the payments as they come due."

It all added up to a tough, circular bind for Elliott. He needed funds to complete his work, but none would be forthcoming until the completion of more work. Under this intense pressure, he spent the following weeks doing what business was in his control: conducting inspections at the yard, seeking a buyer for the hull under construction, trying to purchase anchors and chains from venders, and looking after Colonel Martin's home, mother, rental properties, and slave holdings.

Then on February 7–8, General Burnside's amphibious forces took Roanoke Island for the Union. Just two days later, a fleet of thirteen federal gunboats steamed up the Pasquotank River, overwhelming Elizabeth City's naval defenses with vastly superior numbers and firepower. Among the Confederate vessels captured was the CSS *Ellis*.

The city burned that day, many of the blazes started by federal troops, others lit by residents fleeing their homes, shops, and offices in carriages, taking what possessions they could before torching anything of value left behind. The Martin shipyard went up in flames, black smoke rising thickly over its workshops, the unfinished hull and floating battery on its docks nourishing the conflagration with their timbers.

Elliott nevertheless managed to avoid suffering a total loss. Weeks before, as the Union fleet had made deeper and deeper incursions from the Sounds, he'd scouted out a new location for the shipyard in Norfolk, near the heavily protected Gosport naval headquarters. That same foresight had extended to his contingency plans for his family. Anticipating full-scale attacks on Roanoke Island and Elizabeth City, he had brought his mother and younger brother to the relative safety of Oxford, a town outside the state capital with a strong military presence.

By early February, Elliott's shipyard was on the move. He instructed his laborers to transport its equipment, tools, and materials to the Norfolk site, where he meant to quickly resume operations. If he was to have any chance of meeting his deadline for the three gunboats, he could not afford a long shutdown.

Unfortunately, it was difficult to get operations up to speed. With construction materials in scant supply, many of his bills outstanding, and wartime transport slow and filled with obstacles, Elliott fell increasingly behind schedule. But Mallory showed continued support for his efforts. In fact, he would now direct another offer to the shipyard. An especially important one that reflected a major shift in the secretary's priorities.

The success of the *Merrimack*—or the *Virginia*, as the Confederates rechristened her—against the blockade fleet at Hampton Roads had finally convinced the Raleigh government to loosen its purse strings for the construction of more ironclads. That gave Mallory what he'd long wanted. With another round of lobbying (likely from the Martins), he once again turned to Elliott's shipyard for the work, asking him to pour his resources into building an ironclad with all due haste—and for the healthy sum of twenty-three thousand dollars. This time, however, if the enemy interrupted work, Elliott would be compensated. His gunboat delivery would wait.

Elliott recognized he'd been handed an excellent opportunity. Ironclads were the future of naval shipbuilding. If he could deliver on his agreement, this guaranteed his firm's success.

In April, the awarding of the contract came with a desperately needed $5000 advance. But he'd barely started his preparations before the shipyard made another sudden change of location. The previous month, Mallory had grown convinced that Norfolk was under mounting threat of a Northern offensive. He knew Gosport was highly desired by the enemy and with that in mind, he ordered all machinery and stores at the yard removed "without attracting special attention or notice."

Within two weeks of issuing the ironclad contract to Elliott, Mallory reiterated his warnings of an imminent attack to Gosport's yard commander, Captain Sidney Smith Lee. Though the *Virginia* was stationed near the yard for protection, her skipper had informed Mallory that the federals could "at any time send a force so superior" that it would be unstoppable. After receiving this statement, Mallory wrote Captain Lee on May 1 that "Norfolk is in serious peril" and "all valuable machinery not needed for service must be boxed or secured and sent away from Norfolk at once." Two days later, he sent Captain Lee withdrawal instructions.

Elliott was close enough to the heart of this action to notice things were astir at Gosport and concluded Norfolk would be abandoned. He could no longer risk staying there. In early May, he disbanded his workmen, hoping they could earn a living elsewhere until he found another site. Meanwhile, he suspended his shipbuilding career and enlisted with Colonel Martin's reformed unit, called the 17th Regiment (2nd Organization). While his motives are still unknown, First Lieutenant and Adjutant Gilbert Elliott was soon with the regiment at Camp Johnson outside Kinston, North Carolina. But thanks to Secretary Mallory, his active military career would be a brief one, lasting only two months.

A variety of factors contributed to Mallory's intervention, including the increasing brashness and frequency of Lieutenant Commander

Charles Flusser's incursions into the North Carolina Sounds, and the need for more ironclads. A July 26 letter to North Carolina's governor Henry T. Clark from Mr. Jones W. J. Muse of Wilmington suggested "the building of an ironclad gunboat on the Roanoke for the purpose of ridding the waters of the Yankees." Muse had included a drawing of this proposed gunboat, designed by a mysterious "Mr. Scott" of Louisiana—perhaps by no coincidence the home state of John A. Stevenson, the entrepreneurial commission merchant who submitted his own plan to Mallory back in 1861—and requested that receipt of the sketch be acknowledged because of Scott's concern that it might fall into unintended hands.

Whether the letter or sketch found its way to Secretary Mallory is unknown. But it landed on the governor's desk right around the time the Martin brothers, eager to get the family business back up and running, had been working quietly to persuade Mallory that Elliott's organizational skills would be put to better use as a naval contractor than in filling out routine requisitions for field rations and replacement uniforms.

In July or August, Mallory asked the Confederate War Department to grant Elliott a furlough so he could turn his "business capacity and energy to undertake the building of another gunboat." On August 18, a terse communique titled Special Order 192 was issued from the highest levels of the Confederate military: "A leave of absence for thirty days is granted Lieutenant Gilbert Elliott, Adjutant, 17th Regiment North Carolina Infantry, by Command of the Secretary of War."

On September 17, Special Order 218 extended Elliott's leave to two years "for special naval service." On the same day, Mallory's fourth contract with the Martin & Elliott shipyard reached Elliott, fully signed and executed. By then a new site for the yard was found on the Tar River, an inland waterway well beyond Union penetration, in a town where shipbuilding had been going on for close to two decades and existing construction facilities were available to Elliott. Mallory wanted him to get cracking on the ship—a larger and more powerful ironclad than the two already on order. And this time, eager to build up his fleet, the secretary had deliberately included a contractual clause provision encouraging simultaneous construction of other vessels, contingent on his approval.

Quick to take advantage of the clause, Elliott proposed yet another armored warship. By October 10, after some back and forth with the secretary, he sent a final draft to his office. Based on Mallory's input, the latest ship design was different from the others in one very major respect. "We have the honor to propose to construct for your Department one ironclad gunboat *and ram* at Tillory's Farm on the Roanoke River.... Said boat to be of the same plans and dimensions as the one we are now building at Tarboro, N.C.," Elliott wrote, adding, "It is conceded by everyone that the defense of Tarboro involves as a necessity the defense of the Roanoke River at or below the town of Hamilton."

In other words, this ironclad would run on the waters of Albemarle and Pamlico Sounds, where Charles Flusser's blockading squadron had been wreaking chaos and destruction on rebel maritime interests.

Tillery Farm was about thirty miles north of Martin & Elliott's Tarboro shipyard, and seven miles below the town of Halifax, at which the Confederate government ran its own small yard for the construction of war vessels. The Halifax facility was hardly spacious, but its rail station, commissary, medical facilities, forge and furnace buildings, and defensive battery, offered many benefits.

For Gilbert Elliott, things had changed tremendously in a brief time. Just three months before, he had been without a place to build anything. Now, in October, he oversaw two shipyards with enough contracts to produce a small armada. Due for completion by April 1, 1863, the Tillery Farm ram would be nothing less than his crown jewel.

CHAPTER TWELVE

DISTINCTION OR AN HONORABLE GRAVE

I t was 7:00 a.m. on Friday, October 3, 1862, when the first musket shots cracked from the woods below Crumpler's Bluff at a sudden bend of the Blackwater River in southeastern Virginia. On the sluggish river, a trio of Union gunboats strained to out-race the enemy fire.

Leading the way was the twenty-eight-man USS *Commodore Perry*, skippered by Lieutenant Commander Charles Flusser, with Lieutenant William Barker Cushing serving as his executive officer. Following behind were two light gunboats: the USS *Hunchback*, commanded by acting Lieutenant Edmund R. Calhoun, and the diminutive USS *Whitehead* under the command of Lieutenant Charles A. French.

Their destination was a small town called Franklin, a transportation hub of the Seaboard and Roanoke Railway of great logistical value to Confederate general Robert E. Lee. On a joint mission to destroy the rail bridge with Major General John A. Dix, Flusser's job was to cut off the seven thousand Confederate soldiers in and around Franklin as they retreated, driven from town by Dix's 7th Army Corps.

The evening before, Flusser had brought the group to a point three miles south of Franklin, where the gunboats stopped to wait out the darkness in company. Morning broke surprisingly clear and mild for autumn, and after 5:45 a.m. breakfast, the men pushed slowly upriver, shelling the banks as they went.

The Blackwater River, which fed into the Albemarle Sound, was narrow and crooked, and as the ships moved upstream, their crews had to run hawsers ashore at the bends, "making them fast to the trees to haul their bows around."

Three-quarters of a mile below Franklin, the *Perry* came to the first of several sharp turns in the channel. Flusser ordered a line hauled out to shore...and that was when the rebels sprung their trap. Riflemen concealed high on the bluff sheeted the gunboats with fire.

Flusser reacted quickly, trying to steam past the ambush—but the river was so narrow the *Perry* ran hard into the bank.

As she thumped to a halt, Will, in charge of her forward gun, looked over the ship's side and saw a large group of infantry emerge from the woods. Their leader and standard-bearer, a "splendid fellow with long curly hair" rushed toward the ship waving his sword, cheering on his men, urging them to board the steamer.

He was unaware that his comrades had not followed him down the bank. Muskets fired from the *Perry's* deck, and he fell dead into the mud not ten feet from her rail.

Within a few minutes, Flusser had the boat off the bank and steamed ahead, Will's bow gun ripping into the treeline with nine-inch grape, shell, canister, and shrapnel. "This fire covered the *Hunchback* as she rounded the bend, and she in turn covered the *Whitehead*."

But the *Commodore Perry* was first around the bend—and first to come close to the barricade ahead. Made of trees "felled from both banks," it reached "right across the stream" to impede the gunboats' progress.

Her crew no sooner realized they were caught in an ambush than "every tree and bush and log sent forth a storm of lead—and a yell burst forth that seemed to come from all directions."

Flusser normally would have had the barricade cleared away, but the intense fire made sending anyone ashore out of the question. Instead he ordered his few men to take cover below. "It seemed madness to fight [them] on an open deck," Will recalled. The rebels vastly outnumbered them and held the high ground atop the bluff to the right. Howling like demons, they poured torrents of musket fire down on the *Perry's* deck.

The situation worsened. With one side of the boat still against the land, her decks level with the elevated bank, and not twelve feet of water on the other side, Will "saw a mass of infantry rushing to board us under cover of their comrades' fire."

There was no place to hide. The choice, he knew, was to fight or die.

His instincts took over at once. "Calling for volunteers, I dashed out [into the open], cast loose the howitzer (on field carriage), and assisted by six men and an officer, Mr. [John] Lynch, wheeled it to the [right] side of the deck," he recalled vividly. Under withering fire, Lynch, a master's mate, took a rifle ball to the heart and fell dead on the spot. The rest of the men also became quick casualties under the hail of fire. "I was again alone, all the volunteers being dead or wounded at my feet. Without waiting a minute, I sighted the piece, and sent the canister crashing against the dense mass [of rebels], now about thirty yards away."

As Flusser reported, Will, "amid a storm of bullets, took sure and deliberate aim at the enemy…and completely silenced their fire at that point."

But it was only a brief lull. The rebel snipers kept shooting down from the bluff, their infantrymen resuming their charge until Flusser had to call his men back on deck to fend them off. "[We] were now sent to quarters and a general fight commenced." Will remembered. "The sailors working the great guns, throwing grape and canister, and our marines shielded by the hammocks [placed against the rails for cover] picking the sharpshooters out of the treetops—from whence they fell with a crash and shriek [at] every moment. Our only hope was now to fight our way out—as no army force appeared to aid us."

In fact, Dix's troops were nowhere near the action. On September 30, the general had sent a messenger to inform Flusser he intended to delay the attack on Franklin a week because of "unexpected obstacles," but the messenger missed the departure of the *Perry* and her companions by five hours, and the dispatch went undelivered. Surrounded by thousands of rebel troops, Flusser's little fleet with its two hundred men—their numbers depleted by the typhoid epidemic—was on its own.

"For four hours we fought them at the barricade," Will wrote, "and in that time routed them five times." Flusser kept "hoping to hear the guns of the land force" but was disappointed. "No such welcome sound" reached his ears.

At 10:15 a.m., he abandoned any lingering hopes that help might arrive and ordered his vessels to turn downstream, keeping up "a fire of great guns and musketry." As they made hard back toward the Chowan, the order of the boats reversed—the *Hunchback* now leading the way at a heavy steam, followed by the *Whitehead*, with the *Commodore Perry* bringing up the rear.

But the Confederates continued springing their ambush. To block the gunboats' retreat "trees were cut down below [them] and rifle pits thrown up on every bluff and wooded point." Flusser and his crew were trapped.

Will remembered the harrowing passage years later. "The leading vessels, rounding a bend, caught the fire of about a thousand infantry concealed in [one of the rifle pits]—and after suffering severely, ran by. We were some distance behind, and when we came around were entirely unexpected by the butternuts...right on their flank and only two hundred yards [away]."

The rebels meant to sweep the crews of the first two gunboats with fire from either shore, wiping them out to a man before they could pass through the log barrier. But the *Perry*, coming on from some distance behind, caught the ambushers with "an awful raking fire," pouring "a terrific fire of shrapnel and grape shot through their trench till we could actually hear the bones crack, and see the limbs fly from the mangled bodies. In five minutes, the place was in our possession and that of the dead."

But Flusser's gunboats still needed to escape before enemy reinforcements arrived—and their one path to safety remained closed off by the fallen trees. Unable to get around them, they plunged straight on through, the *Hunchback* leading the trio of vessels on a full head of steam.

Its skipper, Lieutenant Colhoun, must have had his prayers answered. Somehow the barrier gave way before the *Hunchback's* bow. Crashing past it, the boats were soon out of danger and into the Chowan.

"At last, tired and feeble, we fired our last shot, and were clear once more, but with decks covered with the dead and wounded, and slippery with blood—and the whole ship like a sieve, so full of bullet holes was she," Will recalled. "We had done our duty and could only regret that the army had failed us, and that our blue jackets had fallen in vain."

Casualties aboard the *Perry* were bearable. Of her twenty-eight hands, two were dead, and ten wounded—two mortally, Flusser believed. In his post-action report, he cited several officers and crewmen for meritorious conduct, but reserved his most detailed comments for his former student.

"I desire to mention as worthy of praise for great gallantry Lieutenant William B. Cushing, who ran the fieldpiece out amid a storm of bullets, took a sure and deliberate aim at the rebels, and sent a charge of canister among them that completely silenced their fire." He did not fail to commend John Lynch, who "assisted Mr. Cushing, and here met his death like a brave fellow, as he was."

All in all, the outcome could have been worse. "Bullets seemed to miss our small party purposely," Will later wrote Cousin Mary. "There are more than a thousand bullet marks on our vessel."

He understandably believed the mission a "fortunate action" for himself. Though he was no stranger to naval combat, the close-up fighting on the Blackwater River was a baptism of fire. He had taken charge of a deadly situation to save his boat under Lieutenant Flusser's supportive eye. It was the first time in his career that Will gained proper recognition for his bold leadership qualities and was rewarded in a manner he'd only dreamed of in the past.

Will was maturing under fire. "The official report will probably be published, in which case you will see it," he informed Mary. "I could tell you what it says, but will not do so, for fear you might think me too set up." Whether "set up" or not, he delivered his news in a subdued tone that distinguished him from the prankish adolescent booted out of Annapolis. "I will only say that I have since been given command of [a] gunboat for my services. I can justly be proud of [this] at the age of nineteen. It is a thing before unheard of in the service."

The name of Will's gunboat was the *Ellis*, the rebel steamer seized off Roanoke back in February after her captain, James W. Cooke, defiantly met the Union boarding party with an upraised cutlass. As federal sailors poured over the *Ellis*'s sides, Cooke had ordered his men to blow up the ship, but a coal heaver discovered them trying to ignite her magazine and quickly alerted the boarders. Thwarted in his explosive designs, the sword-waving Cooke had resisted capture until shot in the right arm, bayoneted, and thrown down to the deck.

If Will heard about Cook's tigerish defense of his ship, he certainly would have thought him a man after his own heart. In any event, Will was impressed by the gunboat's capabilities. As he informed Cousin Mary about the *Ellis*, "She was of iron—three eighths of an inch in thickness, measured about one hundred tons, [mounting] an eighty-pounder rifle gun forward and a twelve-pounder howitzer aft." Most importantly, the *Ellis* was small and light-drafted, a vessel that "could penetrate every little nook and corner" and enable him to stage the kind of opportunistic cutting-out expeditions in which Charles Flusser had adeptly schooled him.

"I was of course delighted, and made up my mind to gain distinction or an honorable grave before many months should go by," Will wrote.

Those were no mere words, as he was quick to demonstrate.

•   •   •

Located about thirty miles south of Beaufort, Bogue Inlet was an opening into the Atlantic, where, "the bar is shallow, the breakers usually high, a tall bluff guards the entrance, and the little town of Swansboro nestles in the rear, about three miles from the mouth."

In early-to-mid October, Rear Admiral Samuel Phillips Lee, supreme commander of the North Atlantic Blockading Squadron, received information that blockade runners were taking advantage of the inlet "by means of small schooners to Nassau." He informed Flag Officer Davenport of his concerns, who, in turn, ordered "Lieutenant W. B. Cushing to proceed to that point with the USS *Ellis* under his command, and use all available power...to ascertain whether any trade is being carried on through that inlet with or by the rebels."

The *Ellis* was the only vessel in Davenport's fleet of sufficiently light draft to send to the inlet, and even then, he expected the ship to anchor outside the channel on reaching Beaufort. Will's orders were to do his best under the circumstances.

As they pulled up to Swansboro, Will's men exchanged a few rounds of musket fire with a company of enemy soldiers at the shore's edge. But the rebels quickly raised the white flag and hightailed it, leaving the town to its small population of civilians and slaves. Will saw no sign of Confederate trade, and locals denied it occurred; though he was told he might have better luck at nearby inlets, especially New Topsail about thirty miles down the coast.

Following through on the tip without delay, Will steamed southward. The closest his men had come to any real action at Bogue was to poach "a hog, a cow or a sheep" from Southern farmers, giving the ship's cook a chance to add some fresh meat to their otherwise bland meals.

"I have a sort of roving commission, and can run around to suit myself. For the present, I am my own master," Will wrote his cousin Mary, exaggerating. He had no such license but was eager to follow Lieutenant Flusser's lead, attacking enemy shipping whenever and wherever possible. "If under these circumstances I cannot stir the rebels up in more places than one it will be strange indeed."

On October 22, he entered the inlet and found it unfortified—but by no means unoccupied. A large steam ship lay at anchor about a mile from the inlet's mouth. Will had no pilot aboard the *Ellis* familiar with local waters—few blockaders did, which rebels knew and used to their advantage. Undeterred, he made for the steamer at full speed, coming within a hundred yards of her before bumping up against a sandbar.

The steamer's crew, meanwhile, had set a fire on the quarterdeck and abandoned ship, spooked as the *Ellis* dashed heedlessly toward them. But Will's boarding party extinguished the flames before any real damage was done.

After a hurried search, they discovered their prize was the *Adelaide* out of Halifax, England. Her papers revealed a Southern captain was in command, ready to sail for Bermuda with six-hundred barrels of spirits of turpentine in the hold, and thirty-six bales of cotton and some tobacco for a deck load. Altogether the value of the cargo was around a hundred thousand dollars, a handsome catch.

Will immediately ordered lines run to the prize. But with darkness falling, he had to wait until first light before trying to maneuver off the bar. At 4:00 a.m., he tried hauling off with the *Adelaide* in tow, but the schooner drew even more water than the *Ellis* and "grounded incessantly."

Finally, at 8:00 a.m., with the tide low, Will gave up. Waiting for high water was too risky. Unable to pull the vessel out to sea, he decided to destroy her instead, setting fire to the hold full of turpentine.

Unlike the *Adelaide's* rebel crew, he succeeded in setting her ablaze. Before he left the inlet, flames were lapping at her mastheads, the barrels exploding with a roar heard for miles around.

Although Will was not pleased with losing his prize, he hadn't finished with New Topsail Inlet. In his report to Flag Officer Davenport, he laid out strong reasons for concluding illicit trade was happening along the North Carolina coast. Davenport replied three days later, "Continue to act in accordance with your best judgment and discretion, and carry out to the extent of your ability the views of the Government and the admiral."

Will must have found the note enormously gratifying. Davenport could have admonished him for leaving his station without orders. But instead he'd rewarded the very "imaginative and speculative" qualities that Silas Stringham used to smother and Commandant Raymond Perry

Rodgers of Annapolis had insisted gave him "no promise of usefulness" in the Navy.

At last Will had earned the freedom to stalk the enemy at will. He went to it like a wolf on the prowl.

PART II

THE RAM

CHAPTER THIRTEEN

THE IRONMONGER CAPTAIN

In late October 1862, Lieutenant Gilbert Elliott, C.S.A., and Commander James Wallace Cooke, C.S.N., the former captain of the *Ellis*, met for the first time in Rocky Mount, North Carolina, a coastal city seventeen miles east of Tarboro, on the Tar River, where the Martin & Elliott shipyard had relocated that past July. It was the yard's second move in half a year.

Recently paroled in a prisoner exchange, Cooke was appointed the Confederate Navy Department's official liaison with its shipbuilders. He now wished to meet Elliott as he needed the shipyard's bond to authorize an advance payment for the ironclad.

Elliott delivered it to him by hand. With that done, Cooke informed the young shipbuilder that General Walter Gwynn, a West Point graduate and preeminent civil engineer, had been ordered by the C.S.A.'s secretary of war to inspect the fortifications on the Neuse, Tar, Roanoke, and Chowan rivers, report on what improvements could be made to their existing defenses, and determine whether added measures might be needed to obstruct the waterways from federal incursions. Cooke also told Elliott that the secretary had promised "to keep all troops in

North Carolina within the state" rather than redeploy them should forces in Virginia or elsewhere ask for reinforcements.

For Elliott, this was particularly good news. He'd had his full share of uprooting and needed to work consistently and without interruption if he was to build ironclads by their appointed dates. The better protected the Tarboro and Tillery's Farm sites, the more confident he was that he could deliver as promised.

Meanwhile, Cooke had another subject he wanted to raise, and that was the Navy Department's concern about the availability of iron needed for the armored ships. Elliott, who had run up against shortages while still in Elizabeth City, was a step ahead of him. He explained that he'd been making inquiries of distributors in the area, one of whom had collected "several miles of railroad iron from the tracks between Kinston and New Bern without detriment to the public interest."

But Elliott stopped short of claiming that it would be easy to find enough for his purposes. The Confederacy had prioritized the railroad system that transported its troops and kept their supply lines open. Locomotive engines needed copious quantities of iron, and iron rail ties were manufactured by the thousands and held in reserve. That left Mallory and his plans for an armored Navy much lower in the government's overall pecking order.

Cooke had known all this when he arrived at Rocky Point. Based on the precious metal's scarcity, he may have been skeptical of Elliott's ability to fulfill his end of the deal. But the young shipbuilder's energy and industriousness impressed him. From their first meeting, he became single-mindedly determined to get him the iron he needed.

Not that he'd needed much impetus. With his deep-set eyes, dour face, and grey-threaded mustache and beard, Cooke was an angry man, and the source of his anger made him ripe for a crusade.

A native North Carolinian, career seaman, and slaveholder, the fifty-year-old former U.S. Navy lieutenant had been assigned to Washington, D.C.'s Naval Observatory and Hydrographical Office in 1853. He had bought a farm in nearby Langley, Virginia, and lived a peaceful existence there with his wife and only son, cultivating grain and corn, tending a peach orchard of five hundred trees, keeping dairy cows, cattle, horses, sheep, and hogs, and looking forward to his eventual retirement. As the national crisis deepened in 1860, Cooke had been torn about resigning his naval commission. But after the fall of Fort Sumter and his home state's secession a few weeks later, he felt honor-bound to submit his resignation and accept a commission in the Virginia State Navy.

In May 1861, Union troops raided his Langley farm and turned it into a regimental headquarters. Though Cooke had moved his family out earlier, fearing for their safety, the federals' ransacking of his abandoned home and flattening of the fields and orchard left him embittered and vengeful. He spent the next several months aboard Confederate warships, first command-ing the steamer *Weldon N. Edwards*, and then the *Ellis* before his capture, fighting in defense of Roanoke and Elizabeth City.

Cooke was no longer undecided about his future. The Yankees had forced his family from their home, vandalized and confiscated it, defeated him at Elizabeth City, taken his ship, shot, and bayoneted him. His dream of life as a gentleman farmer lay in ashes.

No longer conflicted, Cooke was now a proud defender of the South by loyalty and circumstance. And having met Elliott, Cooke could envi-sion his ram looming large and powerful over the Union fleet. The young man was intrepid and determined. He could build her. Cooke would do everything possible to help the project, find every scrap of iron to cover her with, and supervise her construction down to the last bolt. Pursuing his goal with a single-minded determination, he earned the nickname "the Ironmonger Captain."

If the responsibility fell his way, Cooke would do more than just see the vessel afloat. Given command of a leviathan like that and a crew of brave men, he would clean the enemy from the Sounds and assure the waters of North Carolina once again belonged to the Confederacy.

CHAPTER FOURTEEN

A ROVING COMMISSION

Within a week of burning the *Adelaide*, on October 29, 1862, Will again brought the *Ellis* into New Topsail Inlet. About three-quarters of a mile from its mouth, he spotted a brick saltworks "large enough to have furnished all of Wilmington with salt." Salt to cure beef, pork, and fish for consumption by rebel troops; salt for tanning leather and fixing dyes in their uniforms; and salt as an essential additive to the feed of Southern cattle.

This was exactly the sort of target Will had hoped to find with his "roving commission." There was no staple scarcer—or more valuable—than salt to a Confederate military force.

He was quick to lead a party ashore to demolish the plant. Undertaking their business with alacrity, they "tore down the brickwork, destroyed [the] large copper and iron kettles and pans [for boiling the salt crystals from seawater], cut holes in their flatboats and lighters [or heavy barges used to transfer the salt to larger ships], cut through the cisterns and waterworks, and burned the buildings."

When the party finished reducing the works to rubble, they tossed ten or fifteen freshly made bushels of salt into a ditch and burned the

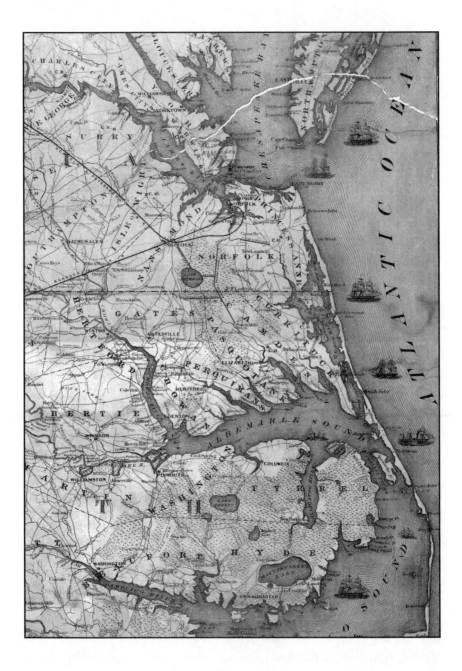

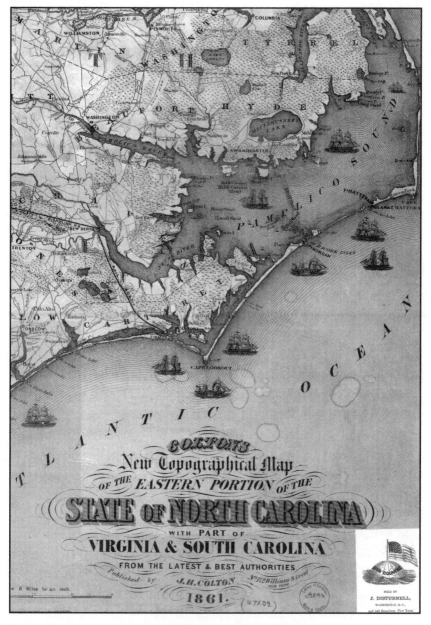

In late 1862, the coastal waters of North Carolina and Virginia became Will Cushing's stalking grounds. *Library of Congress, Geography and Map Division*

remaining buildings. But just as they were ready to leave, the enemy opened fire from a hill about a mile away.

Will peered through his glasses. Even from a distance, he could see they had two artillery pieces and a large supporting infantry force. Their volleys were well aimed; the shells crashed down all around his men. Thankfully, their landing boats were out of range, and they were soon rowing back to the *Ellis*.

Once on the gunboat, Will returned the enemy fire and "silenced them by exploding a shell in their midst." The rebels mounted their artillery on carts and fled.

Will had learned from his experience with the *Adelaide*. This time, he would not risk bumping up on a sandbar. He sounded for a channel, "found that vessels drawing nine feet of water can go up the inlet for three-fourths of a mile."

"I shall keep a bright lookout for rebel trade," he reported to New Berne.

•   •   •

A narrow, shallow waterway bounded by weathered granite ridges and ledges, "The Rocks," as it was known, snaked by gradual curves into the New River Inlet. At about 9:00 a.m. on the sharp, chilly morning of Sunday, November 23, Cushing's gunship USS *Ellis,* guided by two local pilots of solid recommendation, succeeded in passing its low stone walls and started up the river toward the quaint little town of Jacksonville, North Carolina.

Lieutenant William B. Cushing had ambitious goals for his expedition. Weeks before, "in looking at the coast chart," his eye had fallen on New River, which emptied into the Atlantic about forty miles below Beaufort. He'd observed that it was wide and deep after the bar was crossed, and that the county seat, Onslow Courthouse, could be found on its banks some twenty miles from its mouth. It seemed "just the place for a nest of Nassau vessels," and he was determined to "make a dash for it." Like someone reaching his hand into a carnival grab bag, he meant to have his pick of sparkling prizes to carry away with him.

"My object was to sweep the river, capture any vessels there, capture the town of Jacksonville, or Onslow Courthouse, take the Wilmington mail, and destroy any saltworks that I might find on the banks," he reported later, adding that he "expected to surprise the enemy in going up and then to fight my way out."

Will was clearly feeling adventurous—but for all his plans, he would not catch the rebels by surprise. As she neared the river's mouth, the pickets of Captain Edward W. Ward noticed the *Ellis*. Ward had made his home in Jacksonville and commanded over a hundred state guardsmen. He, in turn, sent couriers to alert Captain Abraham Newkirk of Company A, New Hanover County, 41st Regiment—also known as the "Rebel Rangers" and "Newkirk's Coast Guard Cavalry." Newkirk immediately set himself to mustering two saddle companies and a battery of field guns, though not all the artillery pieces would arrive at once.

Meanwhile, Will crossed the shoal without difficulty and went steaming through the inlet. A *New York Herald* naval correspondent along for the mission described the river as "wide and beautiful" in the morning brightness, adding that it was "inviting for navigation."

Five miles upriver, Will sighted an outward-bound schooner carrying a load of cotton and turpentine—and sending up thick clouds of smoke. Probably warned of his approach, the rebels had fired her to prevent their cargo from falling into Union hands and abandoned ship, scattering off toward shore in their rowboats. Will ran alongside the vessel, observed the rampant flames, and decided her crew were better arsonists than the men who had set fire to the merchant vessel at Topsail Inlet. Satisfied the enemy would be unable to extinguish the blaze, he went on toward his destination.

With fewer than sixty residents—mostly hog farmers, fishermen, turpentine makers, and shippers—Jacksonville was situated on the right bank of the river, about forty miles from its mouth. As they approached the town at 1:00 p.m., Will and his men saw a Southern cavalry outfit spring onto their saddles and ride off on the road to Wilmington. Captain Ward and a company were also in town, and they, wrote the *Herald* correspondent, "skedaddled like the rest. He was out driving in a buggy, heard that the Yankees were coming, cut the horse loose from the buggy, mounted horse, harness and all—and left for dear life."

Or perhaps he'd left to summon and organize a defense. Whatever Ward's purpose, Will knew there were 12,000 enemy soldiers occupying Wilmington and its two nearby forts. He needed to hurry.

Dropping anchor in the harbor, he and his two best men, Master's Mates Valentine and Barton, brought a landing party ashore and took swift possession of the town "courthouse, post office, and other public buildings." They also took possession of Ward's buggy, but did not use it, finding the roads in poor condition. With only a handful of locals in town, they met little or no resistance, carried off all the mail, papers, and records they could find, and appropriated twenty-five stand of muskets and bayonets, along with boxes of Confederate uniforms. They also seized "two fine schooners in sailing trim" and "confiscated" the postmaster's slaves, intending to free them.

Before taking leave of Jacksonville, Will stationed several pickets on its outskirts and raised the American flag high atop the courthouse "for the first time in Onslow since the commencement of the struggle." Then he ordered his men back onto the *Ellis*, concerned the rebels who'd fled town had already sounded the alarm.

At 2:15 p.m., he steamed off with the prize schooners in tow; only ninety minutes had elapsed since his party stepped ashore. The ship he'd passed that morning was still burning on the water, and as Will once again neared her at dusk, he drew musket and cannon fire from the wooded riverbank. But the volleys did not injure anyone aboard the *Ellis* nor penetrate her iron hull, limiting damage to parts of the woodwork before her guns pounded the rebels into silence.

The silence did not mean defeat, however. Under Captain Newkirk's command, the Confederates had fallen back from the shore and sent a courier to request another field piece from Captain Zacharia Adams's

Company G, 2nd North Carolina Artillery. Once his added firepower arrived, Newkirk hoped to engage the gunboat from the bluffs closer to the river's mouth.

Soon the *Ellis* came within three miles of the outer bar and slowed down. With the sun lowering in the sky, Will's pilots suggested he stop to wait out the night. High water and daylight, they warned, were needed to make it through The Rocks.

As the *Herald*'s naval correspondent described the treacherous waterway, "[I]t is quite crooked. The channel lies directly through a sandbar, and approaches in one place to within one hundred yards of a high bluff. This channel was one dredged out to accommodate mercantile vessels in their progress towards town, but it is evident it was never intended for the benefit of Yankee warfare. Once a vessel enters this channel it cannot turn around. It has to either back out or to proceed onward until it comes to the point within one hundred yards of the bluff."

Will now faced a serious dilemma. He could see rebel troops swarming on both banks. But he had not hired Southern pilots only to ignore them.

After concluding the channel was impassable in the darkness, he reluctantly heeded their advice, dropped anchor, took his prizes alongside, and rallied his men to "make every preparation to repel an attack." By sundown they had pushed their hammocks against the rail and were standing on watch armed with boarding pikes.

It was a long, tense night on the deck of the *Ellis*. Shivering in their pea coats, men peered uneasily across the water to either side, where they could see the enemy rustling about signal fires in the gloom. But the hours passed without incident, and with daylight the gunboat got back underway.

She had come within fifty yards of the channel's mouth when two field pieces opened fire from the bluff. Will ordered the battle flag hoisted, and with three cheers his crew went into action, swinging their own guns toward the rebel artillery.

The exchange lasted about an hour. In the end, the Confederates fled, Will and his men passing within a hundred yards of their nest, lobbing occasional shells at it without drawing fire. But "the fortunes of the day" were about to change. In the confusion of the fight, the gunboat's pilots had left the man-made channel and mistaken another one for it. As they approached the entrance to The Rocks at high water, they ran "hard and fast" aground, scraping bottom with a jolt that staggered everyone onboard.

Will stayed cool. Taking hurried stock of his predicament, he put all hands to work dumping unnecessary ballast to lighten the ship, and then used anchors and steam to try and get her back afloat. But she had been moving along at a good clip, her own headway forcing her "over a shoal and into a position where, as the center of a circle, we had a circumference of shoal all around." When Will looked over the sides, it seemed to him that the *Ellis* had washed up on a small island.

And that wasn't all. He had another predicament on his hands.

As the sun again began to sink, and the tide ran out, Will "sent a party ashore to take possession of the abandoned Confederate artillery." If they came upon the guns, they were to man them overnight, providing cover for the *Ellis* until the morning flood tide, while keeping the rebels from moving another battery into position. But there were only ten whaleboats and some saltworks in the little camp, all of which the sailors destroyed. The cannons were gone, hauled away on carriages, leaving only the faintest wheel marks in the dirt.

But where were they taken? The question preyed on Will's thoughts.

He was right to be troubled. Though he did not know it, Captain Newark's extra guns had finally come, giving him enough artillery to set up strong points on both sides of the river. As darkness fell over the bluffs, his men had begun readying an ambush.

Will, meanwhile, was far from idle that night. Certain the enemy would attack, he had decided to remove more weight from the gunboat and make another attempt to clear the shoal. This time he "took one of [his] prize schooners alongside" and proceeded to empty the *Ellis*'s holds and decks of everything except her pivot gun, some ammunition, two tons of coal, and enough small arms for a half dozen men."[But] steam and anchor again failed to get [the *Ellis*] afloat," leaving him with only one real option.

His foremost priority was to save his men.

Calling all hands on deck, he addressed them with words that gave proof the nineteen-year-old captain had not let Charles Flusser's book of naval heroism sit unopened in his sea chest.

"Officers and men, I see no chance of getting this vessel off," he said. "We will probably be attacked in the morning, and that, too, by an overwhelming force. I will try to get her off at the next high tide if I am not attacked in the interim. In the meantime it becomes necessary and my duty to provide for the safety of you all. If we are attacked by the enemy in the morning and he overpowers us, either by boarding or otherwise, the only alternative is to go up with the vessel or submit to an unconditional surrender. To do the latter is neither my desire nor intention. I will not do the former except as an absolute and last resort. I wish all the men except five or six—and there must be volunteers—to go on board the schooner. I wish the schooner to be dropped down the river to a point without the range of the enemy's shot from the bluff. It is my intention, with the five or six who may wish to remain with me, in the event of an attack, to work the pivot gun in the morning, and fight her to the last. I will not surrender the *Ellis* to the enemy while a magazine or a match remains onboard."

According to the naval reporter, every member of the crew stepped forward knowing it "was almost certain death," for the ship's magazine was almost entirely unprotected," lacking the sort of armored box that enclosed it on some vessels.

Filled with pride, Will had to choose from among them. Valentine and Barton accounted for two, and after he quickly selected three more volunteers, the rest of the men made their sober goodbyes. As they climbed aboard a gig in the early light, the dedicated *Herald* correspondent also decided to stay on and chronicle whatever followed.

"Thus it was we were left alone," he wrote later.

There was a brief interlude of perfect stillness, and then the thunder of heavy rifled guns cracked from four points on the bluffs. When the rebels spotted the rowboat rowing down toward the schooner, they turned some of their fire in its direction, raising great, fanning sprays of water that splashed over the gunwales to drench the men at the oars. But to the consternation of the artillerymen, the volleys failed to sink them.

Meanwhile, the trapped *Ellis* was in a destructive crossfire. Will and his group answered as best they could, aiming load after load of grape at the bluff. But in a short time, the ship was riddled with holes from front to back, its engine disabled and spewing up hot jets of steam. Crouched behind defensive earthen banks, the rebel gunners saw flames eating at her woodwork, then a bright eruption inside the cabin. They knew they had succeeded in making her a goner.

On the deck of the *Ellis*, Will staunchly resisted the idea of surrender. It was plain to him that "there was no chance to save the vessel, not even the slightest degree of a hope to do so." But he had resolved, even without hope or a possibility of success, to "battle on for the honor of the flag as long as there was anything left of the ship to stand on." He was driven "not by a desire for a display of bravery," the *Herald* reporter observed, "but an actual regret to leave his vessel."

"This is the toughest fight I've ever been through . . . and I've been in eight others," he told one of his small band.

As the onslaught from the bluffs continued, Will acknowledged that continued fighting would serve no purpose, leaving him with two alternatives: he could either let himself, his men, and the *Ellis* be captured, or row a mile and a half downstream toward the schooner, under a hail of withering fire, in his small gig.

He refused to consider the first possibility.

"I cannot surrender her, and to a rebel," he said, then went about the ship dousing her with turpentine, by his own hand setting fires in five places.

Now he needed to make haste; the rebels were rowing from shore in small boats, coming on toward the doomed vessel in force. But he wanted to leave them a message. Before quitting the ship, he, and the men "made sure the battle flag was still flying," loaded the pivot gun, and then trained it upon the bluffs.

Their escape, complete with a defiant farewell, was extremely risky. "When the boat had been thoroughly fired, Lieutenant Cushing, with all on board, left in the gig for the schooner, and the men had to pull their oars through an apparent hailstorm of shell, the shells bursting in the air and scattering in every conceivable direction," wrote the naval correspondent.

Shortly after Will and crew abandoned the *Ellis*, the flames reached her magazine and ignited a thunderous explosion. The newspaperman offered a vivid account of what happened next:

"Portions of the vessel rose in the air to a great height, and then spread in all directions. Some shells which were left forward also burst in the air. The whole scene was one of terrific grandeur. The reverberating echoes, the bursting bombs, the scattering timbers, the roar of the enemy's cannon, the escape in the gig, the evidence of being watched from the shore, and the hard and fast row toward the schooner, rendered the whole scene too exciting and peculiar for a newspaper paragraph."

As soon as Will and his men reached the schooner, they were underway. On approaching the bar, one of the pilots warned that it was low water, that a heavy surf was rolling in, and that they would be unable to get over it.

Will could see the breakers for himself—high and rough, they reared, humpbacked, over the shoal before crashing down against it with white sprays of foam. But several companies of enemy cavalrymen had followed the schooner along the riverbank. He insisted the pilot force her over the bar.

"The schooner was then put into the breakers and struck four times," wrote the correspondent. On the fifth attempt, a stiff breeze caught her stern and pushed her into the open sea.

She had made it through just in time. The Confederate horsemen had come within six hundred yards of the vessel down the beach, trying to reach the mouth of the inlet and cut off her escape. As the wind took her over the swells, they fired a volley, but to no effect. Will's party hoisted their flag, gave three cheers, and broke into the *Star Spangled Banner.*

Behind the vessel the rebels on the shore, some watching with spy-glasses, saw and heard their patriotic celebration. When Will and his men noticed them looking on, they responded by singing in emphatically louder voices.

In four hours, they reached Beaufort. Will had brought away all his men, his rifled howitzer, the ship's stores and clothing, its bags and hammocks, and some of its small arms. Left behind on the *Ellis*'s deck were a small collection of muskets, pikes, and pistols.

Safely at New Berne on November 26, the *New York Herald* naval correspondent wrote his impressively detailed account of the raid, summarizing it in a single well-packed sentence at the article's conclusion: "In this affair, Captain Cushing penetrated forty miles up a 'New' river, where no United States vessel had ever been before since the commencement of the rebellion, took a town and waved over it the United States flag, captured three schooners, forty-five stand of arms, and destroyed the saltworks and ten whaleboats besides sustaining a three days' flight and avoiding the capture of either himself or his vessel."

Will believed his haul from the Jacksonville post office had yielded some potentially useful intelligence. While the captured mail was lost with the *Ellis*, he'd read a fair amount of it before the enemy ambush. Several from the men of Confederate General James Longstreet's corps, postmarked in North Carolina, revealed that the general's troops, which previously centered their operations in Virginia, had expanded their operations into the state, supported by a letter from an "educated lady" who wrote, as Will clearly recalled, "Now that you have the noble Longstreet to command in your State and to protect you, you need have no fear of the Yankees." The captured letters convinced him the rebels were not only willing to yield the eastern part of the state to Union forces but saw that as a foregone conclusion. He also took away that a "bitter feeling had grown up in regard to the conscript law, and all soldiers complained of a want of clothing and shoes." Salt was twenty dollars a bushel and sole leather seven dollars per pound—both commodities inflated in price because of wartime shortages. Finally, he noted, yellow fever had nearly disappeared from the city of Wilmington.

Whatever consolation Will took from the raid's successes, he had fallen short of his own chivalric standards by leaving his ship behind and even wondered whether he was accountable for its destruction. In his report to Commander Davenport, he wrote, "I respectfully request that a Court of Inquiry may be ordered to investigate the facts of the case, and to see if the honor of the flag has suffered in my hands."

Will's request made its way through the chain of command to Assistant Secretary Gustavus Fox at the Navy Department. Fox eventually replied, "We don't care for the loss of a vessel when fought so gallantly as that."

While taking a short leave of absence at New Berne, Will received a letter from Major General John G. Foster, commander of the United States Army's Department of North Carolina, complimenting him for his actions. It arrived with a copy of a separate letter to Admiral Lee requesting that he be detailed to command a squadron of five Army gunboats. Lee and the general had formed a close working relationship, and it was through their connection that Foster would have seen Will's after-action report.

Though flattered by the invitation, Will declined the offer. The young man who had twice wanted to resign from naval service and join the Army now "desired one vessel of the navy more than a fleet of army boats."

Will had at last found his place. He had only to await his next command.

CHAPTER FIFTEEN

BREAKERS AHEAD!

A t 8:00 p.m. on January 5, 1863, a small schooner, rigged out and painted leaden grey to appear of English provenance, entered the mouth of the Little River, some thirty miles below the Confederate held Fort Caswell, near the border between North and South Carolina. Dropping anchor at the bar, the ship lowered three cutters into the water with a party of twenty-five sailors, some borrowed from the government schooner *Martha Vassar*.

They pushed over the bar and upstream. The river was narrow, its banks close and thickly wooded with cypress and pine, their tangled limbs reaching out beyond the water's edge to hang low over the men's heads.

In the lead boat, Will Cushing, steam puffing from his mouth, peered through his glass by the dim light of the moon and stars. He'd heard reliably that a Southern pilot station was found a mile or two up…and a good thing too. On the prowl for seasoned pilots, he meant to snatch a few from their warm bunks.

So far that day, things had failed to go according to plan. But it was not as if Will had been remiss in carefully working out what old Admiral Lee skeptically called his "scheme." He had, in fact, formulated its rough outlines back in late November, while still on leave at New Berne following the *Ellis* affair.

Around that time, Lee and General Foster had been plotting out a cooperative Army-Navy attack on Wilmington with a mind toward approaching the harbor from the south with a fleet of low-draft gunboats. If they could launch into the Cape Fear River from the Sounds, Lee reasoned, they might slip up behind Fort Fisher and avoid its formidable artillery.

The hurdle, or *hurdles*, were the river's sandbars, swamps, marshes, and sudden drop-offs where its deceptively calm surface hid swift and powerful underwater flows. Only men familiar with the waterway could navigate these treacherous passages, and Will had the idea of snatching some Wilmington pilots for the job. But that required stealth and a means of eluding Confederate batteries certain to raise bloody hell if they spotted him.

But how to avoid them? He'd pondered it for a while and then an idea struck. It involved the prize he had claimed in Jacksonville, the same vessel that carried him and the men to safety after the *Ellis*'s destruction. Called the *Home*, it might be altered to slip past the rebels in plain sight of their defenses.

On November 26, Will had sent a letter to Commodore Davenport proposing that "I may receive orders to take the prize schooner *Home* for the purpose of capturing some Wilmington pilots." He went on to suggest disguising her as an English blockade runner, and then took the ruse a step further. "By boldly entering New Inlet chased by one of the blockading fleet, I can succeed. When I get under the guns of the forts, I will wait for pilots or boats from the shore. All persons that come aboard I will make prisoners, and stand out from under the fire of the forts. If an armed tug should come alongside I will take her by boarding."

To Davenport, it was a shrewd, bold ploy that would make Cushing's vessel bait. But it was also perilous and unconventional enough for the flag officer to have reservations about committing to it. He wanted his higher-ups to sign off before going ahead.

Three days after reading Will's request, Davenport ordered Will to present his idea to Admiral Lee at Hampton Roads at his "first opportunity." Will sailed there at once aboard the *Home*, meeting with Lee in early December. The admiral, like Davenport, was intrigued, thinking the plan might "succeed if not leaked out." Knowing the risk, he reached still higher up the ladder of command, sending Will to Washington to see Gustavus Fox. "Young Cushing's scheme ventures more than it promises," he told Fox. "[B]ut liking the morale of the thing, I would not stop the project."

At the Navy Department, a typically decisive Fox spared Will any added rigmarole. "Rashness in a young officer is rather commendable," he told Admiral Lee.

Having obtained the assistant secretary's authorization, Will requested a few days' leave so he might have a new uniform tailored in New York. His clothes, he said, were lost with the *Ellis*, except what he wore that day.

Fox gave his okay, promising to inform the admiral. But he was suspicious. With Christmas only days away, he concluded a uniform wasn't the only reason for Will's swing into his home state. "[He] went off to New York," he wrote Lee in good humor, "not to get clothes, but to see his sweetheart."

Lee was half-right in terms of Will's affections. For Will was keen on seeing Cousin Mary, who was on a holiday trip to Fredonia with her husband Charles Smith and their newborn baby. Traveling there straight from the capital, he stayed at his mother's home for two days, visiting with Mary and other members of his clan, and catching up on news of friends and family. On his last night in town, he even managed, true to character, to get into a quarrel with Smith, who had suggested the national conflict was near its end, much to Will's annoyance as someone intimately acquainted with the fighting. But Mary defused things by playing on the piano, and they had made peace ironically singing war songs "old and new."

For Will, back aboard the *Home*, Fredonia was now some thousand miles away, a joyful holiday season behind him, the ashes of his mother's Yuletide log long ago swept from her hearth. His original plan had been to run in under the forts, take a pilot on board and run out, trusting to the element of surprise to carry him clear. But at both the east and west bars of the harbor, the wind unexpectedly quieted, and his vessel becalmed even while under false pursuit by the squadron's men-o'-war. This had exposed their charade to Confederate shore watchers, leading to Will's abrupt change of plans and dash upriver.

His glass raised again, he looked out ahead and noticed the ground elevating to a low, muddy bluff on the left bank. There he saw a flagstaff in relief against the night sky.

Before he could wonder if he'd reached the pilot house, the sound of musket fire cracked the silence—a volley that knocked over two of the men in the boats. If the rest weren't also to go down, Will knew he would need to take decisive action.

He sprang to his feet. *"Follow me in!"* he shouted, ordering the cutters turned toward shore and beached. In moments, the men were leaping onto the bank under heavy fire.

Will lead his group up the bluff, calling a double-quick charge at the top of his lungs, and then howling like the rebel troopers Alonzo had remembered from Bull's Run. The men followed suit, yelling madly in the darkness as they scampered up the rise with their outthrust rifles and bayonets. Will had no idea how many Confederates he might be facing. But twenty howling jack tars would sound like fifty to their ears.

At the top of the bluff, he saw an earthwork looming beyond a ditch, and then a blockhouse behind its low parapet, all of it visible in the light of a burning, abandoned campfire. The enemy had taken to their heels.

Another frenzied yell, and Will and his men bound through the ditch and over the parapet, sole possessors of the fort and blockhouse, which had been pierced so the Confederate riflemen could fire from within. A quick search convinced Will the garrison had been five times their number, more than large enough to handle them, especially from cover behind the blockhouse walls. But the rebels had bolted as if they, and not his little party, were the ones caught by surprise—fleeing in such haste they not only left behind their arms, ammunition, stores, and clothes, but a supper of pork and beans on the table for the tired, hungry sailors to consume. Before the feast was over, they took some gunshots from outside the encampment's wall, but their return fire put an end to it, and the enemy holdouts scattered into the night.

Soon Will's men brought everything they could lug back to their boats, destroyed whatever was too large and cumbersome for them, and then rowed back to their schooner. Midnight arrived with an ominous roof of clouds, turning the night pitch black. Despite the threat of a storm, Will decided to remain at anchor until daylight, when his men would be able to see their way out of the narrow waterway.

But morning brought throbbing swells from the southwest. The little schooner swayed precariously atop them, her masts rocking, her boards creaking and groaning in the wind. In what seemed the latest and worst stroke of bad luck in his thwarted pilot hunt, a monster storm was coming on.

Will was in an untenable spot. In that area off Cape Fear, the Frying Pan Shoals ran out into the Atlantic Ocean from the North Carolina coast for about thirty miles at a right angle, creating a bight, or windward shore, into which the gale was about to blow full force. He now found himself in that pocket of water, on a small four-ton schooner, its single anchor and chain stretched taut by the rising, agitated waters. If he tried to wait out the storm, the wind would surely wrench the anchor free of the bottom and drive him hard into the rocky coast. But the Frying Pan's treacherous, shifting sandbars, formed by silt from the Cape Fear River, had been a dreaded threat to generations of seafarers, littering the ocean bottom with shipwrecks. To reach Beaufort, he would have to make his way across it, and in a bad sea, no less.

"I had my choice of two alternatives," he later wrote. "I might bear up for the beach and go ashore at Fort Caswell as a prisoner of war, [joining] our poor fellows in the hell at Andersonville, or I might run the thirty miles that separated us from the shoal."

In fact, Will saw no real choice at all. He would not willingly cast himself or his men into the verminous filth and deprivation of the Andersonville prisoner-of-war camp. That left him to head for the Frying Pan and run the chance of striking a narrow channel that threaded across it into the open sea—and he estimated the odds at five hundred to one against the *Home* finding that channel and making it through. If his ship missed her way by even a hundred yards in the fog, she would be dashed to pieces.

Will decided to let no one but Master's Mate Valentine know the terrible risk, placing him at the schooner's helm with his instructions, and providing a compass course that he himself had determined.

They bore east for some time, the gale worsening around them, lashing them with wind, rain, and spray. Valentine steered through the whiteness, the *Home* swaying from side to side, seawater pouring over her gunwales. Several times she angled over and almost capsized.

And then, as Will would later write, he "saw the old quartermaster at the lead turn deathly pale as he cried out, 'Breakers ahead! For God's sake, sir, go about!' In an instant that cry was 'Breakers on the lee bow!' 'Breakers on the weather bow!'"

They were into them, the waves rearing up as high as the spars and crashing down over the deck. Then a shock ran through the hull. *She had struck.*

"All seemed over," Will recalled. He stood beside staunch Valentine, determined to control the ship to the end.

But the shock only lasted for second. With Valentine grasping the wheel, the *Home* "fairly flew through the great white breakers." Despite striking again, and again, "but never hard," she somehow found the channel.

Twenty minutes later, she was safe and scudding for Beaufort. By daybreak, the men were ashore again.

"And not, Thank God, on traitor's ground," Will wrote.

•   •   •

After losing the *Ellis* to an ambush and a disastrous attempted grab of Confederate pilots, Will might have easily qualified as foolhardy, lucky, and gallant all at once. But the courage and ability he showed during those escapades outweighed his shortcomings to those for whom it mattered, namely Welles and Lee. On his return to Beaufort, Will learned he was going to the Capital, where he hoped the secretary would assign him another command.

But first there was a twelve-day leave of absence. Traveling to Washington with an attendant named Elijah—one of the liberated slaves from the Jacksonville raid—Will decided to pay his brother Milton an unannounced visit, only to learn he was in Boston for the wedding of a relative. But when Cousin Joe Smith at the Navy Department told him Milt would return in a couple of days, Will asked Milt's landlady at the Twelfth Street boarding house if he could stay there until his return.

Although hesitant, the landlady recognized Will from his visit the year before and with a sternly raised eyebrow and forbidding frown handed him a spare set of keys. He had no fondness for the woman or her three resident daughters, grumbling to Mary that "in ancient times [they] would have been described as fiery dragons, but who are now called old maids, or ancient angels, and these angels had bad tempers." Not content to leave the insults right there, he added, "They assist their mother, the boarding-house keeper, and preside at the table, one at a time. The consequence is the boarders have poor appetites and the old lady makes money."

Whatever his gripes about "the keepers of the castle," Will had no trouble enjoying his break from the war. For all the nation's turmoil, 1863 was a frenetic boom year for the growth of housing and infrastructure to support Washington's expanding military, government, and civilian population. "Mud and contractors were thick on the streets," he wrote Cousin Mary of its busy atmosphere. While waiting on Milton, he met up with his old Fredonia schoolmate David Parker, who was now superintendent of the mails for the Army of the Potomac and made frequent trips to Washington in that position. They dined together, reminisced, and enjoyed each other's company.

In two days, Milton returned from the family nuptials. As Will wrote his cousin, "[W]e at once commenced to be as jolly as circumstances would permit. There are three regular theaters in the city now, and the star actors don't shirk it as they used to, so I patronized them extensively, laughing at the farces and comedies, and looking grave, sometimes, at the tragedies. Sometimes, I say, for that brother of mine was almost sure to set me off into convulsing laughter by some absurd remark just in the thrilling part, much to the amazement, and sometimes indignation, of the surrounding multitude."

Soon Milton and Will were joined by the honeymooning Boston newlyweds, who stayed at Brown's Indian Queen Hotel, one of the most luxurious hotels in the city—despite the sheep, pigs, horses, and mud outside its porticoed Pennsylvania Avenue entrance.

Will went on to explain to Cousin Mary his tribulations trying to connect with Alonzo while in Washington, the thing he had most set his heart on before the trip. That winter, Lon had encamped with the hundred-thousand-strong Army of the Potomac in Falmouth, Virginia, fifty miles south of the city. After trying to walk, swim, and sail there, which ended in a mud-soaked return to Milt's boarding house, Will had found his fondest hope of seeing Alonzo dashed, and he returned to Washington feeling thwarted.

When next Will traveled to see him, it would be to find his mortal remains.

•   •   •

Riled by his failed attempt to visit Lon, Will decided to vent his frustrations by doing sword exercises in his room, with Elijah standing in for the instructor—who, according *The Boy's Manual of Seamanship and Gunnery*, a standard naval training manual of the time, "would direct his students to face him to afford them a target."

Elijah was hardly thrilled to play that role, with the exercises "scaring him out of a year's growth," Will wrote. "I am afraid that if you were ever to consult [him] as to the events of the day, he would complain of terrible hardships."

But according to David Parker, the door to Milt's quarters got the worst of Will's foul temper, pierced by his cutlass in several places...and even that did not calm him. Heading off with Elijah to the Navy Department after a late breakfast, he "smoked a quiet cigar" and then paid a respectful call to Commander Smith. While in his office, a man entered with two purebred Newfoundland puppies. One had been purchased by Smith, the other was up for sale. Deciding the pup would make a nice gift for Milton, Will bought it for five dollars and had Elijah bring it back to the boarding house.

Elijah was climbing the stairs to Milt's quarters, the dog cradled in his arms, when one of the landlady's daughters crossed his path on her way down. Refusing to allow the dog on the premises, she ordered him to deposit it in the lower hall, where she opened the door and offered it, free, to passersby. It did not take long before someone carried the pup off.

"I was angry, I confess it, I was angry," Will wrote his cousin. "I think that if Congress had been in session, I would have petitioned it to change the sex of the guardians of the castle, in order that I might have used my muscles as in the days of happy youth."

Absent that sort of magical spell, he was of course far too much the gentleman to ever lift a finger to a woman. But he would hold a grudge over the canine's eviction.

One afternoon after dining with Parker, he strolled back to the rooming house to find an organ grinder on the street outside the front door. "Play all the tunes you have!" he said, pulling a handful of change from his pocket.

The organ grinder noisily obliged to the predictable irritation of the landlady and her daughters. Will's revenge was in progress.

Later, when Milton returned from his job at the Navy Department, the women complained that they found the street musician's music offensive and warned that his brother was to refrain from inviting him to play at their front door. When Will was told about their aggravation, he again sought out the organ grinder, asking if he knew of any other local practitioners of his craft.

"Yes," he said happily, sensing work for his friends. "There are three more of us in town!"

Will hired them to come to the rooming house at 8:30 that evening. When they arrived, he asked them to carry their barrel organs up to Milt's quarters and crank out their tunes indoors. The landladies had, after all, only objected to the organ grinder playing *outside* the premises.

Their racket brought the infuriated women up the stairs as fast they could climb them. Chasing the three from the premises, they angrily let Will know he was on the verge of making himself likewise unwelcome. His stunt caused "an open rupture" with them, which must have left poor Milton at a flustered loss.

But Will continued his revenge. The next morning, he opened his window, leaned outside and noticed a cluster of pigeons on a wall behind the building. Deciding some target practice would nicely complement the other day's swordsmanship drill, he fetched his revolver. Perhaps, he thought, the ladies would find the gunshots less horrible than the organ grinder's music!

Bang, bang, bang! The birds launched into flight with startled squawks and a flurry of feathers.

Then Will heard a window raised on the floor below. Looking down, he saw a white-haired head poke out. It was the landlady—no surprise, since she lived directly beneath Milt. In her hand was a stick of the sort she would use to keep the window propped open. The temptation was too much to resist.

He shot, hit the stick, and knocked it out of her grasp. Will would have his revenge on behalf of the Newfoundland pup; never mind that the stunt could have serious ramifications for his brother. Milt was a tenant in good standing, and he meant to keep that status after Will left Washington. Lucky for him, the women pinned responsibility where it belonged. They had no quarrel with Milton, but the younger Cushing would have to clear out. He was no longer allowed to set foot in their house.

Will did not argue. His leave was nearly over, and he expected a new command after meeting with Gideon Welles. Packing his bags, he and Elijah carried them to a nearby hotel and checked in for what would be a very brief stay.

•   •   •

As it turned out, the secretary offered Will his choice of two vessels. The *Violet* was a little steam-driven gunboat measuring eighty-five feet from stem to stern, a fast blockader meant for capturing prize ships off Wilmington. The *Commodore Barney*, a five hundred-ton sidewheel steamer, carried a crew of a hundred men and thirteen officers, and mounted five hundred-pounder smoothbore guns, a hundred-pounder Parrot rifle, and a twelve-pound howitzer.

Will had earned a reputation conducting small-scale raids behind enemy lines. But he was tired of chasing blockade runners and, moreover, had heard that Confederate General Longstreet—Robert E. Lee's "Old Warhorse"—had assumed command of three Virginia regiments totaling about 30,000 men, viewed as a sign he was gathering his forces to retake Norfolk. Meanwhile, General John J. Peck, whom Will had proudly met at Harrison's Landing, was now in charge all the U.S. troops in the state below the James River. Headquartered in the city of Suffolk, Peck and his 15,000-strong 7th Corps were tasked with guarding the land approaches to the Norfolk and Portsmouth shipyards. If Longstreet moved to wrest those sites from Union control, he would use his two-to-one advantage over Peck's forces to throttle them at Suffolk.

Will expected a major naval operation launched against those Southern troops. And he knew the *Barney,* with her large, powerful battery, was suited to that sort of action. Given a choice, he wanted to be part of it. But, he asked, could he take Master's Mate Valentine with him? And some of his other best men from the *Ellis*?

Welles agreed. Will left his office "proud as a peacock" to be captaining the *Barney*." As he wrote Mary, "The command of her belongs to some officer of a higher grade than myself, but they (the powers that be) are pleased to think I have earned the distinction."

And so, tired of muddy Washington, Will set out for Fort Monroe via the Baltimore Railroad. With a fight brewing in Virginia, the coming weeks promised to be anything but dull.

CHAPTER SIXTEEN

ANOTHER FIGHT, ANOTHER VICTORY!

A t first, a restless Will found command of the *Barney* a letdown. The waters of Hampton Roads were quiet, as if the blockade runners were waiting for spring to escalate their clandestine trade—though it may have been that smaller, swifter boats than the *Barney* were keeping their traffic in check.

In the Virginia countryside, meanwhile, Longstreet's divisions were "in mud up to their eyes." The winter of 1863 had been cold and sleety in southeastern Virginia, and with Southern commissaries depleted, his men lacked the most basic provisions and were suffering from malnutrition and scurvy. "Every exertion should be made to put the Army...on the strongest footing for vigorous work in the spring," wrote General Robert E. Lee. For Longstreet's hungry troops, they spent February and March foraging corn, bacon, and grain to feed themselves, and sassafras buds and wild onions to keep their thousands of starving horses from succumbing to starvation.

With the April thaw, their deprivations eased, and Longstreet made his long-anticipated move against General Peck's garrison. Suffolk was on the Nansemond River, a twenty-mile, northerly flowing tributary of the Union-controlled James River, and on April 11, three heavy columns of gray-clad infantry and cavalry, with hundreds of artillery and siege pieces, thrust through the western woods from the distant Blackwater River. Longstreet's plan was to form a line of troops from the Dismal Swamp to the Nanesmond River and then execute a rear flank movement, crossing the Nanesmond to cut off the garrison from the James and its vital ports. At the same time, he meant to capture the Norfolk and Petersburg rail station southwest of the garrison, cutting its main overland supply route and laying siege to the town. "Thus surrounded, General Peck's entire army and the city of Norfolk were to fall an easy prize into his hands," wrote one federal Army historian.

Longstreet himself was so concerned he would be open to an amphibious attack from the James that he had asked for naval support to be sent down from Richmond. But his request was denied. There were too many sunken obstacles that the Confederacy had placed to deter enemy warships from reaching its capital. He made the rapid march down to the Nansemond despite his misgivings.

Before light on the morning of April 12, the federal Navy's Rear Admiral Lee—who was third cousin of the Confederate general—received an urgent message from Lieutenant Roswell Lamson, commander of the river steamer USS *Mount Washington*. He had sent Lamson up the Nansemond on a scouting mission based on multiple dispatches that "the enemy was about to attack Suffolk in large force."

Tall and gangling, with short hair and a neatly cropped black beard, Lieutenant Lamson brought word from Peck that the rebels were on the march and preparing to cross the Nansemond. Lee at once dispatched several vessels to the river—the twin-gunned tugs *Alert* and *Cohasset* and the converted ferryboat *Stepping Stones* carrying a battery of howitzers. Lee also decided to pull Will Cushing and the *Commodore Barney* from a reconnaissance, sending him to the lower Nansemond.

The admiral assigned joint command of the mission to his two young lieutenants. Though Lamson was Will's lower-classman, he had more command experience and a detailed topographical map of the river borrowed from another vessel. He was also captain of a small, lightweight boat that could pass over the sandbar and other obstacles. For these reasons, he was to insert the *Mount Washington* upriver and apprise Lee of the changing situation around Suffolk when necessary.

As the senior officer, Will had overall command of the ad hoc flotilla. His responsibility was to anchor in the lower Nansemond with several of the other vessels, guarding the two likely crossing points, standing ready to intercept any enemy ships trying to flee or enter the river. Because Lee felt the *Barney*'s size and weight prohibited her from traversing the bar, Will received strict orders not to attempt it.

Naturally, Will bucked at any check on his movements. "If the enemy make a fair attack...am I at liberty to lighten my vessel to cross the bar?" he telegraphed the admiral. "At high [tide] I can get in at seven feet [of] water, and then there is deep water all the way up. If it comes to a fight, it will be a hard task to remain at anchor within sight of rebel cannon."

But Lee held firm: Will would remain in the lower Nanesemond with the *Cohasset* at his disposal. "It will not be proper for the *Barney*, with her draft of water, to go over the bar," he wrote.

On the first day, the flotilla remained watchful. While off Suffolk, Lamson sent the *Stepping Stones* to investigate a dispatch from General Peck that the rebels were constructing an earthwork at Deep Creek, on the Nansemond's left bank. Later in the morning, the general's pickets reported a large enemy force showing themselves on Somerton Road, about three miles south of the city. Another rebel detachment several miles to the southeast was on Whitemarsh Road, at the edge of the Dismal Swamp. By mid-afternoon, both groups had faded into the woods, making Peck suspect they were moving their front to draw a complete noose around him.

Increasingly nervous, Peck moved his batteries from his rear flank to the front, leaving all defense of the river to, in his words, "the boats."

Admiral Lee was infuriated after receiving news of Lamson's redeployment. His fleet was stretched thin throughout the Sounds, and the little gunboats he'd mustered under Lawson and Cushing were highly vulnerable to Confederate sharpshooters and field artillery. "The truth is the Army should cease the impolicy of occupying so many detached and weak positions, and relying upon what are called ferryboats in New York and gunboats here to make such positions tenable," he seethed in response. He then wrote this message: "Lieutenant Lamson will please say to General Peck that I have done all I can, and hope to hear soon that all is quiet near Suffolk."

For his part, Will would remain vigilant at the bar, ready to act on a moment's notice if the rebels made their much-anticipated move.

●   ●   ●

That same day on the upper river, Lieutenant Lamson's patrol boats were involved in several exchanges of artillery and musket fire. At two o'clock in the morning, two shots went flying across the *Mount Washington*'s deck from some bushes on the bank. The watch had their weapons in their hands and returned fire immediately, scattering the sharpshooters. Later, the enemy made its second appearance on Somerton Road, prompting another skirmish. Then General Peck sent Lamson a dispatch to let him know Confederate infantrymen were coming down Providence Church Road on Suffolk's outskirts, and Lamson sent orders to the *Alert* to shell them. In a later incident, the butternuts showed themselves coming out of the woods, and Lamson opened fire from the *Mount Washington,* the *Cohasset,* and the *Alert,* sending them into a swift retreat.

Lamson spent the rest of his time preparing to wage an extended river battle, getting coaled, provisioned, and resupplied with ammunition.

"[Y]ou may depend, sir, upon us to do all that is possible to assist General Peck in any emergency," he telegraphed Admiral Lee near evening.

•   •   •

At daylight on April 14, Lamson was heading upstream, leading the Army steamer *West End* and *Stepping Stones* toward Suffolk, when they turned the bend below Norfleet's Point, spotted a fresh earthwork, and shelled it with assorted guns. Seeing nothing but a handful of riflemen crouched behind its banks, Lamson signaled his group to run past, only to be taken by surprise. Suddenly, the enemy rolled seven concealed pieces of artillery from the woods—one a massive twenty-pounder Parrott rifle—and opened up with a thunderous barrage.

The flotilla was overwhelmed. The first shot from the Parrott plowed into the *Mount Washington*'s boilers. Other shots struck in quick succession, raking the vessel's bows and foredecks.

Within seconds her engines jerked and stopped. She drifted against the bank and grounded, crewmen scrambling across her deck, leaping ashore to avoid the jets of steam and hot water shrieking from her boilers. But Lamson ordered them back onto the ship, and they were soon at their guns returning the rebel battery's fire.

The fleet's problems quickly compounded as the *West End* also ran aground, leaving two of its three ships disabled. Lamson sent a man onto the *Stepping Stones* with an order to tow him out of range of the artillery, dropped anchor, and then sent the *Stepping Stones* back to cast its lines to the *West End*.

The group limped slowly downriver, the *Stepping Stones* towing the *Mount Washington* behind her, enemy sharpshooters firing from every point on the shore. It was now low tide, making their flight increasingly treacherous as they tried to cross the bar and obstructions near the mouth of Western Branch to escape into the lower Nansemond.

Once again the *Mount Washington* grounded, and the enemy opened up on her with ten pieces of artillery, trapping the stranded federal vessels in a crossfire.

Lamson knew his ship would be immovable till the next high tide, putting every man aboard in dire jeopardy. Unwilling to let the rebels use them for target practice, he ordered the engineers, firemen, and all others except his gun crew onto the *Stepping Stones*, then instructed her captain, Lieutenant T. A. Harris, to go down to a safer position and return to tow him off the bar at high water.

As a reluctant Harris chugged off toward the inlet, Lamson and his gunners were left stranded, alone, and overmatched by the shore guns' cutting fire.

Or so they thought.

•   •   •

On the deck of the *Barney*, Will saw the *Mount Washington* run aground about a hundred yards from the Hill's Point bluff and about three hundred yards from where he sat anchored at the bar. Then he saw the rebels unmask their battery of rifled guns from the woods behind the earthworks and open fire from both banks.

Two days after the battle, he would write his mother at length about what happened next, sparing poor Mrs. Cushing no grisly detail, with an eye toward the letter's reprinting in the Fredonia *Censor*. As usual, Will's letter contained a few dashes of inaccuracy and smatterings of embellishment—the *Barney*, notably, had been raked by fire, but came through in better shape than he suggested—but the combat was as fierce and bloody as his depiction, and the admiration between Lamson and Will, genuine. In his after-action report, Lamson made sure to mention, "Lieutenant Cushing, in the *Commodore Barney*, remained as near the *Mount Washington* as the depth of water would permit, and it was owing in a great measure to his well-directed fire, causing the enemy to shift his position, that the *Mount Washington* was not entirely destroyed. His vessel was fought in the most effective manner, and he sent his gig to me to ask if he could do anything more."

With the firefight over and his gunboat out of commission, Lamson assumed command of the *Stepping Stones*, and alongside the *Barney* and other vessels continued harrying the Confederate positions for days afterward. The fighting was sometimes intense, and the fleet suffered casualties, but attrition gradually took a severe toll on Longstreet's troops. Hunkered down within their fortifications, using up stores and ammunition to fend off the naval attacks, the Confederates were thwarted in their plans to move against Suffolk.

Meanwhile, General Peck and his garrison remained in the city with Peck claiming he needed every man for its defense and giving parsimonious support to the naval efforts. This did nothing to endear him to Lieutenants Cushing and Lamson, nor anyone else in the fleet, who grew increasingly disgusted with his inaction and timidity. Will himself would later tell his friend David Parker that he referred to Peck as "old granny" in an official report, claiming his "reflections on General Peck" were found so offensive to the War Department that "he was ordered to Washington to explain the matter" to President Lincoln. Will claimed Lincoln "reprimanded him severely" for insulting an "honorable officer of the army," but that he persisted in his defense.

"Let me explain it fully, and I can prove that he is an old granny," he supposedly told Lincoln.

The amused president heard him out, laughed, and said finally, "You go back and tend to your business."

Whether Will's encounter with Lincoln was true or not, on April 22, he vented some of his frustration on an entire Confederate detachment. He needed no prodding, though they gave him plenty.

At 11:00 a.m. the previous day, the *Stepping Stones*, back under Lieutenant Harris's command, had been patrolling near Chuckatuck Village on the south side of the Nansemond when the lookout spotted a black man in civilian clothes waving a white handkerchief on the rebel shore. Thinking he might be a slave or freeman wanting to share information about "what was going on in the country," Harris had sent a boat with five men to bring him back to the ship.

He had been a decoy. As soon as the boat reached the beach, riflemen crouched in the brush fired on her. Will seethed when Harris reported the ambush. He considered it treachery to use the flag of truce as a lure, a base violation of the codes of warfare. Though it was too near sundown to launch a retaliatory strike, he would punish the offenders in generous measure the next day. His men would not "suffer so" again in the future.

On the morning of April 22, Will moved the *Barney* down from Western Branch with the armed tug *Yankee* in company and anchored near the *Stepping Stones*. At once, he organized a boat expedition, and at 1:45 p.m., seven boats rowed from the side of the *Barney*—two of them hers, three from the *Yankee*, and two from the Army's *West End*. Made up of details from all three gunships, the crews numbered about ninety men and brought a twelve-pounder howitzer on one of the boats.

With Will in command, they pulled abreast and, covered by their ships' guns, landed on the beach where the decoy had stood with his white handkerchief. The boat sent in the day before was secured, together with four muskets, and the body of a seaman named Rietchurch. Will had brought along a crewman from the *Stepping Stones,* Master's Mate G. M. Lawrence, who was familiar with the area and could serve as a guide. He left one of his own men, John Aspinwall, in charge of the boats, instructing him to take all citizens who ventured onto the beach prisoner, "in order that no information of [their party's] movements might be taken to the enemy."

Then he was ready to march. His band pushed inland, torching three houses and their adjoining barns. They were not randomly burned. All were on the point of land from which the enemy had fired on the *Stepping Stone*'s luckless crew. And all were owned by civilians Will had been told gave active assistance to the rebels. He would see they paid dearly for that support.

Flames crackling and spitting at their rear, Will lead the men towards Chuckatuck Village three miles distant, where Union scouts estimated four hundred rebel cavalrymen had been posted. About a mile and a half toward town, they came upon their pickets and drove them off with a fusillade of musket fire. As they fled, the soldiers left behind a wagon and pair of mules likely used to haul supplies.

Will had a single—and single-minded—goal for his raid: "If possible, to recapture our men and to punish the rebels for their cowardly conduct." Now a thought struck him. Tethering the howitzer to the back of the cart, and then placing its ammunition inside, he smacked the animals' rumps to start them into a trot. Next he boosted forward his men with a shouted order instead of a slap:

"Forward, double quick!"

The sailors drove away two more squads of pickets as they moved on at a rapid, determined pace. By late afternoon, they reached a crossroads outside town, and Will left about half his men there to guard his rear, entering Chuckatuck with the rest.

Reaching it late in the afternoon, they started up the main street only to see about forty mounted Confederates come galloping around a corner about two hundred yards away, shouting like madmen "with raised sabres and horses at a gallup." One of Will's men, landsman Daniel Oonlow, moving slightly ahead of the rest, fired his musket squarely at the onrushing force and was shot twice in returned fire, falling dead on the spot.

As the cavalry pounded toward his little band, Will hurried around to the back of the mule cart with a gunner named Birtwistle on loan from the flagship. They quickly got the howitzer positioned for firing, poured in a round of grape, "and blazed away," the sailors firing their muskets at the men and horses. "[B]ut the artillery piece was difficult to aim at that close range," and "the shrapnel just went over them and burst in their rear."

Then the unexpected happened. At the sound of the discharging cannon, the mules panicked and "dashed off at a run—right against the advancing cavalry," with the bowed, rattling old cart "swinging first to one side, and then the other of the road." Before the rebels could react, the bolting mules plowed directly into them, cart and all, spreading their panic to the horses. They reared and broke rank, the cavalrymen clinging to their reins.

"Load with canister!" Will shouted, quick to take advantage of the disarray.

"All gone with the cart!" was Birtwistle's answer.

Will understood instantly: Sure enough! It was all gone. He had not an ounce of ammunition for the howitzer. Except, he thought, for the canister already loaded. Something had to be done.

Ordering the gunner to fire that last round, Will ran straight at the Confederates, howling at the top of his lungs, the men picking up his revenant's cry as they joined the charge. The ploy had worked at Little River, why not again? The rebels scattered in retreat as the screaming, apparently lunatic, sailors beat toward them.

When the brief clash ended, two of the rebels were dead, and three of their horses captured, fully equipped, with six cavalry pistols in their saddle loops. The landing party also recovered the cart and mules.

Taking control of the town, Will and the men questioned its terrified civilians about the prisoners from the *Stepping Stone* and learned they were no longer in Chuckatuck, but had been brought to a Confederate encampment across Reid's Ferry, near Longstreet's headquarters on Western Branch.

They were out of reach.

Will left the village around sunset, having done all he could there. He rode one of the captured mounts, another of his officers a second. Will thought the third horse a "fine" animal, and had a veteran crewman climb atop its saddle.

His band was headed toward the beach when they were attacked by sharpshooters. As the rebels fired at them through the woods, Will again made use of his howitzer and shot off a round—and was surprised (though he should not have been) when it had the same effect on the old sailor's horse as it had had on the mules. Its eyes huge with fear, it "went about and shaped a course right back for town," storming off at a mad gallop, crashing through the brush, the sailor pulling hard at the reigns to no avail. The panicked horse would not slow down.

But the old sailor kept his wits about him. Quickly pulling one of the cavalry pistols from the saddle holsters, he lifted the muzzle to the horse's ear and pulled the trigger. As Will later recalled, "The speed of the runaway was great, so that it took about a dozen bounds, end over end to satisfy his momentum."

Thrown from his saddle, the sailor flew through the air and landed in a ditch "with the wreck alongside."

Moments later he got back on his feet, stripped the saddle and pistols off the dead horse's back, and returned to his comrades, hurling angry curses at the unfortunate creature. He was dirty and bruised, but otherwise unharmed.

They reached their boats without further incident at seven o'clock, two hours after setting out of Chuckatuck. Will was disappointed to return without the four sailors but considered his foray a "most important reconnaissance." One of the things the locals had revealed was that Chuckatuck had been the headquarters of Longstreet's left wing until just four hours before his arrival. Their pullout, Will wrote in his report, "demonstrated that the rebel flanking force had drawn back" from Suffolk and was moving off to reinforce Robert E. Lee's regiments for an expected battle at Chancellorsville. It was information he intended to communicate to General Peck without delay.

But Peck would continue to infuriate him with his inaction.

The fighting in the waters off Suffolk went on for another two weeks, with Will and Lamson cruising the river and opportunistically poking at enemy defenses. But Will noted that for the most part "all was quiet on the Nansemond," which he considered mounting evidence that the Confederate garrisons were pulled off elsewhere.

He did recall one narrow escape in his memoir. On May 1, before attacking two batteries, he sent a group of five men into the woods on the rebel shore "to conceal themselves and keep a bright lookout." The *Barney* was about a quarter mile from the further emplacement, and only twelve hundred yards from the closer one, an earthworks near a manor called Le Compte's house that stood on a high bluff at Western

Branch Creek and served as General Longstreet's headquarters. If the infantry came down to the shore, the pickets were to fire once and retreat under the bluff, leaving the rebels to the *Barney*, which had two heavy guns loaded with grape ready to meet them.

"As our ship in her movements neared the woods," Will wrote, "I saw one [crew]man under the bank, at the water's edge, waving his hat as if to warn us back. But as no musket had been fired, and he was not twenty yards away, I sang out to him in an angry tone to know what it meant. As I hailed, a crashing volley of musketry came from amongst the trees, and there was no need of further inquiry."

Will was standing on the hurricane deck in full uniform, his speaking trumpet and marine glass in hand, when three discharges of buckshot penetrated his clothing to the skin, and the hair at the crown of his head was "cut off close to the scalp." Miraculously, he otherwise escaped unharmed, and shouted for his broadsides to open fire on the shore.

After about ten minutes the *Barney*'s attackers fled, unable to withstand its heavy guns for long. But the exchange was ferocious and left some of Will's best men dead on the deck.

He would later discover that Longstreet's men had moved stealthily upon his pickets, coming down the bluff through a patch of swamp to take them "so suddenly that there was no time to alarm us in the matter indicated. [But] this one brave sailor placed himself right under the muzzles of their rifles and tried to warn me.

"As soon as the firing commenced," Will concluded, "he jumped into a boat on the beach, sculled on a short distance, took up his rifle and fired; a few yards further on he loaded and fired again, and continued to in that way until the Confederates withdrew. Strange to say, he was not hit, though the boat in which he escaped was riddled by sixty balls."

Will would reflect on the Suffolk campaign with a scathing condemnation of Peck's performance. "It is my opinion," he wrote, "that very bad generalship was shown by the commanding officer of our army—General Peck.... That Longstreet knew Peck's [superior] defenses, I cannot doubt; for I captured an engineer officer of his force, with the plans of our works, their names, and the number and position of our men in his possession, and it was mere madness with such information to think of storming our front. They must then have been in retreat, leaving but two or three thousand men to amuse our general. And it was with this information that I rode on a dark night and drenching rain to urge an advance of our forces.

"I wrote to Admiral Lee at the same time, the state of the case, and did not hesitate to say that Peck had it in his power to either capture what men remained, or keep Longstreet's main body north of the Blackwater. But the general was convinced that the enemy was massing on his front and did not advance for a week—when as I predicted a mere shell [of a force] was found—a skirmish line—that went off like a puff of smoke before our regiments."

On May 3, 1863, Longstreet began withdrawing from Suffolk in earnest. Within twenty-four hours his regiments were falling back toward the village of Chancellorsville to the north, where General Joseph Hooker, crossing the Rappahannock River with the 130,000-strong Army of the Potomac, had attacked Robert E. Lee's numerically disadvantaged force of 60,000. There was some bloody fighting with Union troops at Longstreet's rear as he tried to reach Lee with reinforcements, but that in essence marked the end of the siege

The next day, May 4, Admiral Lee relieved Lieutenants Cushing and Lamson of duty on the Nansemond, ordering Lamson to bring the *Mount Washington* to Hampton Roads for reassignment. The battle-damaged *Commodore Barney* sailed to the Baltimore navy yard to undergo extensive repairs.

Gideon Welles would send both officers letters of glowing commendation. To Will, he wrote:

Sir,

Your gallantry and meritorious services during the recent demonstration of the enemy upon the Nansemond and in cooperating with the army are entitled to the especial notice and commendation of the Department. Your conduct on this occasion adds additional luster to the character you had already established for valor in the face of the enemy. The energy and ability displayed by yourself and the officers and men under your command in the defense of the lower Nansemond are most creditable and are appreciated by the Department. The Department desires to express to you more especially its admiration of your gallantry and enterprise in conducting an important armed reconnaissance with a party from the gunboats some miles into the enemy's country to the village of Chuckatuck and putting to flight a body of rebel cavalry and safely returning to your vessel. Accept my congratulations for yourself and the officers and men that were under your command.

> Very respectfully, etc.,
> Gideon Welles
> Secretary of the Navy

Welles telegraphed Lamson a similar letter of praise, adding, "The Department...is proud to see in the younger members of the corps such evidence of energy and gallantry, and execution and ability scarcely surpassed by those of more age and experience."

Coming from no lesser figure than the secretary, these words of praise were deeply appreciated. Will was so flattered, he waxed on about it in a letter to his favorite cousin, "I was three weeks on the river, and had a fight great or small nearly every day. I have since received some very handsome letters from the Secretary of the Navy, and the admiral, in acknowledgement of my services. I am in high favor with the department...."

For all his penchant for hyperbole, William Barker Cushing was not exaggerating this time. He had become the brightest of rising stars in the United States Navy.

With the *Barney* headed for Baltimore, he was slated for three weeks' shore leave while she was "again put in fighting trim." This meant Will could look forward to visits with his brother Milton, Commodore Smith, David Parker, and Old Neptune himself in the capital.

It would be fair to say, however, that the honor of again being "privately presented" to President Abraham Lincoln at the White House was at the top of his list of engagements.

•   •   •

Lieutenant David Parker was in Washington on May 5 or 6 when he received a telegram from General Hooker on the Potomac. Having met with the general at his tent camp a day before, he had not thought to hear from him again so soon.

The Chancellorsville campaign had not gone well. Though half the size of Hooker's army, the Southern force commanded by Robert E. Lee had outmaneuvered and outflanked his divisions, cutting them up like a giant scissors, inflicting 14,000 casualties in a few bloody days to force their retreat across the Rappahannock. Lee also suffered major losses—an estimated 10,000 men, General Stonewall Jackson among them—but it had been the federals that came away pummeled and dispirited.

In charge of the mail of Hooker's command, Parker had a unique talent for slicing through bureaucratic red tape, and he had ferried across to the general's tent camp after the battle to assure the battered, weary men could send and receive their posts. But his unexpected telegram had nothing to do with mail arrangements. Rather, General Hooker was asking Parker to bring him a new uniform coat.

Lieutenant Parker took pride in being a master facilitator. Indeed, he was the architect of an entirely new and expedited mail distribution system for Hooker's troops. But he was never asked to hand deliver a coat to anyone—not that the general didn't have good reason to ask. President Lincoln was coming to review the troops, as he had done during McClellan's Peninsular Campaign. Beyond knowing his presence would be a morale boost to the men, the president would want Hooker to look him in the eye and explain his ignominious defeat at Chancellorsville. Hooker, fresh from battle, wanted his best coat, and Parker informed him it was at his tailor's shop in Washington.

Parker obligingly went to pick up the coat, bringing it back to his room in a paper box. He intended to get a good night's sleep and return to the army in the morning. However, Will knocked on his door that afternoon, saying he'd brought his ship to Baltimore for repairs, and planned to be in town for several weeks.

As Will entered the room, his gaze wandered to the box sitting atop a piece of furniture. "What is this here?" he asked…and without waiting for a response, opened the box, took out the coat, examined it, and then started unbuttoning his *own* naval officer's coat.

Parker stared at him, incredulous. "That belongs to General Hooker," he said. "I'm to bring it to him tomorrow."

Will hung up his own coat and shrugged into it. "I will see how the General's coat feels on me," he said, then offered Parker the mischievous smile he remembered from childhood. "I dare you to put mine on, and we go to the theater!"

Parker laughed and played along. With its gold lace and epaulettes, Will's double-breasted tailcoat was quite showy. But Parker thought General Hooker's coat, two stars and all, looked "overpowering" on a young man of twenty.

And so, they ventured out on the town that evening. Will attracted attention wherever they went, people leaning over in their seats at the theater, or glancing over their shoulders on the street. "No doubt many [of them] asked their neighbors if they knew who that young major general was," Parker recalled with amusement years later.

Parker half-thought they would be questioned by other officers; or, worse, taken into custody by the military police. But no harm came, "and a couple of days later, at Falmouth, General Hooker wore the coat at the great review of the Army of the Potomac as he sat beside President Lincoln."

Will thoroughly enjoyed his three weeks in the capital. On his third day in town, he visited Gideon Welles at the Navy Department. Would he be interested in meeting the commander in chief, Welles asked?

"I have spoken to him about the good work you and Lieutenant Lamson have done for us," Welles said.

Will was speechless, his expression of astonishment and delight obvious to Welles, who arranged for them to meet the following week.

The next several days could not have passed quickly enough for Will as he awaited his reception at the White House. Each morning he took the train to Baltimore to check on work on the *Commodore Barney*, then returned to Washington to spend time with Parker and Milton. Unable to sleep the night before his meeting with Lincoln, he penned and memorized some eloquent words he meant to recite in his presence, voicing his patriotic loyalty to the country, and his willingness to fight to his last breath if necessary.

But when they finally met, the president was "rather subdued and sad—and did not talk about the war," Will wrote. "It is said that Chancellorsville was a blow to everyone here, and that [he] was very depressed by it."

Abandoning his planned speech, Will let Lincoln guide the direction of their conversation. They spoke for over an hour, and though Will never revealed what they discussed, he did say the president was pleased to compliment him "heartily" on his success. Despite Lincoln's pensive mood, Will left the meeting in high spirits about his future in the Navy.

When the *Barney*'s overhaul was incomplete after three weeks, another three weeks was added to his leave, which proved ideal. His mother, he learned, was visiting family in Boston, giving him a chance to see her outside drowsy Fredonia, while also enjoying the company of his female cousins and their pretty friends.

Will revived his love affair with Boston, where he had "a dozen different engagements a day, laughed, talked, smoked, enjoyed the society of the ladies, and had some grand rides, good fishing, and some splendid dinners on the sea beach." Then, toward the end of June, he left to check on the *Barney*'s progress.

On May 21, he sent Mary word from Baltimore that the ship was finally ready to leave the yard. "My good time is over now, and I have hauled aboard my 'dignity tacks' and become 'Captain Cushing' instead of 'Will'," he said. "My vessel is in good repair, and my crew is replenished, my battery is heavier than before; and I am prepared to pay upon sight all that I owe the rebels in the shape of shell, grape, and canister. It is not going to be a dull summer as near as I can find out."

Within days, Will was back in command of the *Barney* and off on another operation. General John Dix and about 10,000 troops were moving toward a town called White House, Virginia, to probe the Confederate defensive lines around Richmond. In the weeks after Chancellorsville, Robert E. Lee's army had moved relentlessly north toward Pennsylvania, drawing men and supplies from around the Southern capital. Now a scouting report had revealed that most rebel troops had left the vicinity. According to Dix's intelligence, the fortifications just two miles outside the city had reduced garrisons and only a few mounted guns.

Will's orders were to bring his ship up the York River to its intersection with its tributary the Pamunkey, conveying the fleet commander, Captain Pierce Crosby, to White House, Virginia, where Crosby would link up with Dix and his men, "take command of the United States naval vessels in the York River and its tributaries, and cooperate with the army under General Dix, giving all practicable assistance."

Accompanied by the gunboats *Commodore Morris* and *Morse,* and the transport steamer *Western World,* Will was also to aid in the landing of three hundred cavalry and supplies.

Soon after the cavalry went ashore, it launched a raid against a smaller Confederate mounted force, capturing Brigadier General William H. F. Lee, a son of Robert E. Lee, along with seven captains, two lieutenants, and a hundred privates. The raiders also seized a railroad bridge, thirty-five mule teams, a hundred additional mules, between seventy-five and a hundred horses, and about $20,000 in rebel bonds—a tidy haul taken with only light casualties.

Will continued to patrol the Pamunkey until June 29, when he received urgent new instructions from the admiral to "proceed immediately to Washington City, D.C., with the *Commodore Barney*...and report promptly to the Department for orders."

Robert E. Lee and his men had pushed far across Maryland toward Northern territory. Although General Hooker and the Army of the Potomac were in hot pursuit, Lee's army stayed several steps ahead of them. Fearing an imminent attack on Washington or Baltimore, Secretary Welles considered how best to deploy his naval forces.

Will steamed off toward the capital, even as General Lee reached the Pennsylvania border. Philadelphia was his actual target, but Lee had realized he would never be able to penetrate that far—not with Union forces close at his heels.

Gathering his troops, the Confederate general prepared to make a stand near a town called Gettysburg.

CHAPTER SEVENTEEN

I WILL GIVE THEM ONE MORE SHOT!

From the *New York Times*:

DETAILS FROM OUR SPECIAL CORRESPONDENT
Headquarters, Army of the Potomac, Saturday night, July 4, [1863]

The Battle of Gettysburg! I am told that it commenced, on the 1st of July, a mile north of the town, between two weak brigades of infantry and some doomed artillery and the whole force of the rebel arm....

Its value was priceless; however, though priceless was the young and the old blood with which it was bought. The error put us on the defensive, and gave us the choice of position.

THE PLAN OF BATTLE

From the moment that our artillery and infantry rolled back through the main street of Gettysburg and rolled out of the town to the circle of eminences south of it, we were not to attack but to be attacked. The risks, difficulties, and the disadvantages of the coming battle were the enemy's. Ours were the heights for artillery; ours the short, inside lines for maneuvering and reinforcing; ours the cover of stonewalls, fences, and the crests of hills. The ground upon which we were driven to accept battle was wonderfully favorable to us. A popular description of it would be to say that it was in form an elongated and somewhat sharpened horseshoe, with the toe to Gettysburg and the heel to the south.

Lee's plan of battle was simple. He massed his troops upon the east side of this shoe of position, and thundered on it obstinately to break it. The spelling of our batteries from the nearest overlooking hill, and the unflinching courage and complete discipline of the army of the Potomac repelled the attack. It was renewed at the point of the shoe—renewed desperately at the southwest heel—renewed on the western side with an effort...on which the fate of the invasion of Pennsylvania was fully put at stake.

Only a perfect infantry and an artillery educated in the midst of charges of hostile brigades could possibly have sustained this assault. [General Winfield Scott] Hancock's corps did sustain it, and has covered itself with immortal honors by its constancy and courage. The total wreck of Cushing's battery, [and] the list of its killed and wounded; the losses of officers, men and horses [Captain Andrew] Cowan sustained; and the marvelous outspread upon the board of death of dead soldiers and dead animals—dead soldiers in blue, and dead soldiers in gray, more marvelous to me than anything I have ever seen in war—are a ghastly and shocking testimony to the terrible fight of the Second Corps that none will gainsay.

That corps will ever have the distinction of breaking the pride and power of the rebel invasion....

•   •   •

Will Cushing arrived at Gettysburg days after the battle ended. His brother Lon was dead. He may have learned about the destruction of Alonzo's battery from the telegraph wire, from the *New York Times* report picked up by newspapers throughout the country, or possibly from some other source. Granted a leave of absence, he hoped to obtain his brother's body and, "if permitted," take command of his guns in the Army's next battle since Lon's entire officer cadre had been killed.

Unknown to Will, however, his brother Milton had already rushed to the scene, found Lon's remains, obtained a plain wooden soldier's casket, and escorted the body aboard a train to West Point for burial.

Will later described the field as "a sickening sight." Even with the army having begun its gruesome cleanup, "[t]hirty thousand wounded men, and thousands of unburied dead lay on the earth—in road, field, wood, and orchard and under the scorching sun on the bare hillside amid all the wreck of a great battle. Dismounted cannon, dead horses, exploded caissons, and broken muskets were everywhere—and the artillery position on Cemetery Hill [defended by Alonzo's Battery A, Fourth Artillery, on the north side of the battlefield] was almost paved with the rebel iron that had been hurled by the hundred and fifty guns massed against it previous to the final charge." Picking his way through the horrific carnage, Will found the battery wiped out. "Five out of the six guns were dismounted—all the officers and most of the men were shot, and seventy of its horses stiffened upon the wooded knoll where they were placed for shelter."

Will would eventually learn the details of Lon's heroic final hours and minutes from the accounts of his battery's survivors. Beginning on the second day of the offensive, when General Longstreet arrived to bolster Lee's strength with his artillery, Battery A's one hundred twenty-five men and six cannons had taken a concentrated pounding atop the cemetery heights. One after another, Lon's cannons were blown apart, his men falling dead and wounded on all sides. By the third day of battle, July 3, he had only a handful of working guns and bloodied artillerymen, as a rain of incoming shells poured continuously down on the hilltop. The sun an angry red ball visible through clouds of sulfurous yellow smoke, his exhausted, weakened men fought on in the ninety-degree heat and humidity. Critically low on ammunition, he had ordered those still at the guns to search for rocks, bullets, shell fragments, "even a bayonet" to jam into their barrels as shot.

Lon himself was in desperate shape. During one ferocious enemy barrage, shrapnel tore into his right shoulder, and, moments later, his leg and genitals. In horrible pain, blood dripping from his tattered shell jacket and breeches, he refused to let his sergeant, a burly German named Fuger, bring him to the rear for medical attention.

"No," he protested, "I stay right here and fight it out or die in the attempt!"

That same day, General Longstreet reluctantly ordered a charge of 13,000 troops through the Union's defenses. Convinced it would result in an unnecessary number of casualties, Longstreet had expressed his reservations. But with Robert E. Lee ordering the charge, Longstreet prepared for action. General George Pickett would lead his division through the federal center, where Lon's ragged Battery A was holding the line. About three o'clock that afternoon, Pickett's brigades began to advance. Lon would have seen them marching up the slope in columns half a mile long, the red flags of rebellion waving high above their heads. He would have heard their fifes and drums rattling "Dixie" into the air as they came on in a human tide.

At Lon's command, his gunners tore into the enemy ranks. But at once, the Confederate artillery answered, shelling his battery with volley after murderous volley from behind the charge. Meanwhile, the rebels kept coming in the face of the Union barrage, stepping over their own dead and dying as they relentlessly ascended the hill.

Sick and bleeding profusely from his wounds, Lon had stayed at the guns to assist his "tired, powder-burned and bruised" artillerymen until the head of the enemy column was within three hundred yards of them.

One of his men later recalled him pressing his thumb to the vent of a gun without a thumb pad and burning it down to the bone. Thumbing the vent was required on each reload to stop air from entering the breech and igniting embers in the tube; with the leather pad lost or worn out, Lon would have needed to press his bare finger to the vent, holding it steady against the red-hot gun barrel as his flesh was excruciatingly charred and seared.

The enemy charge continued amid the earsplitting thunder of battle, the Southern boys enveloped in smoke and flying dust, many of them "bent in a half stoop...as if to protect their faces and dodge the balls." With just two workable guns left, Lon had them moved up to an angular rock wall at the very summit of the hill, peered through his field glasses, and saw the rebels closing in, "a mingled mass, from fifteen to thirty deep." So weak he could barely keep his legs under him, Lon told Sergeant Fuger to relay his orders to the men and had them load the guns. They hurriedly scavenged for ammunition, pushed whatever they could find into the muzzles, and then tensely waited for Lon to give the firing order.

His glasses to his eyes, he stuck to his gun and let the enemy draw close enough for him to make out their faces through the swirling dust...and then closer still, so they were practically staring down the canon's muzzle. At last he shouted "Fire!"

Fuger echoed his command, and the cannons disgorged a hailstorm of flame and improvised canister, smashing through the rebel wave. Then one of the men, Corporal Thomas Moon, saw Armistead drop to the ground on one side of Lon's gun, and Lon crumple at his knees on the other side. The devoted Sergeant Fuger, standing some three feet away, also noticed Lon falling forwards and rushed over to catch his body in his arms. A musket ball had struck him below the nose and traveled through his upper jaw into his brain, killing him instantly. Moon would later reflect that if he had remained at the gun like Cushing, he would have died there with him.

Left in command of the battery, Fuger had ordered two men to carry Lon to the rear and shouted for the rest of them to obey his orders—not only the cannoneers, but the drivers who had brought the guns to the front, and whose horses were dead. As the rebels came swarming over the wall, the artillerymen of Battery A stood their ground, "fighting hand-to-hand with pistols, sabers, handspikes, or rammers, until, with the help of [General Alexander] Webb's Pennsylvanians (four regiments), who had rushed from the rear" to support the artillery batteries on the heights, the enemy were all killed or disabled. "Not one" of the party that came over the stone wall ever returned to a rebel camp.

That night the only sound on the hill was the hiss of rain drilling into the field below. The Confederates had pulled back in defeat, General Lee ordering a retreat over the Potomac into Maryland.

Corporal Moon was on guard duty through the downpour, with three men under him. But all they had to guard at the wall were "a few dead men." They pushed the bodies together, forming a macabre bed, and remained atop them until dawn, so they would not have to lay on the soaked, muddied ground.

The next morning, Moon and another man took off Lon's bloodied uniform blouse and shoulder straps. Moon would carry them with him until the next winter and give them to Howard Cushing at Brandy Railroad Station in Virginia.

When Will Cushing came to Gettysburg, he knew very few of the circumstances of his brother's death. But he did know Lon had fought to the last breath. He had been brave, gallant, and sacrificed himself for his men and country. Will knew Alonzo had died proudly.

With his body already on its way to New York, Will took the rail back to Washington feeling empty and lost. He would return to his ship, still mourning for his beloved Lon. But deep within him, nestled in pain and grief, was a desire for revenge.

If the rebels should kill him, I don't think that I would be a man any longer. I should become a fiend.

Over the next twelve months, Will would prove those words—written to Mary long before from the deck of the *Minnesota*—eerily prophetic.

CHAPTER EIGHTEEN

GOOD CONDUCT

From a report to Congress:

DESTRUCTION OF THE BLOCKADE RUNNER *HEBE*,
ANGLO-REBEL STEAMER

S. P. Lee, Acting Rear-Admiral, Commanding North America Blockading Squadron
United States Flagship Minnesota
Off Wilmington, N.C., August 24, 1863.

Sirs,

At daylight on the 18th instant, the [Confederate] steamer *Hebe* attempted to run into Wilmington by the New Inlet entrance. Being headed off by the [USS] *Niphon*, Acting Ensign Breck commanding, she chose to head ashore a few miles above Fort Fisher (on Federal Point), and her crew escaped in boats....

As there was no prospect of getting the *Hebe* off, she was
set on fire by a boarding party from the *Niphon*, or by the
shells of the *Niphon* and [USS] *Shokokon*, Lieutenant W. B.
Cushing commanding, after the boarding party had been
captured by the enemy—who, with two pieces of artillery
and riflemen, well protected by the sand hills close by, fired
sharply upon the boarding party and upon the vessels....

Lieutenant Cushing and Acting Ensign Breck deserve
credit for their good conduct on this occasion.

Will's second command, the USS *Shokokon,* was by his own
description "an experiment of the Navy Department," a large, fast,
light-draft ferryboat with a "built out" or strengthened hull that "pos-
sessed many advantages in maneuvering amongst the shoals of Wilmington Harbor."

Admiral Lee had major reservations about the sidewheel steamer's
ability to endure the rough waters around the Capes, and the captain
originally assigned to her had considered her unseaworthy without a trial.
But when the *Barney* was again sent for repairs, the admiral opted to let
Will have a crack at giving the new vessel a run as a blockader. Will could
then decide for himself whether it was up to the task. If he concluded
otherwise, he could sail it back to Hampton Roads and have another ship.

It was good for Will to get back on active duty. He had spent July in
Washington with Milton, the two brothers doing their best to console
each other over Lon's death, trying to overcome their grief to whatever
extent they could manage. His loss took a psychological and emotional
toll on the entire family. At the end of that month, Will had written his
mother that he was about to be assigned the *Shokokon*, calling it a ship
with a "jaw-breaking Indian name," mentioning that he would be stalking "anglo-rebel steamers" off Wilmington, and telling her to "look out
for prize money."

But he had known his talk of blockading and prizes would be
faint comfort in her sorrow. "I long to hear from you, dear Mother,

and know that you do not feel utterly lonely and sad," he concluded. "Think how many children you have left, and how dearly they love you."

On August 11, Will reported to Captain Augustus Ludlow Case, who assigned him to "the southern end of the line, to watch the shores of Smith's Island and the shoals along which vessels often pass in and out." Bringing the ship to her station, Will would also develop "serious doubts as to whether she would survive a good, stiff gale." But he resolved to find out.

Within a week, Will and Breck engaged the *Hebe* at New Inlet. It was the *Niphon* that initially spotted her burning black smoke en route to Wilmington, and moved in to head her off, driving her aground. When Breck saw the blockade runner's crew fleeing in boats, he sent out a party in one of his dinghies with orders to set her afire.

Breck knew he would be unable to put her in tow. A gale wind was blowing, and the sea was too heavy.

On the schooner, the boarding party found a valuable cargo of drugs, coffee, clothing, provisions, some bales of silk, and several cases of liquor. One of their leaders, Ensign Dewey, later praised his men for working "with alacrity" to gather combustibles and start the ship burning. Mentioning the liquor in his after-action report, he proudly wrote that "instead of drinking it, they broke the bottles and poured the contents upon the fuel."

Given that they would soon find themselves leaping overboard into a stormy sea, it was good thing they did not pause to imbibe.

As they tried to start their fires, failing twice because of the water and wind slamming the deck, the *Shokokon* arrived at the scene. Bolstered by added manpower, Breck sent out two other dinghies to assist his boarding party, Will providing a third to go with them. But the whitecaps drove one of the *Niphon*'s boats onto the sand, where rebel cavalry suddenly appeared from the wooded embankment behind the beach and took its crew prisoner at gunpoint. His other dinghy succeeded in bringing a couple of men off the schooner.

The *Shokokon*'s boat, meanwhile, was lowered with a line running back to the ship. When Dewey realized it aboard the schooner, he took a small rope from the deck and jumped overboard, thinking he could cast it out so those he'd left behind could leap from the schooner and grab hold of it. But the sea twice knocked him against the *Hebe*'s propeller, and he would do nothing but make for the rescue boat along with one other man.

After Breck's remaining dinghy brought the men back to the *Niphon,* he sent it out again to rescue the rest of the boarding party. It never reached the schooner. The waves broke over it, swamping it until it capsized, forcing its crew to jump overboard into the turbulent water. All swam to shore and were captured.

On the deck of the *Shokokon*, meanwhile, Will saw fifty more butternuts, all infantrymen, rush down from the bank to join the mounted troops, spouting ammunition at the two federal steamers from muskets and two British artillery pieces—Whitworth twelve-pounders. That sped a decision for him. He and Breck could not remain exposed to such intense fire for long without sustaining severe damage. The *Hebe* had to be destroyed.

Will sent a single shot wide of the schooner to warn the three members of the boarding party still onboard to abandon ship. Then, as they splashed onto the beach, he riddled her with fire. Twice his shells set her ablaze and twice the seawater spraying across her deck smothered the flames. But at last an explosive projectile detonated behind the smokestack and she started to burn, the flames spreading from stern to bow, raging on until she was a charred wreck.

Zigzagging around the schooner at distances between one and three hundred yards, Will kept his fire for four hours, Breck's ship joining him in the barrage, the rebels in turn harassing them with their Whitworths the entire time. All the Confederate artillery shells passed harmlessly over Will's gunship; when she finally pulled off, she was scored by musket shells but otherwise unmarked. Breck would report almost the same thing. "Strange to say," he wrote, "no one was hurt by either rifles or large shot. Our running rigging was somewhat cut up, and we have a great many marks of bullets about our masts and bulwarks, but no damage of consequence, except the loss of our three boats."

There could have been no better antidote to Will's grief—or outlet for his wrath—than the schooner's destruction. But the loss of the rebel cargo, the *Niphon*'s dinghies, and most of her men left a gnawing frustration inside him.

Then he had a thought.

Back on August 12, he'd lead a small boat reconnaissance into New Topsail Inlet and was driven out by the fire of four rebel artillery pieces stationed opposite the inlet's mouth. But that had not occurred before he discovered a schooner, the *Alexander Cooper*, moored at a wharf some six miles up the sound and protected by a battery of six guns.

Will now grew determined to destroy the ship. And as it was so well guarded, he concluded he would need a strategy.

*   *   *

The only snag was that Will's senior officer, Captain Case, "declined to permit" his request to cut out the schooner on grounds that it would involve an irresponsible "risk of life," although Will offered another theory for the refusal in his memoir, speculating that "the great fish present could not surrender so dainty a morsel to a 'youngster.'"

He refused to take "no" for an answer.

On the evening of August 22, he moved ahead with the expedition in outright contradiction of orders, anchoring the *Shokokon* close in to the ocean beach about a mile downstream from the schooner and sending two boatloads of men ashore with a dinghy. That put them a fair distance to the rear of the artillery force guarding the mouth of the sound.

Will's instructions were clear. Acting under his executive officer, Acting Ensign Joseph S. Cony, the half dozen crewmen were to seek out and capture anything that could be of use to the enemy.

The dinghy hefted onto their shoulders, the men began crossing the neck of land that divided the sea from the sound. Although only a half mile wide, the neck was covered with dense scrub oak, which would make for a halting, strenuous hike.

The *Shokokon*, meanwhile, remained anchored well off to the south, her stack pouring out coal smoke that curled up above the treetops and was spotted by lookouts high on the schooner's mastheads.

Will had calculated the distraction in advance. The rebels, he hoped, would assume he was preparing to launch an expedition up the mouth of the inlet, and "make every preparation for [his] reception."

His plan worked like a charm. Near nightfall, while the lookouts "strained their eyes" gazing in the wrong direction, Cony reached the reeds at the edge of the sound, boarded the dinghy with six men, and launched into the water, rowing toward the schooner with muted oars. A short while later, they landed unnoticed about fifty yards from the wharf. A trusted master-at-arms named Clifford, sent out alone as an advance scout, crept toward the rebel camp in the darkness, took a head count, made note of its Whitford twelve-pounder, and returned to his shipmates saying they were outnumbered, three to one.

Cony was versed in Will's tactics of surprise and deception. He ordered a charge of the enemy camp, and his group bore down on the rebels with a collective shout. Convinced they were facing more than just seven men, the bulk of the Confederate detachment fled without a fight, leaving behind ten prisoners, and abandoning the *Alexander Cooper*, their twelve-pounder, eighteen horses, and some extensive saltworks. The sailors spiked the gun and burned the vessel and the buildings with the help of some slaves.

That left them with something of a problem. Their dinghy was too small to accommodate more than three prisoners; at the same time, it would be impossible to guard the group of them while returning overland to their boats in the brush and darkness.

Again, Cony used a ploy Will would later appreciate. After signaling to boats out upon the water, he told seven of their captives to walk a quarter mile up the bank and report to a Lieutenant Jones, who was supposed to be waiting there to take them into custody. Before they started, there was a warning: do not stray too far from the path Cony laid out or pickets would shoot them. As to the question of which prisoners to bring back to the *Shokokon*...

"The rebel officers and privates were dressed alike, and Mr. Cony was at a loss to know what three to retain," Will told the admiral. "He settled the matter, however, by picking out the three best looking ones, who all turned out to be privates. So the officers owed their safety to their lack of physique, a new feature in military strategy."

Though still in terrible anguish over Lon's death, Will was at least showing a bit of his old humor. He was also justifiably proud of his men. In his report, he praised Cony and the rest effusively, while saving his highest praise for Clifford. "[He] has volunteered upon no less than four occasions of danger since I have been aboard and never fails to do his duty," Will wrote. "He is qualified for promotion to master's mate."

Later Clifford received a medal and promotion at Admiral Lee's request. Cony was promoted that same day, in his case to acting Master's Mate. As for the *Shokokon's* young captain, it was particularly good that Lee tailored the facts retroactively, stating he had sanctioned the foray.

There could have been no greater sign that Will had made his mark in the United States Navy than having a rear-admiral cover up his insubordination.

•   •   •

In the last week of August, the *Shokokon* was removed from service not because of damage sustained in battle but because of a nor'easter of hurricane strength. The blow ran every Union blockade ship in flotilla out to sea as they fled its destructive winds, forcing Will seek cover on the lee side of Frying Pan Shoals.

His ship barely survived. During the gale, "her wood ends opened about half an inch" and she began to leak "to the extent of 450 gallons a minute." When struck by a surging wave, "she seemed to give and bend like India rubber." The wind tore the boiler from her hull, the sea carried away her forward ports, and both conspired to split her sternpost.

Will was convinced that if she had been ten miles further out in the Atlantic, she would have gone down. As he reflected, "it was close work, and quite experiment enough" for the gunboat. Admiral Lee concurred.

After the storm, the *Shokokon* went to Hampton Roads for comprehensive repairs. Meanwhile, Will's orders sent him to Washington, D.C., as a bearer of dispatches. He would spend several months ashore fighting boredom and trying to stay out of trouble.

CHAPTER NINETEEN

THE *ALBEMARLE*

The dispatch arrived for Captain Cooke as he was enjoying tea with Mrs. Catherine Ann Edmonston and her family at Hascosea, her summer home and the smaller of two plantations owned by the Edmonstons, who ranked among the wealthiest and most influential of North Carolina's planter aristocrats.

It was Saturday, August 1, 1863. Earlier that day, Mrs. Edmonston had been down to visit Edwards Ferry, the site of Gilbert Elliot's shipbuilding operation since the spring of that year. While Tillery's Farm had certainly benefited from its nearness to the well-serviced and protected Halifax shipyard, Elliot's move to Edwards Ferry, twenty-odd miles downriver on the south bank of the Roanoke, was all about the ironclad ram.

At first, Elliot held some doubts about it. There were no existing yard facilities on the property offered to him by William Ruffin Smith, a wealthy slaveholder and long-time proponent of Southern rebellion. In fact, it was an active cornfield, the ground "already marked out and planted for the coming crop." Elliott had supposed he might find "a portable sawmill, blacksmith's forge, or other apparatus" scattered about the area, but it was clear preparing the site for his use would be a challenge.

Captain Cooke had been quicker to see its advantages, pointing out that the 2,600-acre location was about the size of Tillery's Farm and the Tarboro site combined, giving Elliott enough room to build his own machine shops and house a labor force for the ironclad's construction—a force Smith offered to bolster by letting Elliott choose all the men he needed from among his plantation workers. Also, Elliott had repeatedly petitioned the army to assign a guard detail to his yards and was rejected for several reasons, including a lack of space to accommodate the troops. The larger site, Cooke suggested, might ease resistance to his appeals.

Elliott was eventually swayed, placing no small value on the enthusiasm Smith and his son Peter showed toward his greatest enterprise. "In hearty sympathy" with it, they promised to aid him "in a thousand ways to accomplish the end [he] had in view." Peter Smith and his wife Rebecca even invited him to lodge at their home for the duration of the project, opening its doors wide to him.

The move was clinched in the early spring when Smith gave Elliott a horseback tour of the plantation to scout out a suitable spot for a shipyard. Elliott had noticed "a field gently sloping north towards the river, while nestled between slightly higher banks."

Being familiar with the river's seasonal rise and fall, Elliott recognized that the site would be "sufficiently free from overflow to admit of uninterrupted work for at least twelve months." He also believed—with good reason—that Union spies had been keeping track of the ram's construction and was convinced the relative year-round shallowness of the water would make it difficult for the enemy to send down gunships to prevent its completion. Finally, the field bordered stands of oak and yellow pine, timbers of an ideal strength for the ironclad's frame and planking. Elliott had envisioned building a sawmill so the wood could be cut easily, milled, and transported over to the stocks.

The young shipbuilder made his decision. In March, he'd transferred his operations to Edwards Ferry and never voiced a single word of regret. Despite its remoteness and crude conditions, the new site's advantages far outweighed its drawbacks.

But four months had passed since the relocation, and for all the support Elliot had gotten from the Smiths and local populace, the ironclad's delivery still lagged behind schedule. To some extent, the delay was an inevitable consequence of the move itself; the month of May was spent readying ground for the stocks, which had needed the right combination of stability and slope to support a vessel calculated to weigh 376 prodigious tons at launch, and make it possible to move something that big and heavy down the slipway into the water. There were other logistical problems, but the main impediment to progress was the same.

Elliott needed more iron.

Iron for the ship's machinery, iron for her armor, and iron for the guns.

As project superintendent, the indefatigable Commander Cooke had done everything he could to advance its acquisition from sources everywhere. His friendship with the Edmonstons, socially prominent neighbors of the Smith family, arose in part from the simple hospitality they had extended to him, his wife, and ten-year-old son, who would sometimes stay at their home for extended visits. But it did not lack for canny pragmatism. An obsessive diarist and passionate anti-abolitionist, Catherine Edmonston enjoyed chronicling the ram's progress at Edwards Ferry, while observing and logging troop and naval movements of the "deplorable" Northerners. She also loved to entertain and made Cooke a regular at her frequent lunches and dinner soirees with influential friends.

"Captain Cooke still with us," she wrote in one journal entry. "I hope he will construct such a boat as will deter the Yankees from an advance up our river."

He certainly shared that hope and took full advantage of Mrs. Edmonston's gatherings to lubricate voucher approvals at the Navy Department and hasten deliveries of precious iron. But he did not stop there. Throughout that summer, Cooke had scoured the state for scrap iron, pulling broken boilers from junk piles, asking women and children to donate old pots and pans, and leading raiding parties to ransack farm tools, tear up railroad ties, and even gather buckets of bolts that would be brought to Tredegar Ironworks to be melted down for the ram's armor plating. Whether through finesse, force, charm, or intimidation, knocking on doors or knocking them down, Cooke was singlemindedly resolved to see the project through to a successful conclusion.

But the "shreds and patches" of iron he accumulated would only take things so far along. As the Ironmonger Captain led his raiding parties around the countryside, he had joined Elliott in pressing the Department for more of what they needed. If the ram's existing machinery and armor was built with a "determined will that mastered doubt," that "will" would not be enough to keep production from sputtering to a halt without a substantial bulk shipment of the critical metal.

Meanwhile, Cooke and Elliott had diligently kept the good graces of Catherine Edmonston by continuing to attend her socials, updating her about the vessel's construction, and, on occasion, inviting her to inspect it. Earlier on the day of their tea, Cooke had brought her down to the stocks for a viewing, and she'd returned to Hascosea impressed.

"I rode down to the boat…with Capt. Cooke to see the object of so much care and anxiety, and found a negro force employed throwing up entrenchments & preparing to mount small cannon which the Department have sent her to defend it," she entered in her journal. "The boat is much larger than I had supposed & seems a strong & substantial piece of work."

Mrs. Edmonston had asked Cooke to return to Hascosea with her afterward, and he gladly took her up on the offer. He was sipping from his teacup amid a pleasant late afternoon breeze when a servant brought Elliott's telegram out to the garden.

His expression grew anxious as he read, telling the Edmonstons something was wrong.

"The federals are at Rich Square," he said at last. "They have come in force."

The group fell silent. Rich Square was just seven miles northeast across the Roanoke.

Cooke hesitated. "They are inquiring for the gunboat," he said, confirming their fears.

He hastily excused himself, mounted his horse, and rode off with a promise to return with any further news.

On his arrival at Rich Square late that night, he learned from Confederate troops that the rising river was a godsend, its height preventing the enemy from moving their artillery "near enough to its north bank to allow a clear shot at the yard." Cooke was also informed that another Federal troop detachment, either from Murfreesboro or Winton, had been moving behind the advance column. But when Union forces at the north bank realized they'd pushed too far ahead of the rest, they had withdrawn and turned around to join them.

Cooke was back at Hascosea around dawn, "worn and wearied out" after having been in the saddle all night. The word he brought the Edmonstons was a relief, but they knew the short-lived Union troop buildup had been a warning. The yard at Edwards Ferry needed greater protection.

Lieutenant William F. Martin, who had a vested interest in its safety, was quick to ensure it. On his recommendation, Lieutenant Colonel Stephen D. Pool's battalion composed of Companies B, G, and H of the Tenth Regiment was sent to Fort Branch on the Roanoke, some miles below the shipyard near Union-controlled territory. Their orders were "to garrison and strengthen" the fortification and "prevent the enemy's gunboats from ascending the river and destroying the ironclad at Edwards Ferry." With Pool assigned elsewhere, Captain J. L. Manney was in charge of the battalion, which remained at Fort Branch until year's end.

Commander Cooke was pleased with the reinforcements. But his mind kept its abiding, relentless focus. Iron was paramount. The scraps he'd gathered were not enough to meet his needs; he desired, beyond all else, a major shipment.

It would not be long before he got his wish.

•   •   •

On August 24, Gilbert Elliott welcomed a notable visitor to Edwards Ferry. Adam Tredwell, the assistant paymaster of the Confederate States

Navy, had made the trip down from Richmond to present him with a $10,000 voucher for the transport of iron stored at a place called Besse's Station on the Atlantic and North Carolina Railroad line between Morehead City and busy Goldsboro junction.

How much iron was waiting there, Elliott enquired?

Four hundred and fifty tons, Tredwell told him.

The shipbuilder was euphoric. For close to a year, North Carolina's governor Zebulon Vance and Flag Officer William. F. Lynch—the former commander of the naval defenses at Roanoke Island and now the leader of all the Confederate naval force's state waters—had been in negotiations to obtain railroad iron from the mostly government-owned rail company. At last, those talks had yielded fruit.

With Tredwell's funds at his disposal, Commander Cooke hurriedly pulled together a caravan of men and wagons to cart the iron to Trefelgar. Brought there in the form of track ties, it would be hot-rolled into plates and then transported overland from Richmond to the shipyard.

Four hundred-fifty tons of iron was easily enough to finish armoring the ram. Their elusive dream was close to becoming a reality.

CHAPTER TWENTY

ZEALOUS AND ABLE

In early September 1863, Will Cushing conveyed his packet of assorted naval documents to Gideon Welles in Washington, thinking he would return to the North Atlantic squadron before too long. After all, one of the dispatches from Admiral Lee concerned Will, recommending that he was to be removed from the leaky *Shokokan* and given a new command. The message praised him as "a zealous and able young officer" sent to the capital "in the belief that the Department will cheerfully assign him to a swift and staunch steamer...and return him for present duty on the blockade of Wilmington."

Will soon received his command. He was to take the helm of the USS *Monticello,* the same screw steamer that had taken part in the attack on Hatteras Inlet under Admiral Silas Stringham. One of the Navy's crown jewels, she was "a real war vessel," sleek, black, and low-lying in the water, capable of "well over twelve knots under steam and canvas," with two masts, "an intricate curling decoration painted in gold alongside her bows," and her name set off in the same brilliant gold.

Eager to inspect her, Will rode the train to the Philadelphia navy yard where she was docked for repairs and a full overhaul. He thought her the most beautiful ship he'd ever seen, a true reward for his service. Still, the extensive work being done on her was projected to take weeks, and he saw no point in hanging around to wait. Requesting a leave of absence, he traveled up to Fredonia to visit his mother.

Will had not seen her since Alonzo's death and was stunned by how much she had aged. Grieving and forlorn, Mary Barker Cushing sat alone in a house that was cheerless and quiet as a tomb. It occurred to him that Lon would have been the one to brighten her spirits. But he was gone, buried deep in the soil at West Point.

Will stayed on at his family home for about a week. His old bedroom felt small and confining, and while it pleased him to learn that his letters were regularly published in the *Censor*, and that reading his exploits had become quite the popular diversion to his former neighbors, he felt bored and out of place among them.

At night, his mother would ask him to join her in praying at her bedside. She would kneel and close her eyes, asking God to forgive those who took Lon from her, then imploring Him to protect Howard, her oldest son, who was off to the war in Illinois. No one had heard from Howard for over a month, and she worried for his safety. She could not bear to lose another of her boys and prayed that he had not fallen to harm.

His head bowed, Will would do the same, quietly mouthing words of entreaty, words his mother wanted to hear, thinking they would bring her a measure of peace. But his heart seethed like a furnace over Lon's death. His true prayers were for vengeance.

After about a week, edgy and restless, Will was ready to leave for Philadelphia. Though she never said it aloud, his mother wanted him to stay. But he wanted to return to battle. Promising he would try to find out about Howard, he hopped aboard the train to Washington and then went on to Philadelphia to superintend the progress of his ship.

Much to his frustration, he learned the *Monticello* would be stuck at the dock a while longer. The work seemed interminable, and he was bored and irritated from prolonged inactivity. Moreover, a contentious gubernatorial race had divided the people of Philadelphia. The city's

Democrats stridently opposed the war and wanted a quick settlement with the South. Their candidate, a man named George Washington Woodard, was running hard to unseat the abolitionist Republican incumbent and Lincoln ally Governor Curtin.

Arriving in town, Will checked into the Continental Hotel at the corner of Chestnut and Ninth Streets, a short walk from the yard where the *Monticello* docked. With electioneering at its overheated peak, the Democratic newspapers had alleged that Lincoln looked to "carry the election of the country" by using soldiers to cow potential Woodard voters. In full uniform, Will caught the eye of a Copperhead in the busy hotel rotunda. He was not only a soldier, but a naval officer, and a ready target.

Will was signing his name in the register when the man jostled against him and shouted, *"Here's another one of Lincoln's hirelings come to intimidate us at the election!"*

He had taunted the wrong officer. Canes were fashionable at the time, and Will was carrying one. He swung the cane at the troublemaker and opened a deep cut in his face.

As the man's hands flew up to the bloody gash, the people in the rotunda separated according to their political sympathies, lining up for a brawl—but someone must have alerted the police. Pushing through the crowd from the hotel entrance, they arrested Will "under the complaint of the man he had struck" and tossed him behind bars.

But he had his supporters among the eyewitnesses. Soon, as many as fifteen or twenty wealthy citizens showed up at the station house to pay his bail. The next morning, Will appeared in court, paid a fine and was released from custody.

The matter did not end there. A couple of days later, his penchant for carrying a grudge—and the seething anger he carried over Lon's death—overrode his better judgement.

Will had learned the instigator of the fight owned a drugstore near the Philadelphia, Wilmington, and Baltimore Railroad station at Broad and Pine Streets. Deciding to take a trip to Hampton Roads, he checked the train schedule, timed the ride from the store to the station, and took a cab over to the drugstore with his luggage aboard. Asking the driver to wait, he leaped out of his coach, ran into the drugstore, pulled the man from behind the counter, and handed him a severe beating. Then he jumped back out into the cab "and reached the station as the train was beginning to move."

Will considered the incident "closed." It is unknown how the pharmacist felt about it. But Will would spend some weeks away from Philadelphia as the *Monticello*'s overhaul wore on.

On November 19, he headed back to Pennsylvania, but stopped in Gettysburg for the dedication of the military cemetery. It was a sobering day, and Will's heart was heavy with loss. Far toward the rear of the crowd, he could barely hear President Lincoln's historic speech but would read his words in the newspaper the next day.

•   •   •

It was February 17, 1864. The USS *Monticello*, finally seaworthy, arrived for blockade duty at the mouth of the Cape Fear River, taking her station some thirty miles south of Wilmington. Five long months had passed since Will's last raid aboard the *Shokokon*, and not even Christmas in Washington with Cousin Mary and her father or Commodore Smith had done much to brighten the cold, dreary winter for him. The family had done its best to celebrate the holiday in a spirit of joyful togetherness. But Lon's death, and the death of Smith's son Joe at Hampton Roads the previous year, cast a pall of sadness and depression over their celebrations.

Will craved action to take his mind off his grief and satisfy his hunger for revenge.

His first week on the Wilmington blockade was routine. During the day, his squadron remained anchored at the sand bar, beyond the range of Confederate guns, watching for the smoke of escaping steamers. During the night, the blockade ships would creep close to the bar and form a line, their leaden grey hulls blending with the fog and foam. Will would catch what little sleep he could in the late-morning hours.

On February 21, he decided to break up the tedium and launch a cutting-out expedition—in honor of Washington's birthday, he claimed. The scheme was pure Will Cushing. He intended to anchor the *Monticello* inshore under the guns of Fort Caswell and then slip into Wilmington harbor with three small boats, passing between Caswell and Fort Campbell on the opposite shore. The goal was to find a prize in the harbor, "capture her by boarding, and run her out, by their guns, to the squadron."

At 9:30 p.m., however, the *Monticello* was spotted from the forts and driven back down toward the river's entrance by their guns. Will was not deterred. Thirty minutes later, he left the ship in an armed gig and went ahead to lead the boats up the channel with forty sailors. Their oars muffled, the men rowed past the forts undetected but found no vessels in the anchorage.

Disappointed, Will considered dashing ashore onto Smith's Island on the eastern side of the inlet and tearing the rebel flag from its battery. But as he rowed close to reconnoiter the fortification, an oar accidentally grazed its earthwork wall.

Thinking the noise a dead giveaway, he braced for a challenge—but none came. To his astonishment, the loud knocking of the oar did not draw a sentry. The enemy was overconfident and careless, he concluded. A new plan hatched in his mind, but it would require reinforcements.

Benjamin Sands was fleet commander and captain of the sidewheel steamer USS *Fort Jackson*. At age fifty-three, the long-bearded Sands was known more for his hydrographic inventions than battle experience. Which made him precisely the type of senior officer Will disliked.

Returning to the squadron, Will approached Sands with his plan. If the rebels were so careless as to miss the sound of his oar, it seemed certain they would be vulnerable to a surprise attack.

"I request your permission to take the island," he said. "With two hundred men, I could hold it until relieved by the army."

Sands was reluctant. He thought the mission too risky absent more detailed intelligence. But Will pressed his case, explaining it would close to the enemy one of the troublesome entrances to the Cape Fear River.

The commander refused to bend. "Can't take the responsibility," he said dismissively.

Will had gotten such responses before—and he would later confess this one provoked him. It was known that Fort Caswell's commanding officer, Brigadier General Louis Hébert, made his headquarters in the village of Smithville on the island.

Take responsibility?

"I can not only do that, but if you want the Confederate general off to breakfast, I will bring him," he said.

Will left Sand's cabin without another word and returned to his ship. He wanted to begin his preparations and fully intended to deliver on his promise. He would capture Hébert and board any vessels found at anchor.

On the night of February 29, the *Monticello* lowered two boats into the chop, Will in the lead aboard the gig, with acting Master's Mate W. L. Howorth serving as his second-in-command. Acting Ensign J. E. Jones was in charge of the second boat, a cutter.

Their oars dipping into the water, the boats started toward the harbor. Will knew nothing about Smithville besides its position on the charts and importance to the rebels. But he thought his plan "too bold to fail."

A short while after setting out, Will succeeded in landing directly in front of Smithville's only hotel. He was in the center of town, not thirty yards from the angle of the fort at the island's point.

Moving stealthily in the shadows of the elevated bank, Will noticed a saltworks with a pair of slaves hard at work, took them prisoner at gunpoint, and questioned them about the island's layout and troop dispositions. They supplied all the information he needed. The general's residence and command center, a large house with a southern veranda, was just up the street from the hotel in the town center. Opposite the house was a barracks with about twelve hundred sleeping troops inside it. No more than fifty feet separated the buildings.

Leaving most of his men behind to guard the boats, Will took How-arth, Jones, a seaman, and one of the slaves into town with him. With the slave serving as their guide, they crept up the street, reached the large house, and stole across the veranda to a door.

Will pressed his shoulder against the door, and it swung open. Leading his men inside, he found he was in a large, darkened mess room—there were tables, chairs, and dishes, but it seemed unoccupied. A flight of stairs led up to the second story, and Will climbed it on the balls of his feet, striking a match when he reached the top. In its pale, flickery glow, he saw several doors that opened off the landing. He chose the nearest one, reached for the handle, pushed it inward—and then hearing a loud, sudden crash below him, froze where he stood.

"Captain! Captain!"

Will turned, raced back downstairs, and heard someone bumping around behind a door. Pushing it open, he simultaneously lit another match, and by its flash saw a half-clothed man facing him, holding an upraised chair in his hands as if to strike.

There was no time to hesitate. Barreling through the entryway, Will pounced on the man and wrestled him down on his back, his hand over his throat, the muzzle of his revolver at his temple.

"Say one word, and I will kill you," Will said. He assumed the man was General Hébert. His pistol held steady, he rose, motioning him to his feet. Then he struck a third match and lit the room's candle.

Questioning the man on the spot, Will realized that he had not snared his desired prize, but Captain Patrick Kelly, the chief engineer of the lower Cape Fear defenses. General Hébert, it turned out, was in Wilmington.

Will did nothing to betray his disappointment. "Is anyone else in the house?" he asked.

Kelly was too terrified to lie. The adjutant general, Hardman—he had just fled the place. His bed was close to the window, and he'd heard suspicious noises out in the veranda. Tossing off his blankets, he had opened the window, stuck his head out, and peered into the gloom.

The first sight to meet his eyes was the muzzle of a navy revolver about two inches from his nose—Master's Mate Howarth's gun, Will would learn. With his free hand, Howarth had reached out and grabbed Hardman's arm, trying to drag him out the window. But fear endowed Hardman with quickness and strength. Slamming the window down hard on his own hand, he felt a jolt of agony, wrenched his arm back inside, and dashed out the back door in his nightshirt and stockinged feet.

It is a good joke, but not exactly the time to laugh, Will thought. In a minute, soldiers would be swarming like angry bees from the barracks.

Hurrying his prisoner into his "most necessary garments," Will pocketed the papers of the absconding adjutant, gathered the men, and hastened down toward his boat. The town was alive by this time, but "like the old gent with the spectacles on his forehead—looking everywhere but in the right place."

As it turned out, Will's party had caught a break. Hardman had not even imagined that Union soldiers would have the audacity to storm into the house. Instead, he thought a mutiny in progress and scrambled off into the woods without alerting the garrison.

Meanwhile, Will arrived at the beach with the adjutant and slaves. He had meant to take the Confederate general out of the harbor in one of his own steamers, which would have been icing on the proverbial cake. But neither general nor steamer were present, so he had to settle for loading the prisoners he'd snagged into his little gig.

The captives aboard, Will shoved off into the cold, black river. His boats were about fifty yards from the Smithville fortification, and a shorter distance from the sentinel at the wharf, but they departed so quietly no one noticed them. Behind them on the island, drums were beating out a roll as the butternuts rushed to their guns. But they were too late. Will was abreast of Fort Caswell before Smithville's signal lights told the sentries Yankee boats were in the harbor. They did not fire a single shot.

It was midnight when Will climbed onto the *Minnesota*'s deck under the light of a high, pale winter moon. An hour later in his quarters, he gave "[his] rebel" a pair of dry socks and a glass of sherry, "laughed at him, and put him to bed."

His escapade was not over, however. Before sunrise the next morning, Will brought the *Minnesota* to anchor near the flagship and rowed over with Captain Kelly, keeping his promise to deliver his "guest" to Commander Sands for breakfast.

Sands was astonished, though he shouldn't have been, given Will's growing reputation in the Navy and the amount of coverage his adventures had received in the newspapers. At any rate, Will, in gentlemanly fashion, asked permission to send ashore a flag of truce for Kelly's clothes and some money "to make his stay in a Northern prison more comfortable."

Sands agreed. Around 11:30 a.m., a rowboat displaying a white flag appeared outside the walls of Fort Caswell. Will had dispatched Ensign Jones with the prisoner, and they were met by another Jones, a Confederate colonel. The Union Jones requested a parlay, and the Confederate Jones sent word to the fort's commander, Major General William H. Whiting, asking his approval. But Whiting was in Smithville that morning, causing a delay in communications, while leaving the ensign, the colonel, and Kelly to await his decision. Although the opposing Joneses were "on their extreme dignity," observing truce etiquette, both were on guard as they paced up and down the beach, suspiciously passing each other several times in cool, watchful silence.

Then Kelly wheeled "sharply and suddenly" around at his fellow Confederate.

"That was a damned splendid affair, sir!" he exclaimed, referring to the previous night's raid.

His enthusiastic review proved the icebreaker, and "a chat ensued." In short order, the adjutant general joined them, arriving "with his arm in a sling, and limping from the effects of his impromptu promenade" through Smithville's woods the night before. Kelly's clothes were brought to him along with "bacon and hard tack for which to regale their guest," Ensign Jones.

Amid all this jollity among foes, Jones the Yankee produced a letter Will had sent for General Hébert. It read:

My Dear General,

I deeply regret that you were not at home when I called. I enclose my card.

Very Respectfully,
W. B. Cushing

CHAPTER TWENTY-ONE

FLUSSER VERSUS THE GOLIATH

On April 12, 1864, Lieutenant Commander W. Charles A. Flusser wrote his younger sister Fanny from the USS *Miami*:

> The rebs promise to fight us this week with the ironclad ram, for which I have been watching so long, and eleven thousand men.
>
> I wish our garrison was one-third as strong. I don't know whether the scamps will come or not, but will be prepared by day after tomorrow to give them a good fight so far as the boats are concerned. The longshore people must look out for themselves while we afloat destroy the Sheep—the name we've given the ironclad because we thought it would not show fight. It will prove to be a formidable antagonist, and we will have our hands full to whip it. Fortunately it will not be many minutes after her appearance before the result of the passage at arms is known.
>
> I wrote the admiral to send me some good shot to penetrate her armor and I should need no more boats. Fact is, I look on her as peculiarly my own. I am prepared for a very

desperate fight, and think unless Fortune frown outrageously on me, my arrangements will defeat her. The plan to fight her was the result of long thought and some anxiety. I was lying sick abed…and trying to read, but was not satisfied with my preparations, and read without understanding, thinking all the while of her.

At 4 o'clock in the morning I had found what I wanted, and turning to a friend who was smoking by my bedside, and who was formerly in the Navy, I gave him my plan. He expressed his delight and his entire confidence of success. The next day it was made known to several officers, and its advantages were so evident that all immediately [gave their support.]

I think there is no instance on record of a fight on the plan I intended to pursue. In fifteen minutes after we get to close quarters my commission as commander is secured or I am a dead man. I am aware that the result of these rests with God. I shall not fail to ask his aid, but do not think the rebel cause so good that we have any reason to fear the end.

•   •   •

That same day, Gilbert Elliott and Commander James Cooke received a surprise visit from General Robert Frederick Hoke, the dashing young commander of a large, seasoned Virginia army brigade.

Hoke had two reasons for his appearance at the shipyard. The first was to conduct an inspection of their ironclad—Cooke had informally named it the *Albemarle* the previous October—and to judge with his own eyes whether reports of its near completion were trustworthy. The second reason was to convey an urgent message from Richmond.

President Jefferson Davis and his chief military advisor, General Braxton Bragg, had determined that the Union's tight clamp on North

Carolina shipping must end. For two long years, the town of Plymouth had been the home base for Flusser's relentless squadron of blockaders, a staging area for too many Yankee incursions into the Sounds and its tributary rivers. The raids grew bolder by the day, penetrating deeper into Confederate territory.

General Bragg had been devising a plan to retake Plymouth from the Yankees with a swift, coordinated, and overwhelming offensive. Under the command of General Henry W. Wessells, the federal garrison's 2,300 troops were scattered around the town in vulnerable earthworks fortifications, none of the detachments larger than 500 men, many isolated by large tracts of forest and marshland. Bragg believed the command insufficient for defending the place against a major expeditionary force—and his sources told him Wessells shared his belief. But Wessells's superiors, Generals Peck and Butler, had repeatedly ignored his appeals for reinforcements, putting their confidence in the protection given his waterfront flanks by Flusser's Plymouth squadron.

This small fleet consisted of four gunboats: the USS *Miami*, commanded by the gallant Flusser himself; the *Southfield*, commanded by Lieutenant Charles French; the USS *Whitehead* (French's former ship) captained by Acting Ensign George W. Barret; and the USS *Ceres,* commanded by Acting Master Henry H. Foster. An army transport, the USS *Bombshell*, was also attached to the squadron.

Summarizing things for Elliott and Cooke at the shipyard, Hoke explained that General Bragg had placed him in command of the land forces to participate in the attack on Plymouth, some seven thousand men from half a dozen Confederate states. His assignment was to encircle Wessells's garrison, wait for the naval patrols to be cleared, and then storm the enemy's landward fortifications. It would be up to the *Albemarle* to carry out the naval assault by drawing off and annihilating Flusser's squadron.

The expedition, Hoke said, was to begin within two weeks, taking advantage of a quiescent Union front. It was essential that the *Albemarle* play her part.

Elliott and Cooke hesitated at first. There was too much work left on the ironclad. Boilers, engines, roofing, and iron shield were to be fitted before she could be ready for service.

But Hoke was adamant, demanding "a careful statement as to the exact time, with increased facilities, that the *Albemarle* could be depended upon for assistance."

As he listened, Cooke recognized a golden opportunity. He had long desired greater military aid. Could he have it now?

"We could do it in fifteen days," he replied, matter-of-factly. "With ten additional mechanics."

Hoke did better. Cooke was ordered to prepare the ram, "and guns, ammunition, and a few men quickly arrived," with a promise of the rest of the crew in short order. On April 16—only a day before the planned attack—Hoke made a return visit to the yard, officially naming Cooke the ironclad's commander, and bringing with him two officers and twenty added volunteers from his brigade, described as "long lank Tar Heels from the piney woods" with little or no training as sailors.

Though Cooke would have preferred more experienced hands, he felt confident that he could whip the North Carolina soldiers into shape. His larger problem, however, was that despite his "herculean exertions," the *Albemarle* was not completed. But Cooke had "named his day for action, and…was not a man to deal in disappointments."

He intended to keep his promise.

It was on the morning of Sunday, April 17, that the newly christened CSS *Albemarle* "began her career as a floating workshop," Cooke atop her pilothouse barking orders to cast off all lines, and Gilbert Elliott aboard as his volunteer aide. Elliott had meant to see the action, firsthand.

To the townspeople on the riverbanks, gathered in small boats and carriages to watch her pass, the ship was a source of great amusement and curiosity as she wound toward her destination. There were ten portable forges on deck, along with a towed forge behind her in case of problems. Mechanics and carpenters thronged her sides, hanging from construction stages and pounding away at her armor plates with huge sledgehammers. Inside her hull, military preparations began amid the clatter, the gun captains drilling their men at the big rifled cannons, shouting commands in a babble of voices.

Years later, Gilbert Elliott would offer this description of his greatest achievement moving down the turbid waters of the Roanoke:

> The *Albemarle* was 152 feet long between perpendiculars.... The shield was sixty feet in length and octagonal in form.... The armament consisted of two rifled Brooke guns mounted on pivot-carriages, each gun working through three portholes.... She had two propellers driven by two engines of 200-horse power each.... The sides were covered from the knuckle, four feet below the deck, with iron plates two inches thick. The prow was built of oak, running eighteen feet back... [and] covered on the outside with iron plating, two inches thick, and tapering off to a four-inch edge [to form] the ram.

Fearsome as the *Albemarle* was, one farmer also saw humor in her as she set sail. "I never conceived of anything more perfectly ridiculous than the appearance of the critter as she slowly passed by my landing," he wrote, laconically.

As with most debuts, it was difficult to impress every critic.

•   •   •

At 10:00 p.m. trouble struck. The bolts that held the main coupling of the *Albemarle*'s center shaft unseated, causing her to grind to a dead halt in the water.

Fortunately, Cooke had the portable forges aboard. His smiths and mechanics labored for six hours to make repairs and were able to get the ship back underway around 3:00 a.m.

But trouble soon struck again. The ironclad had continued some distance downriver when the rudderhead broke off, leading to another halt. Again, workmen scrambled to fix the damage, but four more hours were lost.

Despite these delays, Cooke managed to reach a point about three miles above Plymouth by 10:00 p.m. on Monday. Upon arrival, he became confused. General Hoke's troops were supposed to have moved against Plymouth the day before, setting up siege artillery around the town. But Cooke had yet to hear from them, and knew nothing of their status, the disposition of enemy shore batteries, or the placement of obstructions such as torpedoes, sunken vessels, and wooden piles in the river. He could not continue responsibly without more information, so he lowered anchor and sent a lieutenant and some men out on a scouting expedition.

Two hours later, the party returned with discouraging news. They had found the obstructions and believed them impossible to pass. Frustrated, Cooke saw little choice but to bank the engine fires and order the off-duty officers and crew to rest.

For Elliott, the disappointment was too much to abide in silence.

"If the ram is to accomplish anything, it is now or never, sir," he appealed to Cooke, feeling uncomfortable lying at anchor all night. "It will be foolhardy to attempt passage of the obstructions and batteries in the daytime."

Cooke did not disagree. But what would he suggest they do?

"I request permission to make a personal investigation," Elliott said, without hesitation.

Given the emergency, Cooke assented, admiring Elliott's bravery. For the best assessment, Elliott would have to go downriver as far as Plymouth under enemy guns.

At 11:00 p.m., Elliott rowed from the *Albemarle* in a small lifeboat, Pilot John Luck and two of the few experienced seamen on board having volunteered their services. Arriving at the obstructions in the black of night, the group took soundings with a long pole, and to their "great joy" found there was ten feet of water over and above the obstructions. The oldest seamen said this was due to the remarkable spring melt on the heels of a long, snowy winter.

"Such high water has never before been seen in Roanoke River," he enthused.

But there was more to reconnoiter. Pushing downstream to Plymouth, Elliott and his volunteers took advantage of the shadow of the trees on the north side of the river, opposite the town, and silently watched federal transports taking on women and children, who were being sent to safety ahead of Hoke's anticipated bombardment. After a while, almost afraid to breathe, the party made way their back toward the ram with muffled oars, hugging the river's northern bank.

Reaching the ship about 1:00 a.m., Elliott informed Captain Cooke it would be possible to navigate over the obstructions if the boat were kept in the middle of the stream, where the water was at its highest level.

The indomitable commander was quick to act. At 2:30 a.m., he roused his men, gave the order to get up steam, and in his impatience, slipped the cables and started downriver. He soon passed the fort at Warren's Neck and took several shots from the battery without returning fire. Protected by their ironclad shield, those aboard the ram thought the noise made by the shot and shell striking the boat sounded no louder than pebbles thrown against an empty barrel.

The *Albemarle* continued onward, went safely over the obstructions, and lower down the river passed another fortification at Boyle's Mill. Since its 200-pounder Parrott gun remained silent, Cooke knew his ship went unobserved—fortuitous considering the narrowness of the channel at that point.

Cooke was now less than a mile from Plymouth. Still having heard nothing from the army, he remained unsure what course to pursue. If Hoke's troops had massed around the town according to plan, they would be waiting to move on his arrival. He needed to determine their position and let them know he was close.

What he did not know was that Hoke was not alone in expecting him. For the better part of two years, Commander Charles W. Flusser had received steady intelligence about the construction of the ironclad which he sarcastically called the Sheep. Recently, he'd heard she was poised for an imminent attack, making her a sheep no longer.

He would lay a clever trap.

•   •   •

Flusser's preparations had begun a full month before, in late March, as word of increased rebel military activity near Plymouth and the ram's near completion came filtering out of North Carolina. With snow melting and spring rains raising the river to a depth that would allow the *Albemarle*'s passage, he had anticipated that it would appear at any time and laid his sunken obstructions upriver near Thoroughfare Gap. Though reports of the ironclad's exact size and armaments were contradictory, Flusser had known it would be heavily armored and concluded that his best tactic against the vessel was to immobilize her so she could be blasted to smithereens at close range.

But how to stop her advance?

Over a year earlier, Admiral Lee had proposed that Flusser use a rear assault to fend off a floating battery moving toward Plymouth. His idea was for Flusser's squadron to rush around the battery's flanks to its rear, and "firing all arms…attack it by ramming and firing."

Flusser had believed the admiral's plan suicidal from its earliest mention. The thought of ramming his frail wooden craft against an ironclad—a ship designed to reduce such vessels to splinters—made no naval sense to him. And even if he were mad enough to try it, how were his four fleet boats to sweep past the ram on the Roanoke River, a mere three hundred yards wide in that area, with any hope of success?

No, he would not try this scheme, potentially disobeying superior officers—especially since he had devised what he believed was a far better one.

Of the five warships in his flotilla, the strongest were the *Southfield* and the *Miami*, double-ended gunboats designed to maneuver in narrow riverine waterways. Flusser reasoned that if he lashed them together in a V formation with rope and chain cable across their forecastles, he could lure the *Albemarle* into the V, entangle her, and pound her with the forward deck guns of both ships, while simultaneously bringing to bear the heavy shore guns of Fort Gray and Fort Worth. Then, by having the two warships steam ahead, he could jam the ram's stern into the bank, where she would be at his mercy—helpless against the land and water artillery leveled against her.

Flusser felt confident of the plan's success. In his mind, it was the best possible plan under the circumstances, turning the *Albemarle*'s very size, bulk, and weight against her.

"We will sink her, or I will sink her myself," he told his squadron commanders.

On April 17, Flusser was ready and waiting for the colossus, having received word that she had embarked from Halifax the day before. He did not know of the drive shaft problems that had forced her to stop for repairs following her launch. He did not know of the second breakdown either.

What he did know was that the Confederate siege of Plymouth had begun with a fury. When the *Albemarle* did not arrive on time, General Hoke, thinking Captain Cooke and his ironclad might not show, began pounding the town with artillery fire ahead of his invasion.

Under constant shelling, General Wessells on Sunday night ordered all Plymouth's noncombatants—women, children, slaves, and the sick and disabled—brought to a safer point aboard the Union steamboat *Massasoit*.

Flusser had helped with the evacuation. As he paced the decks of the steamboat, lending a hand where he could, he was wrenched by the anguished groans of the wounded and the hasty farewells of pale, terrified women leaving their men behind to face the fearsome ironclad.

Pausing amid the confusion, he gallantly tried to reassure them.

"Ladies, I have waited two long years for the rebel ram," he said. "The Navy will do its duty. We shall sink, destroy, or capture it, or find our graves in the Roanoke."

On April 18, while repairs were made to the ram upriver, the *Ceres* was at Plymouth, and the *Whitehead* at the Thoroughfare a few miles above town, both vessels serving as scouts for the ironclad's advance. Meanwhile, the *Southfield* was above Plymouth until the Confederate fire stopped for the night around 9:00 p.m.

About half a mile below the town, Flusser himself was back aboard the *Miami* waiting for a report from one or both of his outliers. He received it shortly after midnight on April 19, when the *Whitehead* arrived "by a roundabout passage from below and reported the ram as having passed the Thoroughfare."

Flusser knew the time had come to set his plan in motion. At 1:30 a.m., he ordered the *Southfield* to move onto the port side of the *Miami*. He then made what would prove a critical error in judgement.

In a preliminary report to Flag Officer Davenport, he had written, "I feel confident of success as far as we (the Navy) are concerned. [But] my plan of defense prevents me giving the army what aid I should wish before the ram is whipped."

The suffering that Flusser saw during the evacuation convinced him to change that plan to its detriment. He would not leave the soldiers on shore fighting without naval support any longer than necessary—even if it meant putting himself at increased risk. Based on a dry run, he reasoned that the amount of time needed to release the chain lashings, and then clear the decks for action, was about twice the time required to release the rope lashings. To be ready in the shortest possible time to assist the army, he decided to pass only rope lashings between the two vessels.

At 3:45 a.m., the *Albemarle* finally appeared in the predawn gloom. Just moments earlier, her lookouts had spotted the two Yankee gunboats and sounded the alarm, sending her men to quarters.

In his cabin aboard the *Miami,* Commander Flusser was informed hastily of the ram's appearance by his executive officer, acting Master's Mate William Welles. Coming on deck at once, he peered straight out over his bow and saw an enormous shadow in the middle of the river, bearing straight in his direction.

"Steam ahead as fast as possible and run the ram down!" he shouted.

In less than a minute, obeying his order, the *Miami* and *Southfield* moved up the river, their bells ringing to go ahead, fast.

·   ·   ·

At first, Captain Cooke and John Luck, the pilot, did not see Flusser's snare. But as the ram closed with the vessels, the spars lashing them together suddenly grew visible in the twilight.

Cooke did not take long to recover from his surprise. He knew the steamers would be unable to maneuver in time to avoid a collision, not lashed together as they were. Shouting orders to feint toward the southern shore, he ordered a turn midstream with the throttles wide open. The *Miami* was now closest to the ironclad off her port bow, the *Southfield* slightly behind and dead ahead.

He was turning the Yankees' trap right back on them.

·   ·   ·

The clash was brief and ferocious. Grazing the *Miami* near the waterline, the *Albemarle* tore a ten-foot long gouge into her port bow and then plowed into the *Southfield* at full speed, her ram crunching nine feet into her starboard side. A moment later, she opened fire on both ships with her forward pivot gun and a hail of musketry.

The Yankee steamers had simultaneously brought their batteries to bear on the ironclad as she came on them, but the solid shot from their hundred-pounder Parrott rifles and nine-inch Dahlgren guns did not so much as leave a perceptible dent on her armor. Impaled on her iron tusk, the *Southfield* began sinking at once, water rushing through a gaping hole in her starboard bow. The Confederate ram had pierced clear through to her forward storeroom and boiler.

Then the unexpected happened. The impact of the armored behemoth striking the rope lashings put tremendous stress on them—stress the chains Flusser originally intended to use, might have withstood. As the mortally wounded *Southfield* continued "forging ahead on her own steam," and the straining ropes buckled and snapped, the *Albemarle* wedged apart the two federal gunboats, and the Miami swung wildly around toward the *Southfield*.

Lieutenant French's ship lost, he ordered his crew into their boats. But as the *Miami*'s stern came swinging toward them, he instructed "such men as could do so to jump onto her decks." Some succeeded, while some splashed helplessly into the Roanoke. Still others, unable to get off in time, went down with the ship. French, leaping across the gap, was among those to land on the *Miami* safely.

Meanwhile, the *Miami*'s crewmen were lobbing grenades through the ironclad's portholes. Captain Cooke repeatedly shouted for Luck to reverse engines, but the ram's iron plates were deeply entangled in the frame of the Yankee vessel. The *Southfield* had begun to fill and settle down on the *Albemarle*, forcing her bow to submerge.

"She's taking water!" the ironclad's crewmen shouted. The river came gushing through her portholes as she tilted forward.

Again, Cooke shouted for Luck to back up the ship. And once again, he failed to extricate her from the sinking Union vessel. Unable to use his pivot gun with the bow half underwater, Cooke ordered his entire crew on deck to engage the enemy with small arms. On the *Miami*, a group of Flusser's hands also gathered up top to form a boarding party, firing their muskets, and dueling with the Confederates at close quarters.

By now, the *Southfield* had almost dragged the ironclad beneath the surface. But as the Union gunboat struck bottom, she leaned over on her side and shifted away from the *Albemarle*'s bow, enabling Luck to finally wrench her free. The ironclad bobbed to the surface on an even keel, water sluicing from her foredeck.

She came up under heavy fire. Flusser had been hitting her with "broadside after broadside," firing the first three shots himself. His six great guns belched and roared, but their shells bounced ineffectually off the ram's metal hide.

Flusser thought he saw a desperate opening—*if* one were bold enough to take advantage of it. The *Albemarle* had moved so close to one of his Dahlgrens that her side was almost touching its muzzle. Flusser could see nothing but a wall of iron. At that close range, he hoped a shot from the Dahlgren nine-inch might pierce the vessel's armor.

Rushing to the weapon, he ordered his division officer, acting Ensign Thomas Hargis, to fire.

Hargis was reluctant. *"There's a shell in that gun, captain!"* he warned.

Flusser understood his meaning. The percussion shell was on a ten-second fuse. If it did not penetrate the armor, it was likely to ricochet back at them. But he waved Hargis off, thinking it his last and best chance to destroy the ironclad.

"In fifteen minutes after we get to close quarters, my commission as commander is secured or I am a dead man."

It is possible those words written to his sister just days earlier flashed through Flusser's mind at that instant.

"Never mind, my lad!" he shouted. The side of the iron behemoth filled his vision. "We will give them this first, and solid shot after!"

Pushing the young officer to one side, he sprang to the gun, took hold of its lanyard, and pulled.

It was a courageous but fatal decision. True to Hargis's prediction, the shell rebounded harmlessly off the ironclad's side, and thumped back onto the *Miami*'s deck. Flusser and Hargis barely had time to think before it exploded in a tremendous blast of heat and light.

Flusser died instantly, nearly torn to pieces by shell fragments. Beside him, Ensign Hargis was badly mangled, but he would linger for over a month at the Naval Hospital in Norfolk before dying. Close by, ten others suffered less critical injuries.

Now in command of the *Miami,* Captain French, with Executive Officer Welles in agreement, ordered a retreat. With the *Southfield* sunk in twenty feet of water, the iron ram had straightened and was making directly for them. They considered it useless to sacrifice the ship like the other vessel.

As the *Miami* fled downriver, Captain Cooke was free to turn the *Albemarle*'s guns on the Union shore defenses at Fort Williams.

The battle for Plymouth was practically over. Surrounded by Hoke's troops, battered by "terrible fire," General Wessells capitulated on April 20.

As he extended his sword to Hoke in crestfallen surrender, he remarked, "General Hoke, this is the saddest day of my life."

"General, this is the proudest day of mine," Hoke responded.

After two years, the Confederacy had reclaimed the North Carolina Sounds, taking 1,600 prisoners, and capturing spoils that included twenty-five Union artillery guns, a huge storehouse of food and supplies, and 200 tons of fuel coal. More devastatingly, Gilbert Elliott's ironclad controlled the strategically vital Roanoke. It was one of the Union's worst defeats of the war.

For the next six months, the *Albemarle* reigned supreme over the state's eastern waters.

CHAPTER TWENTY-TWO

"I SHALL NEVER REST UNTIL I HAVE AVENGED HIS DEATH"

The fifth day of July 1864 found Rear Admiral Lee, U.S.N., in a mood that was both pensive and resolute.

Pensive because the CSS *Albemarle*'s continued domination of the Roanoke made it impassable to Union warships and stopped any chance of wresting coastal North Carolina from the Confederacy.

Resolute because Lee had just met with one man who had a chance of bringing down the armored goliath. His official reason for summoning Captain William Barker Cushing to Hampton Roads had been to receive his report on, and give his personal commendation for, a series of successful behind-the-lines raids and reconnaissance expeditions up the Cape Fear River in late June. Aware of Cushing's unconventional methods of penetrating enemy defenses with small, stealthy raiding parties, Lee was convinced those tactics were needed to destroy or capture the *Albemarle*.

There was good reason the *Albemarle*'s reputation for fearsome invincibility had grown to legendary status on both sides of the Mason-Dixon line within three short months. For not long after General Hoke's victory at Plymouth, the federal Navy had brought its assembled might against the ironclad and met, again, with catastrophic results. President Lincoln's wartime leadership was now under intense scrutiny.

The other debacle had occurred in May as Hoke's troops, along with the ram, set out to retake New Berne, on Pamlico Sound, from Union control. With its capture, Hoke meant to route the last Yankee troops in his state.

Receiving intelligence that the *Albemarle* was crossing the Sound to support Hoke's assault, Admiral Lee had sent a full squadron of gunboats—including four of the Navy's most powerful double-enders—to lay in wait for her. Captain Melancton Smith led the strike from aboard the USS *Mattabasett,* accompanied by the USS *Sassacus*, USS *Wyalusing*, the late Commander Flusser's USS *Miami*, and the remnants of Flusser's old squadron.

As Captain Cooke brought the *Albemarle* out of Plymouth on May 5—escorted by the steamers CSS *Bombshell* and CSS *Cotton Plant*—Captain Melancton Smith's fleet assembled in two lines at the mouth of the Neuse River. His plan was for the gunboats to "pass [the ram] and travel around and around her in a terrific grand waltz." They were to "concentrate their fire on the stern... being cautious not to hit their sister ships with shot and shell."

Although Cooke's task force sighted the federal gunboats from a distance, it was too late to avoid them. By 2:00 p.m., they had surrounded him.

The battle raged for three hours as the ram's attackers hammered her with their cannons, shooting away her boats, riddling her smokestack, and knocking her rear pivot gun out of commission. But the incessant fire was unable to breach her armor. As one squadron commander later wrote, it was as though Smith's guns were shooting blanks.

At last the ironclad smashed free of the ambush, and with engines growling plowed through the ring of ships to turn upriver. The Union's mightiest vessels of war were left broken and limping in the water.

All except one. The *Sassacus,* a large, heavily armed sidewheeler commanded by Lieutenant J. L. David, steamed after her at a speed of ten knots and was able to catch up. But her guns remained ineffective.

The *Albemarle* and USS *Sassacus* in combat. Only one ship would survive. *U.S. Naval History and Heritage Command*

In a final, desperate gambit, David ordered the *Albemarle* struck amidships, knowing full well the move would cripple his own vessel, but thinking it the only way to defeat her.

The *Albemarle* heeled over, water washing over her starboard side. Still in contact with the ironclad, *Sassacus* fired three broadsides at her from a hundred-pound rifle. The rounds scored solid hits but shattered harmlessly against her iron flank, fragmenting back onto the deck of the *Sassacus*. At the same time, the *Albermarle* righted herself in the water, firing a shot that penetrated her assailant's boiler.

"In an instant," wrote a *Harper's Weekly* naval correspondent aboard the *Sassacus*, "everything was enveloped in scalding steam. So dense was the cloud that objects were shrouded and invisible within [one yard]." Fleeing the gunboat's interior, badly burned sailors poured onto her deck and were picked off by small arms fire from the *Albemarle*'s portholes.

"The roar of our guns, the crack of musketry, the screams of the scalded and dying now commingled to make the scene most appalling," recalled the correspondent.

That ended the engagement. The *Albemarle* drew off from her disabled attacker and turned back toward Plymouth, "covered with wounds and glory."

As spring turned to summer and the ironclad's immense shadow continued to dominate the Sounds, Lee knew something had to be done, and fast. He and Secretary Welles were receiving intense criticism from Washington, where Congress had started an investigation into why the ram's construction was not prevented, with some legislators expressing consternation over the Navy's ongoing failure to launch a successful attack on the ship. A few in Congress went even as far as to accuse its highest officers of cowardice.

Lee found himself in a tight spot. Nothing was more urgent and crucial than sinking the *Albemarle*. But how? His attempts to overcome her with superior numbers and firepower were costly failures. She had demolished nine of his best ships and killed scores of his best sailors. A different approach was needed if he was going to have any chance of success.

On July 5, Will arrived at the admiral's flagship and was offered a new mission.

It was a bitter wish come true. The ironclad had been in his sights since April, when Charles Flusser died fighting her on the Roanoke River.

"I shall never rest until I have avenged his death," Will had written his mother.

Those words were no mere outpouring of grief and anger, but a blood oath. A consummate naval officer and model of daring and chivalry, Flusser had been Will's inspiration ever since Annapolis. He was the one instructor who had always believed in Will, encouraged him, and supported him even at his lowest ebb. Will would never forget Flusser's giving him *Naval Enterprise: Illustrative of Adventure, Heroism and Endurance*, a book he had treasured and paged through countless times over the years. Nor would he forget Flusser's offering him a spare bed when he had nowhere else to go.

Yes, Will sought revenge against the Confederate ram, even at the cost of his own life. Like Lon's death at Gettysburg, the loss of his beloved friend and mentor had been a great a blow to him.

In Lee's office aboard the flagship, Will "at first proposed an attack on the ram with [the fleet's] gunboats at Plymouth, or a boat expedition, led by himself, with eighty men."

Lee strongly disagreed with using the gunboats, and cited Captain Melancton Smith's failure, along with a recent admonition by the captain, which labeled the approach futile.

"It is Smith's opinion that it would be inexpedient to fight the ram with our long double-enders in that narrow river," Lee said. "I would instead propose a torpedo attack, either by means of an india-rubber boat, which could be transported across the swamp opposite Plymouth, or a light draft, rifle-proof swift steam barge, fitted with a spar torpedo."

Will said he would follow any course the admiral ordered, asking that he be allowed to give up command of the *Monticello* temporarily in order to oversee the fitting of whatever boats were provided for the mission.

Lee agreed to the request. Will was ordered to report to the Navy Department in strict secrecy to deliver the admiral's plan along with his own proposal to Secretary Welles and Gustavus Fox.

He returned to the *Monticello* just long enough to make hurried arrangements for his departure. Four days later, he arrived in the capital to present his plan for a boarding party of a hundred men to carry two inflatable pontoon boats—the very India-rubber boats Lee had mentioned—to a point on shore near the anchored giant, then paddle silently up to her, scale her side, kill the sentries on deck, and cut her out from right under the Confederates' noses. With its wicked piratical flair, the scheme's intentions mirrored those of his raid on Smithville back in February. In Will's mind, it would have delighted old Flusser, who could never resist a good cutting-out expedition.

It was also a plan Will thought less likely to get him killed than Admiral Lee's alternative. The spar torpedo was a marine mine filled with gunpowder and rigged to a long pole, with a percussive blasting cap designed to explode on contact. Intelligence gathered on the *Albemarle* showed her armor did not extend far below the waterline, a necessary vulnerability if she was to be light enough to float. Lee thought that if Will could steal up to the lower part of the ship with a specially rigged torpedo, and ram her with it, he might blast a huge hole in her side. The Roanoke would finish the job on its own, rushing in to drown her.

After considering the two options, Welles and Fox chose the second despite its risk—unless Will had a foolproof plan for cutting her out. Will saw nothing left to discuss, since Welles and Fox were under intense pressure to act decisively against the ironclad. However miniscule his odds of survival, he would carry out his orders.

Over the next three months, he prepared for the brazen escapade as if it were his last hurrah.

•   •   •

In July 1864, William Willis Wylie Wood, a United States naval engineer with a reputation for brilliant invention, was on special duty in New York City, tasked with the construction of a federal ironclad fleet and other vessels. He was also engaged in devising means to destroy Confederate ironclads and to remove the improvised harbor obstructions Southerners employed as deterrents.

Recently, he had been experimenting with launches "having torpedoes fitted to them," and that summer had several prototypes floating in the water at the Brooklyn Navy Yard.

His wild hair and big, bushy beard in full, overgrown display, the forty-six-year-old Wood was sitting at his desk at the ironclad office on Canal Street when a young man—a mere youth, in his eyes—came in and introduced himself as Lieutenant W. B. Cushing.

"I am North on a secret mission under the sanction of the Honorable Secretary of the Navy," he said, insisting on absolute confidence. "The object is to cut out or destroy the rebel ironclad ram *Albemarle*."

Will explained that the ram was lying at Plymouth, North Carolina, something Wood, and most of the country, already knew.

"I am looking for small, swift, low-pressure tugboats for the purpose of throwing a force on board and capturing her," Will said. "So far, however, I have been unable to find just such vessels."

Thoughtfully plucking at his untamed whiskers, Wood said he did not believe he had any boats of the nature described. But the young lieutenant pressed him.

"Sir, I have already visited the Navy Yard," Will said. "There I saw a steam launch being equipped with a torpedo…which is why I have called upon you."

"Oh?"

Will nodded. "I wish to make inquiry as to what is to be accomplished by its use," he said. "And so on, and so forth, if you would be kind enough to share the particulars with me."

Impressed by the lad's determination, the inventor gladly obliged, and Will was soon convinced he'd found what he wanted. Before leaving Wood's office, he sat down at his desk and wrote to the Secretary asking that the Department give him two of the torpedo boats under development.

"I will visit my mother at Fredonia, right here in this proud state of New York," he said. "When the launches are ready, inform me, and I will come down and learn how to use the things."

• • •

One hot afternoon late in July, Carl Schurz, a fifty-five-year-old German immigrant, journalist, and power broker in the Republican party, went to visit President Lincoln at the White House to discuss his upcoming reelection bid. The Democratic National Convention was to be held in Chicago at the end of August, and Schurz believed Lincoln should actively start his campaign before their opposition claimed the political stage.

Schurz had good reasons for his opinion. The war was grinding on with no end in sight; for every bit of progress it seemed there was a demoralizing setback. While Robert E. Lee's recent defeat at Gettysburg had seemed like a turning point for Northern fortunes, the Union army had not been able to break through to Richmond or cut vital Confederate supply lines in Georgia. Meanwhile, General Hoke had kept a firm military grip on Plymouth, with the CSS *Albemarle* still looming over the Sounds to guard the North Carolina coastline and rebel shipping from U.S. Navy blockaders.

Battered, bloodied, and weary, many of the Union's citizens were "wild for peace" at any cost, with Lincoln facing increasing dissatisfaction with his administration's wartime policies from within his own party. A movement was even building to replace him with another candidate, with the names of popular military men like Grant, Butler, and Sherman tossed around.

When Schurz called on Lincoln, the president asked that he wait in his office until the day's business had finished, then ride with him to his summer cottage three miles northeast of the White House.

In the carriage, a haggard Abraham Lincoln grimly shared his frustration and disappointment with those in his party who were wavering in their support and suggesting he was "already beaten." Some even said his compulsory wartime draft was an excuse to build a despotic army that would keep him in office indefinitely, probably the most painful claim against him.

"God knows, I have at least tried very hard to do my duty, to do right to everybody and do wrong to nobody," he told Schurz, speaking for a long time without interruption. "And now to have it said by men who have been my friends, and who ought to know me better, that I have been seduced by that they call the lust of power...that I have been doing this and that unscrupulous thing hurtful to the common cause...have they thought of that common cause when trying to break me down?"

Reaching the cabin, Lincoln went on talking about the war as dusk set in and the oil lamps were lit. In the glow of the lamps, Schurz thought he saw the president's "sad eyes moist and his rugged features working strangely as if under a strong and painful emotion."

At last Lincoln fell silent, waiting for a response. Deeply touched, Schurz didn't know what to say and took some moments to collect his thoughts.

"The people, undisturbed by the bickerings of your critics, believe in you and will faithfully stand by you," he said finally.

He spoke with confidence, and Lincoln seemed cheered. Later that night, the president grew calmer, and even made some humorous remarks.

"Well, things might look better, and they might look worse," he said as Schurz left the cabin, shaking his hand heartily. "Go on, and let us all do the best we can."

In fact, Lincoln was skeptical of his friend's assurance. Over his first term in office, he had learned to share his vision of a reconstructed America by writing public letters to newspapers that he knew thousands would read. He had adopted a policy of leaving the White House whenever possible to inspire the troops and citizens. He had made his impassioned address at Gettysburg.

But the people were tired of war. The people despaired. Now, Lincoln thought, inspiring words would not be enough to preserve their fading trust in his administration. They needed a decisive *success*, and nothing short of it, if they were to stick with him.

He went to bed that night, as he would on many other nights, wondering if that ray of light would come in time for the election.

•   •   •

It was a dark, dreary day when Will arrived home on a brief, unexpected visit and invited Mary Barker Cushing to ride with him to the wooded Arkwright Hills, five miles southeast of town.

Mary was surprised by his request. She had never been into those lonely hills. But something in her son's manner, an intensity in his eyes, convinced her go without asking for explanation.

They were deep in the countryside, where no one could hear or see them, when Will pulled in the reins and stopped the wagon.

"Mother," he said, turning to her, "I have undertaken a great project, and no soul must know until it is accomplished." He paused for a long moment. "I must tell you, for I need your prayers."

He then informed her the Navy Department had commissioned him to destroy the rebel ram *Albemarle*. Told her how, when, and where, while she tried to slow the beating of her heart and listen without interruption.

At last, when he finished, she said, "My son...I believe you will accomplish it. But you cannot come out alive."

There was another silence. Hanging between them was the unspoken knowledge that she had not yet recovered from burying Alonzo at West Point. The prospect of the war taking another of her sons was an insupportable weight on her heart.

It was a while before Will spoke.

"Mother," he said, "it shall be done, or you shall have no son Will. If I die, it will be in a good cause."

After that, Mary knew there would be no dissuading him, and she spoke only words of encouragement. But every hour that passed for her after he left Fredonia was an age of dread and agony.

She would keep their secret, in suspense, until she heard the results of his mission.

●   ●   ●

In late August or early September, Will's close friend David Parker received a letter from him, asking if Parker could spare a few days to come and stay with him in New York, adding that he wanted somebody with whom he could talk.

Parker knew this meant something unusual. Since he was able to get away from Washington at the time, he went straight away.

Joining Will in his room at the Old United States Hotel at the corner of Pearl and Fulton Streets, near the Battery, Parker found him to be under visible, uncharacteristic strain.

"I must tell you something in confidence," Will said. "You must swear to tell no one."

Parker gave his solemn oath, and Will shared his reason for being in New York. With that, some of the pressure he was feeling seemed to siphon off, and he grew more like his usual upbeat self.

Around the time of Parker's visit, the launches had arrived, although not without some frustration. Both came with damaged keels, and one had a large hole in the bottom.

But much had already been accomplished. Will and Wood, the engineer, were busy developing the torpedo and spar assembly together. With the two of them rooming at the Old United States Hotel, they spent many nights getting acquainted and discussing "the resources of the torpedo steam launches."

Early in the process, Will had insisted on alterations to the existing design of the torpedo rigs. Usually, spar torpedoes were fixed to the front of the boat. But Will foresaw needing to raise or lower his torpedo depending on specific conditions and circumstances (the depth of the water, for example) so it could strike below the spot where the *Albermarle*'s iron armor overhung its wooden hull. To this end, he and Wood devised a complex setup after weeks of trial and error. This consisted of a hinged, fourteen-foot-long boom that swung out over the launch's bow, and an iron slide from which the torpedo would detach, each manipulated with rope lifts and rods aboard the launch.

One afternoon, David Parker walked over to the Navy Yard with Will and joined him and the engineer on a test run aboard the more usable of the two launches. Out on the Hudson River, Will detonated several torpedo shells using his modified assembly. There were bugs to be worked out, but its design appealed to Will.

Parker's visit, meanwhile, offered him a distraction from the seriousness of his work. In the evenings, they would visit theaters for amusement. Will seemed more relaxed on the outside, but inside he remained tightly wound. Walking down a deserted Broadway from the Winter Garden Theater late at night, they passed two uniformed firemen in red shirts, black trousers, and patent leather boots.

At the time, the United States Army and Navy were unpopular among some New Yorkers. There had been draft riots among the working class over conscription, and resentment still ran high a year later. The two firemen deliberately stepped in front of Will and Parker to block their path and made insulting remarks.

Parker took hold of Will's arm, hoping to steer him around the men without further incident. But they had not gone more than a step or two when Will turned, chose the biggest one for himself, and told Parker to take the other.

Still the savage fighter Parker remembered from childhood, Will brought his man down to the cobblestones in a moment, and kept beating him even as the other struggled to pry them apart.

Will was fortunate to avoid jail, like he had after his altercation with the Pennsylvania pharmacist. When a policeman ran up to the scene, Parker thought the police and firemen would be in "close accord." But to his surprise, the big fireman seemed apologetic, his friend remained silent, and the policeman made no arrests.

Within a few days, Will and his old friend said their solemn goodbyes and Parker returned to his post in Washington. Will did not appear to doubt the success of his plan, but he also seemed prepared for failure and death. Parker would recall later that his resolution was "unflinching."

•   •   •

Even as Will went about his final preparations at the Brooklyn Navy Yard, Rear Admiral Lee was transferred to the Mississippi River Blockading Squadron and replaced by David Dixon Porter, who shared none of Lee's confidence in Will or his plan. In fact, he believed the whole thing doomed to fail, saying outright he would not have authorized it. The rough condition of the launches deepened his skepticism.

Under increasing pressure to finish their work before Porter withdrew the Navy's support, Cushing and Wood did their best to iron out the rig's problems on the Hudson River, something they were never fully able to do. But Will considered a version tested in mid-September up to the job.

As repairs on the boats were nearing completion, Will was visited by a cousin from Fredonia, George H. White, who was in the city on business. Will was fond of White, and glad to see him, but he could not tell him the details of his mission. Still, White sensed its gravity. He concluded from Will's unusually subdued demeanor that it was something momentous and said so to him before heading home.

Will's expression grew reflective. "Cousin George," he said, "I am going to have a vote of thanks from Congress, or six feet of pine box by the time you hear from me again."

His grave suspicions confirmed, White asked if he had told his mother. Will said yes.

"And her words to you?" White asked.

Will clearly remembered her last encouragements.

"'I know you will do your duty,'" he replied.

CHAPTER TWENTY-THREE

AN IMPORTANT AND PERILOUS UNDERTAKING

B y September 22, 1864, Will's launches were finally patched up and on their way to Virginia via the Delaware River, Chesapeake Bay, and Potomac River.

But his mission was beset with more setbacks in the coming weeks. While en route to its destination, one of the launches, *Picket Boat #2*, broke down and was seized by Confederate soldiers. Angry and dismayed by its capture, Cushing had to implore Admiral Porter to let him continue with the operation with a single launch—a plea his new commander would have strongly denied, were it not for some outstanding political circumstances.

As Lincoln and Schurz had discussed, the president was facing a close election and was under heavy criticism for recent wartime losses. He was in desperate need of a resounding victory to boost public morale and to keep the White House. Moreover, the *Albemarle* had annihilated nine ships and taken the lives of over a thousand men. Politically or practically, however one chose to view the situation, it was an unmitigated disaster for the president and Union.

In late October, a still skeptical Porter asked Cushing to meet Captain W. H. Macomb aboard his flagship, the steamer USS *Shamrock,* and begin operations. Will enrolled a group of fourteen volunteers from different ships in the fleet, including Ensign Howarth, his trusted right-hand man from the *Minnesota.* His only promise to them was "death, glory, or promotion."

On the night of the 26th, Will brought his men into the launch and started his expedition. But a Union picket tug stationed at the mouth of the river overheard the loud noise of her engine. The tug's crew knew nothing of the secret expedition, and brought the launch to bear, thinking it a rebel craft.

Identifying himself to the ship's officer, Will was allowed to go on his way—but he decided to abort the mission for the night. It had occurred to him that if friendly pickets could hear the launch's machinery, so would the rebels. The noise needed his attention.

Returning to the *Shamrock,* he asked the ship's carpenters to box in the engine to mute its rumble. If his idea worked, no sound would come from the launch until she was close to her goal—at which stage he would count on the rebels' being unable to stop her.

Construction of the engine box occurred on October 27. That same day, a group of escaped slaves brought aboard the ship provided eyewitness intelligence that the enemy had stationed pickets on the half-submerged wreckage of *Southfield* in Plymouth Harbor. In addition, they said, there were enemy troops lined along the shore—as many as four thousand in all.

The number of rebels was daunting. Will had known there would be a significant troop detachment and planned on stealth and cover of darkness allowing him to get past them. But the pickets were an unexpected hurdle.

After some hurried thought, he ordered an auxiliary boat's crew to capture the pickets or get themselves captured, it made no difference to him. In either case, the uproar they created would divert attention from Will and his crew, who could then sail undetected to finish their mission.

The *Shamrock*'s Lieutenant Rufus Duer oversaw the choice of volunteers. "I want eleven men and two officers to accompany Lieutenant Cushing on a dangerous expedition, from which probably none will return," he said, addressing them on deck that afternoon. "None but young men without incumbrances will be accepted." His eyes moving between their faces, he motioned to one side of the deck. "Those who wish to volunteer will now move over."

The entire company—275 sailors in all—stepped over as one.

When Lieutenant Duer told Macomb of the number, he said, "I thought so. Pick your men."

Armed with muskets and pistols, thirteen sailors were ordered to lower the second cutter, which by then was fully equipped.

By 8:30 p.m. Will was ready for another try at sinking the *Albemarle*.

A cold drizzle was falling, and his small band of men shivered in the wetness as they climbed into their boats. At 9:00 p.m. they left the *Shamrock*, the second group in tow of Will's thirty-five-foot open steam launch. Half an hour later, the boat pulled up alongside the launch and moored. Only then did Will reveal what was expected of them.

It was a dark and miserable night. The temperature was sixty-six degrees, the Roanoke about ten degrees cooler, with thin sheets of mist fluttering over its low, slow surface.

As the party entered the river, the shadows seemed to thicken around them. The channel was about a hundred fifty yards wide, but its banks seemed much closer, the dense black lines of gum and cypress trees on either side giving the men a sense of acute claustrophobia. Prohibited from uttering so much as a whispered word, they felt the silence to be dense and oppressive.

For the next two and a half hours, they moved upriver "in the midst of darkness, cold, and unknown dangers, for a volley might be fired from either bank, or an obstruction...in the riverbed might strike...at any moment."

In *Picket Boat #1*, Will Cushing and his fourteen volunteers found the foggy conditions an advantage, helping to shield them from enemy eyes. Behind them on a tow rope, water splashing around its keel, was a cutter with thirteen added men aboard.

And eight miles up ahead was the *Albemarle*.

Though she was too distant to see in the night, Cushing could feel her menacing presence deep in his bones.

•   •   •

Sometime after 2:00 a.m., Will spotted the wreckage of the South-field up ahead. The *Albemarle*'s first kill, it sat there like a picked-over carcass, its hurricane deck jutting above the waterline.

Four rebel sentries stood atop its soggy, broken planks, guarding the harbor inlet. If they saw the invaders, they would fire rifles or rockets to alert the soldiers in the earthwork fortifications along both banks.

Will was prepared to cast off the second boat so that its crew could kill the sentries…but so far, so good. The two small vessels moved forward through the darkness, skirting the wreck by about thirty feet, the chugging of its steam plant muffled by a tarpaulin stuffed inside the box around its engine walls.

And then, miraculously, they were past the wreck, undetected.

Silent and erect in the launch's prow, light brown hair flowing down over his shoulders, his expression set, twenty-one-year-old Will Cushing felt determination and something else: a grim, tightly harnessed anger. It was in these very waters that Charles Flusser had died moments after the *Southfield* took her savage hit.

Checking his emotions, Will turned his gaze toward Plymouth's wharves a mile upriver. His right hand clenched three lanyards that allowed him to silently control the launch—one tied around the engineer's ankle at the other end, another attached to the wrist of the boom operator, Ensign Thomas S. Gay, and a third attached to the howitzer in case it had to be fired. In his left hand, two braided ropes allowed him to release and detonate the torpedo.

At almost 3:00 a.m., with the *Southfield*'s wreck left well behind, Will stared out over the prow of his launch into the rainswept darkness. Two days had now passed since his false start. Drenched to his skin, his wet hair plastered to his face and neck, he focused on the harbor ahead.

Suddenly he hitched in a breath, resisting the urge to whoop in exultation, as he'd once done in Fredonia after playing a prank on his brothers to avenge a slight, cutting his rowboat loose from its moorings so it would float off on the lake without them.

The *Albemarle* loomed in sight. *At last.* Her humpbacked bulk rose up and up against the dim, flickering firelights of Plymouth.

Will tugged one of the lanyards in his right hand, signaling his engineer to proceed.

And then he heard the loud, harsh bark of a dog. Coming from the wharf? The riverbank? He would never know.

Whrrrooof!

That was all it took to alert the Confederates.

Within seconds, a voice hailed from the *Albemarle*'s deck. "Who goes there? What boat are you?"

There was tense silence in the launch.

"*What boat are you?*" the guard repeated. "*Who goes there?*"

"We'll soon let you know!" Will shouted back, finally. The element of surprise gone, he saw no point in pretending.

The incoming musket fire started at once—from the ironclad, the shore, everywhere around him.

Will was quick to react. He ordered the cutter to cast off and return to the *Southfield,* thinking his men could overcome the Confederate guards and open a rear escape route. Then he shouted for his engineer to go full speed ahead toward the dark wall of iron in front of them.

He meant to take out the *Albemarle* if it was his last living act on earth.

His launch was shooting forward under heavy fire when a blaze erupted on the shore...then another...and another. Rebel sentries were igniting large wood piles splashed with turpentine and pine tar, illuminating the harbor, and warning their fellows.

But the illumination also aided Will. In the sudden glare of the flames, he saw a barrier up ahead—a circular pen of cypress logs chained together around the *Albemarle*. About thirty feet wide on all sides, it had been built to thwart a torpedo strike of the very sort he was leading against her. If Will had seen it an instant later, his boat might have struck the pen head on in the darkness.

Standing tall in its prow, Confederate bullets screaming through the air around him, Will ordered his pilot to sheer off from the cordon and make a broad sweep of it as he sought out openings and weak spots. But the logs were rigidly connected.

Then Will noticed something in the firelight. A thick growth of moss and river slime on the logs. An idea flashed through his mind.

"Bear away!" he shouted, ordering his pilot to veer off a hundred yards and double back toward the log pen at full speed. If the launch built up enough steam, it might vault over the slick, slippery logs, and land inside the pen with the ironclad.

The pilot followed orders. As the little boat went sharply into its turn, Will was swept by a sheet of fire from the ship. A bullet creased his sleeve, the back of his coat was torn out by buckshot, and the sole of his shoe went sailing off his foot

Will laughed half-crazedly at his predicament as the launch circled about and bore toward the logs, its engine roaring and throbbing, its screw churning up a wide wake of foam...

"*What boat are you?*" someone screamed yet again from atop the ironclad.

The men on the launch shouted comical answers. Will's own response was a blast of grapeshot from his howitzer.

An instant later the launch struck the logs and was over, flying like a sled over a snowbank, then splashing down hard into the water. Four more bullets plunged through Will's clothing in quick succession. Ten feet above his head, a cannon angled down from the *Albemarle*'s porthole, but the gunnery mates could not lower it enough to target the launch.

Will decided he was close enough. With the torpedo release line now in his left hand, and the trigger line in his right, he ordered his torpedoman to lower the boom.

The cylindrical mine dropped into the water.

Will would always remember hearing a cacophony of voices above him.

"*Lower, lower!*" a gunnery officer shouted as his men struggled with the cannon.

Then a call for him to surrender from the ironclad's captain.

He would sooner die.

"Leave the ram, or I'll blow you to pieces!" he replied.

All in a heartbeat, he saw the cannon above him, finally in position, its muzzle staring him in the face no more than ten feet away. He heard one of its officers shout, "*Fire!*", glanced down to confirm the torpedo had dipped under the *Albermarle*'s iron apron, and then felt a burning pain on the back of his left hand as a bullet seared his flesh.

Staying cool and composed, waiting to feel the torpedo knock against the *Albemarle*'s bottom, he hauled in the triggering line.

There was a dull, muffled *whump*, a high column of water shooting up into the air over the launch. The *Albemarle* reared as the explosion blew a hole in her large enough for a horse-drawn wagon. At the same time, her cannon discharged with a thunderous roar. A hundred pounds of grapeshot grazed the heads of Cushing's men as the dense mass of water thrown out by his torpedo came down on them with choking weight.

"*Men, save yourselves!*" Will ordered at the top of his lungs.

Then he tossed off his cutlass, revolver, shoes, and coat, and plunged from his sinking launch into the river.

•   •   •

The next several hours were by far the most harrowing of Will's life.

Bullets and grapeshot plowed the river's surface as he swam toward the log pen, climbed dripping over it, and then struck out toward shore, using the bonfires to orient himself.

LIEUT. CUSHING'S TORPEDO BOAT SINKING THE ALBEMARLE ON ROANOKE RIVER, N. C.

"Men, save yourselves!" Cushing ordered. *U.S. Naval History and Heritage Command*

It was cold, long after the autumn frosts, and the water chilled his blood. In the starless night, his head barely poking above the surface, he was unable to judge the distance to the opposite riverbank. But he swam for it anyway, knowing that his nearest friends, the Union fleet, were over a dozen miles off. Any fate seemed better than falling into Confederate hands.

Shivering, his clothes soaked and heavy, Will was in the water for what felt like hours. He seemed to make little headway but refused to give in to discouragement. All around him, the rebels were out in dinghies, picking up his men as they struggled to stay afloat, questioning some about their captain.

"Give us his name!" one of them demanded.

Will couldn't make out the response.

Time passed. Several yards away, one of his men gave a great, gurgling yell and went under. Moments later a boat crew heard Will splashing in the water and bore in his direction. He dogpaddled in silence, waiting them out, his breath bated as they rowed off without finding him.

Will swam on. Finally, the shoreline was visible. And within reach.

Then he heard a groan somewhere behind him. Another swimmer. Though fatigued and numb from exposure, he turned toward the man and recognized him. It was his acting master's mate, a man named Woodman.

Will noticed he was still wearing his cap.

"This way," Will husked. "I'm over here."

"I can't make it," Woodman replied in a faint voice. "I can swim no longer."

Will stroked toward the crewman, tossed the waterlogged cap off his head, slipped his right arm under his chest, and ordered him to swim toward shore.

For some ten minutes, Woodman managed to stay above water... but then cried out that he could go no further.

"Come on, you can make it!" Will urged.

It was no use. Woodman's strength was gone. Will tried to support him but was too tired. The master's mate sank like a stone. Thankful not to be brought down with him, Will made for the bank.

He almost didn't reach it. As dawn neared, the river took on a high chop, splashing water into his mouth so he gagged on every labored breath. His strokes feeble and mechanical, he was swimming on willpower alone.

Don't give up, he told himself. Don't sink.

Will touched soft mud not a moment too soon. In his excitement he stood up, took a faltering step onto the bank, and then dropped facedown into the mire, his legs still in the water.

He remained there until daybreak, frozen, unable even to crawl on his hands and knees. Exhausted, dizzy, he could hardly think straight. But his determination to escape remained unshaken.

By full morning, the bright, warm sunshine restored his spirits and a large measure of his stamina. But as he slogged uphill toward drier ground, hidden in the reeds, Will realized the area was swarming with soldiers and sailors and gleaned from overheard snippets of conversations that they were combing the shore for *him*.

It pleased him to be the puppet master jerking their strings. But had he succeeded in his mission? Did his torpedo send the *Albemarle* to the bottom? The question plagued his thoughts.

For the next six hours, Will would elude enemy posses, one excruciatingly narrow escape after another. Around midday, still no closer to Union lines, he crawled past a Confederate work party in a cornfield, gained the bordering woods, and disappeared into the trees.

He was pausing for a respite, sprawled on the ground, when an elderly black plantation worker spotted him from the field.

Surprised by the "muddy apparition" in front of him, the slave froze where he stood. Will pushed laboriously to his knees and crouched, ready to spring.

When both realized they had no reason to fear each other, Will got an idea. Something about the old man impressed him as trustworthy. Reaching into his pocket for twenty wet dollars in greenbacks and some soggy verses of scripture, he asked him to go into town for news of the ram.

The man accepted his offer and returned with exactly the word he'd hoped for.

"She's gone dead sunk," he said. And looking him in the eye, added, "They will hang you, massa, if they catch you."

Will would have howled with pride, if he could. The "unsinkable" *Albemarle* was sunk. But he would save his celebration for a safer occasion. He had no wish to find his head in a noose.

Soon he was back on his way, hiding in the swamps, using the sun to guide his direction. Hours passed, and he had more close brushes with rebel search parties. Hungry and bleeding from his wounds, hobbled where the bullet had torn at his heel, he felt on the verge of collapse.

At length, he found a road and near it a creek. On the opposite bank, a rebel patrol had pulled ashore with a small, flat-bottomed fishing skiff.

Hidden in a patch of underbrush, he watched them till sunset... and then saw them stride off with talk of going to eat their supper. When every soldier was gone, he crept down to the creek, dove in, swam across, and cut the skiff loose, swimming downstream behind it.

As it rounded the first bend in the stream, he climbed aboard and grabbed a paddle.

Darkness swallowed him. Famished, worn out, Will paddled for hours, steering by the pale blue stars.

Finally he reached the mouth of the Roanoke. Several more hours passed. He paddled in an enervated daze, moving his arms mechanically, never stopping to rest.

Then . . . a large vessel was ahead, its outline sketched against the stars. Believing he'd reached the point where the Union fleet might be, Will made for it. Though he did not know it, midnight had come and gone.

After ten solid hours of paddling, he came within hailing distance of the ship.

It was, in fact, a friendly gunboat—the USS *Valley City*.

"Ship ahoy!" he shouted, waving arms he couldn't feel. *"Ship ahoy!"*

It was a while before they would pick him up. Many aboard were convinced he was a rebel spy, having heard Lieutenant Cushing had died in Plymouth harbor.

Finally, they threw out a line and hoisted him onto the deck, where he collapsed on his back, half-unconscious from exhaustion and dehydration.

More time passed before he saw familiar face leaning over him. It was an acquaintance, the ship's commander, J. A. J. Brooks.

"My God, Cushing," he said in astonishment. "Is this you?"

"It is I."

"Is it done?"

"It is done," Will replied faintly.

Given a glass of brandy and plenty of water, Cushing was revived and brought to the flagship *Shamrock* to meet with Commander Macomb.

As he set foot on deck, Cushing heard cheers all around him. Rockets were fired into the air, and a hearty meal prepared as he was debriefed in Macomb's cabin.

His return to dry land and recuperation would wait, however. With news of the mighty *Albemarle*'s destruction, Macomb called a meeting of his captains for daybreak the next morning.

They intended to waste no time moving on Plymouth.

PLYMOUTH REGAINED, LINCOLN VICTORIOUS, ELLIOTT SUNK

At precisely 11:00 a.m. on October 29, Macomb's fleet set sail to retake Plymouth from the Confederates. But as they neared the city, they discovered a major obstacle. With the *Albemarle* sunk, the rebels had anticipated an attack and sunk schooners beside the *Southfield*'s wreck to close off the harbor mouth.

Macomb and his ships withdrew, but not for long. A scouting expedition by the *Valley City* determined there was another way into the harbor. Middle River would lead the massive fleet around and above the sunken vessels.

Two days later, on October 31, they formed their line and steamed into Plymouth harbor, shelling the city on their approach.

The battle was fierce, but brief. The *Albemarle* had been the shore batteries' fearsome protection but was now at the bottom of the river. Macomb was free to bring his warships within short range of the enemy defenses and unleash his devastating firepower.

The overwhelmed Confederates soon abandoned their forts, allowing Plymouth to be captured from the rebels.

At Hampton Roads afterward, Will reported on his actions to Rear Admiral Porter. His former harsh critic gave him a hero's welcome, informing him he had sent word of his success to Secretary Welles in Washington, D.C., who quickly told President Lincoln.

The news would spread like wildfire.

CUSHING THE DAREDEVIL, blared one front page headline.

Another read, DESTRUCTION OF THE *ALBEMARLE*: WILL CUSHING'S REPORT ON THE SPLENDID GALLANTRY OF OUR TARS.

In November, Lincoln won the election by six hundred thousand votes, riding a surge of renewed optimism sparked in large part by Cushing's incredible feat. The following month Will received the formal thanks of Congress at the president's written request. It was the nation's highest expression of gratitude during the Civil War.

Will was promoted two grades to lieutenant commander, invited to gala events in his honor, asked to give speeches throughout the United States, and given the wry moniker "Albemarle Cushing." Later, he would gain another nickname: Lincoln's Commando.

•   •   •

William Cushing went on to have many more colorful exploits during and after the Civil War, gaining, as always, new friends and detractors in the Navy, battling pirates in the Caribbean, insurgents in Panama, and eventually going on a diplomatic voyage to the Far East. In 1870 he married Kate Forbes and built a house in his hometown of Fredonia. Will was, however, beset by repeated health problems, which many attributed to the wounds he sustained during his attack on the *Albemarle*.

By the early spring of 1874, the "once dashing young officer ... had become gaunt and walked with a limp." He was curt and touchy, his gray eyes glaring from deep sockets of pain and fatigue.

In May, Will became gravely ill while on leave following squadron exercises in Norfolk. For the next seven months, his health declined until he fell into a state of constant delirium and was transferred from his home to a government hospital.

On December 17, 1874, Commander William Barker Cushing awoke, suddenly lucid, and called for his wife and mother. When they arrived, he embraced them, reciting the Lord's Prayer. He died moments later at age thirty-two. His obituary in the *New York Times* read:

> All through the [Civil War] he distinguished himself by sig-
> nal acts of perilous adventure. He combined coolness and
> sound judgement with a courage unsurpassed, and on all
> occasions proved himself a valuable officer.

Will's burial was on January 7, at Bluff Point, the cemetery of the United States Naval Academy—the school which once ousted him as irredeemable. His tombstone stands there to this day shaded by oaks on a hill overlooking the Academy grounds and the Severn River. A single word is cut above his name: ALBEMARLE.

Will had gone from irredeemable to irreplaceable in the course of his lifetime, his story forever linked to that of the Confederate ram he sank in one of the most unforgettable feats of daring in naval history. In some ways, Will's early life and wartime exploits seemed to lead inevitably toward his encounter with the ironclad terror of the Roanoke—a historic case of the unstoppable force colliding head-on with the immovable object. His often contradictory personality combined kindness and cruelty, loyalty, petty vindictiveness, erratic behavior, and absolute trustworthiness. As a ship's captain stalking Confederate ports and vessels on Albemarle Sound, he was by turns calculating and impulsive, a shrewd tactician and a reckless hothead. His audacious and often hastily planned strikes against superior rebel forces prompted both admiration and consternation among his peers and higher officers.

But his valor was unrivaled, as was his wolf-like ferocity.

As President Abraham Lincoln wrote, "The destruction of so formidable a vessel...is an important event touching our future naval operations, and would reflect honor on any officer."

The famed David Glasgow Farragut, for whom the office of Admiral of the United States had been created, was even more direct in his assessment of Will's contribution to the Union's cause.

"Young Cushing was the hero of the war," he said.

•   •   •

Unlike Will Cushing, Gilbert Elliott spent his later years in near obscurity, his fortunes as a shipbuilder taking a steep downturn with the *Albemarle*'s destruction. At the peak of her reign over the North Carolina coast, Elliott won a lucrative Confederate contract to build a second ironclad—one he promised would be even bigger and stronger.

But Will Cushing's sinking of the ram, and Plymouth's recapture by the Union, prompted him to order the unfinished ship burned to keep it out of enemy hands.

Financially ruined, he abandoned the shipyard, married, and opened a wholesale grocery with his brothers—a partnership that eventually folded.

In 1877, Elliott moved his family to St. Louis, where he quietly practiced law for some years. In 1893, he again moved, this time to Staten Island, New York, opening a new law office with his son, Gilbert Elliott III.

In 1885, he died quietly of an illness at age fifty-two and was interred at Greenwood Cemetery in Brooklyn.

•   •   •

Captain James W. Cooke was not the *Albemarle*'s captain on the night of her destruction. After his decisive victory over Charles Flusser's blockade squadron and escape from Melancton Smith's ambush, Cooke

was detached from the ironclad and given command of North Carolina's inland waters, a post he held until the end of the Civil War.

On May 12, 1865, following the Confederacy's surrender a month earlier, a paroled Cooke retired.

With his wife and three sons, he moved to Portsmouth, Virginia, where he lived quietly for the next three years, until his death at age fifty-seven.

Cooke is considered one of the greatest naval commanders of his era.

•   •   •

After the recapture of Plymouth, the United States Navy raised the CSS *Albemarle* and towed her to the Navy Yard at Norfolk, Virginia, where she was auctioned for scrap to the highest bidder.

J. N. Leonard and Company, a stock investment firm and manufacturer of diverse products, placed a winning bid of $3,200.

The only parts of the once great "Devil of the Cornfield" to survive the Civil War are a cannon and smokestack.

Today, the smokestack is on display at the Museum of the *Albemarle*, in Elizabeth City, North Carolina.

AUTHOR'S NOTE

Will Cushing first stormed into my awareness in 2013. I had recently finished my World War II narrative history *First to Jump* and was looking for an interesting subject for another book-length work of nonfiction.

I use the verb "stormed" very deliberately. It's a good fit. I hadn't planned to write about the American Civil War. The period was a bit too far outside my comfort zone. But then... Will happened.

Will Cushing is a force of nature. He instantly overtakes the imagination with his courage, his passion, his brash intensity, and gallantry. With his sheer *panache*. If I may abruptly switch metaphors, Will doesn't just grab the spotlight. He's the whole show.

Thus, I was left with absolutely no choice but to tell his tale. Or as I came to feel, let Will tell it through me.

As the book took shape, I discovered that a handful of biographies have been written about Will over the decades. The earliest tend to soften the rough parts of his background and over-romanticize his admittedly incredible exploits, and the later ones to overanalyze his psyche in contemporary terms. In my view, none put his acts of audacious daring—and occasional recklessness and self-destructiveness—into full, rich context within the widescreen history of the War between the States

Commander William Barker Cushing, U.S. Navy, wasn't an introspective man in the modern sense. He wasn't one to examine his motivations and impulses. He was always on the move, seeking adventure, on the ferocious hunt. When he launched his vengeful guerrilla raid against the ironclad CSS *Albemarle*, the terror of the Roanoke, it was bound to be a collision of monumental proportions—the irresistible force that was Will meeting the immovable object that was the Confederacy's most dreaded warship. President Abraham Lincoln would write that Will's actions against the juggernaut changed naval tactics forever.

America's first rear admiral, David Glasgow Farragut, went a large step further, saying he was convinced it decisively changed the Union's wartime fortunes.

In the course of my research and writing, I found a number of significant errors and inconsistencies in previous tellings of Will's story. I decided that to set things straight, I would rely almost exclusively on primary nineteenth-century sources—many rare and obscure. I drew heavily from letters, official after-action reports, contemporaneous newspaper and magazine articles, and military histories written about Will, his supporting cast, and the war in general during his life. These original sources fill in certain elusive details and preserve a certain rawness and immediacy of experience that consistently worked their way into the narrative, giving it both a vitality and adherence to the facts I otherwise couldn't have achieved. Eventually I came to feel like one of the wartime newspaper correspondents who tagged along on Will's cutting-out expeditions, only to find themselves in the thick of a riotous shoot 'em up with Confederate ground troops or blockade runners, often outgunned and outnumbered...but never outfought. My goal here was to present pure, unfiltered Will Cushing. To bring him to life as he really was. I'll leave it to you, Kind Reader, to gauge my success.

A list of major sources follows. But first, a few words of thanks:

To Doug Grad, my agent and friend of many years, for his honesty, experience, and determination in getting this project off the ground.

To Alex Novak for buying the book based on my proposal and showing infinite forbearance while awaiting the manuscript's delivery. Alex is a gentleman, an old-school editor in the finest sense. His steady, unflagging belief in my ability to get the job done gave my confidence a lift when I really needed it.

To Stephen Thompson, my editor, for his enthusiastic support, suggestions, and deft hand in helping me improve, refine, and shape the manuscript into its final form.

To my most excellent copyeditor, Laura Spence Swain.

And finally to Regnery Publishing for taking a chance on this book in a tight and highly competitive marketplace.

I believe Will, who was never shy about regaling people with his adventures, would enjoy the result.

Jerome Preisler
Maine
July 2020

BIBLIOGRAPHY

BOOKS, MEMOIRS, AND OFFICIAL GOVERNMENT HISTORIES

Abbot, Willis John. *Battle-fields of '61, A Narrative of the Military Operations of the War for the Union Up to the End of the Peninsular Campaign.* New York: Dodd, Mead and Company, 1889.

Ammen, Daniel. *The Navy in the Civil War, Vol. 2, The Atlantic Coast.* New York: Charles Scribner's Sons, 1883.

Ashe, Samuel A'Court. *Biographical History of North Carolina from Colonial Times to the Present.* Greensboro, North Carolina: Charles L. Van Noppen, 1916.

Benjamin, Park. *The United States Naval Academy, Being the Yarn of the American Midshipman.* New York: G. P. Putnam's Sons, 1900.

Brown, Kent Masterson. *Cushing of Gettysburg, The Story of a Union Artillery Commander.* Lexington, Kentucky: The University Press of Kentucky, 1993.

Buckingham, James, and Mary J. Tilton. *The Ancestors of Ebenezer Buckingham.* R. R. Donnelley & Sons, 1892.

Burrows, E. J. *The Great Rebellion of 1861, Twelve Months' History of the United States, Showing What a Republic Can Do: Skirmishes and Battles, What the Rebels Have Done to Destroy the Union, the Lessons of the Year, Etc., Etc.* Philadelphia: C. Sherman & Son, 1862.

Clark Walter, ed. *Histories of the Several Regiments and Battalions from North Carolina in the Great War 1861-65 Written by Members of their Respective Commands.* Raleigh, North Carolina: E. M. Uzzell, 1901.

Cushing, William B. *The Sea Eagle: The Civil War Memoir of LCdr. William B. Cushing, U.S.N.* edited by Alden Carter. Chicago: Rowman and Littlefield Publishers, 2009.

Dickey, Luther S., and Samuel L. Evans. *History of the 103rd Regiment, Pennsylvania Veteran Volunteer Infantry 1861–1865*. Chicago: L. S. Dickey, 1910.

Doubleday, Abner. *Reminiscences of Forts Sumter and Moultrie in 1860–'61*. New York: Harper & Brothers, 1876.

Edwards, E. M. H. *Commander William Barker Cushing of the United States Navy*. New York: F. Tennyson Neely, 1898.

Elliott, Robert. G. *Ironclad of the Roanoke: Gilbert Elliott's Albemarle*. Pennsylvania: White Mane Publishing, 2005.

Fletcher, Annie. *Within Fort Sumter, Or a View of Major Anderson's Garrison Family for One Hundred and Ten Days*. New York: N. Tibbals & Company, 1861.

Frothingham, Jessie Peabody. *Running the Gantlet (sic), The Daring Exploits of Lieutenant Cushing, U.S.N.* New York: D. Appleton and Company, 1906.

Haight, Theron Wilbur. *Three Wisconsin Cushings: Original Papers*. Wisconsin History Commission, 1910.

Hannings, Bud. *Every Day of the Civil War: A Chronological Encyclopedia*. Jefferson, North Carolina: McFarland and Company, 2000.

Haskell, Franklin Aretas. *The Battle of Gettysburg*. Wisconsin History Commission, 1908.

Headley, J. T. *Farragut, and Our Naval Commanders*. New York: E. B. Treat & Company, 1867.

Lossing, Benson John. *Pictorial History of the Civil War in the United States of America*. Philadelphia: George W. Childs, 1866.

Malanowski, Jamie. *Commander Will Cushing: Daredevil Hero of the Civil War*. New York: W. W. Norton & Company, 2014.

Moore, Frank, ed. *The Rebellion Record, A Diary of American Events*. New York: G. P. Putnam, 1861.

Parker, David B. *A Chautauqua Boy in '61 and Afterward*. Boston: Small, Maynard and Company, 1912.

Parker, Thomas W. *Young Heroes of the American Navy*. Boston: W. A. Wilde Company, 1915.

Preble, George Henry. *History of the Flag of the United States of America, and of the Naval and Yacht Club Signals, Seals and Arms, and Principal National Songs of the United States, with a Chronicle of the Symbols, Standards, Banners and Flags of Ancient and Modern Nations.* Boston: A. Williams and Company, 1880.

Roske, Ralph, and Charles Van Doren. *Lincoln's Commando.* New York: Harper & Brothers, 1957.

Sandburg, Carl. *Abraham Lincoln: The Prairie Years and the War Years.* New York: Harcourt Brace & Company, 1939.

Scharf, John Thomas. *History of the Confederate States Navy from Its Organization to the Surrender of Its Last Vessel, Its Stupendous Struggle with the Great Navy of the United States; The Engagements Fought in the Rivers and Harbors of the South, and upon the High Seas; Blockade-Running, First Use of Iron-clads and Torpedoes, and Privateer History.* New York: Rogers & Sherwood, 1887.

Stempel, Jim. *The CSS* Albemarle *and William Cushing, The Remarkable Confederate Ironclad and the Union Officer Who Sank It.* Jefferson, North Carolina: McFarland & Company, 2011.

Stick, David, ed. *Outer Banks Reader.* Chapel Hill, North Carolina: University of North Carolina Press: 1998.

White, Ellsberry Valentine. *The First Iron-Clad Naval Engagement in the World, History of Facts of the Great Naval Battle Between the* Merrimac-*Virginia, CSN and the Ericsson* Monitor*, USN, Hampton Roads, March 8 and 9, 1862.* Portsmouth, Virginia: self-published, 1902.

Wilson, John Laird. *Battles of America, Sea and Land, Biographies of Naval and Military Commanders, Vol. 3: The Great Civil War.* New York: James S. Virtue, 1878.

GOVERNMENT AND MILITARY RECORDS

Butler, Benjamin Franklin. *Private and Official Correspondence of Gen. Benjamin F. Butler During the Civil War.* Privately Issued, 1917.

House Documents, Printed by Order of the House of Representatives during the First Session of the Thirty-Eighth Congress, 1863–64, in Sixteen Volumes. Washington, D.C.: Government Printing Office, 1864.

Index to the Executive Documents in Nine Volumes, Printed by Order of the Senate of the United States, for the Second Session of the Thirty-Sixth Congress, and of the Special Session 1860–61. Washington, D.C.: George W. Bowman, 1861.

Message from the President of the United States at the Commencement of the First Session of the Thirty-Sixth Congress Vol. 1. Washington, D.C.: George W. Bowman, 1860.

Office of Naval War Records, U.S. Department of the Navy. Index of Official Records of the Union and Confederate Navies in the War of the Rebellion, Series 1, Vols. 1–13. Washington, D.C.: Government Printing Office, 1902.

Official Records of the Union and Confederate Navies in the War of the Rebellion, Series 1, Vol. 5, Operations on the Potomac and Rappahannock Rivers from December 7, 1861, to July 31, 1865, Atlantic Blockading Squadron from April 4 to July 15, 1861. Washington: Government Printing Office, 1897.

———. *Series 1, Vol. 6, Atlantic Blockading Squadron from July 16 to October 29, 1861, North Atlantic Blockading Squadron from October 29, 1861, to March 8, 1862.* Washington: Government Printing Office, 1897.

———. *Series 1, Vol. 8, North Atlantic Blockading Squadron, from September 5, 1862, to May 4, 1863.* Washington, D.C.: Government Printing Office, 1899.

———. *Series 1, Vol. 9, from May 5, 1863–May 5, 1864.* Washington, D.C.: Government Printing Office, 1899.

Steward, William H. ed. *History of Norfolk County, Virginia and Representative Citizens.* Chicago: Biographical Publishing Company, 1902.

The War of the Rebellion, A Compilation of the Official Records of the Union and Confederate Armies, Series 1, Vol. 51 in Two Parts, Part

2 *Confederate Correspondence.* Washington. D.C.: Government Printing Office, 1897.

The War of the Rebellion, A Compilation of the Official Records of the Union and Confederate Armies Series 2, Vol. 3. Washington: Government Printing Office, 1898.

———. *Series 4, Vol. 1, Section 1, Correspondence, Orders, Reports and Returns of the Confederate Authorities, Similar to That Indicated for the Union Officials, as of the Third Series, but Including the Correspondence between the Union and Confederate Authorities.* Washington, D.C.: Government Printing Office, 1900.

———. *Series 1, Vol. 18, Operations in North Carolina and Southeastern Virginia, from August 20, 1862, to June 3, 1863.* Washington, D.C.: Government Printing Office 1887.

Thompson, Robert Means, and Richard Wainwright, eds. *Confidential Correspondence of Gustavus Vasa Fox, Assistant Secretary of the Navy 1861–1865.* New York: Naval History Society, 1920.

MAGAZINE AND NEWSPAPER ARTICLES

"*Albermarle*, The Career of the Confederate Ram." *The Century Illustrated Monthly Magazine* 36 (May 1888): 420–440.

Elliott, Gilbert. "Her Construction and Service, by Her Builder."

Holden, Edgar. "The *Albemarle* and the Sassacus."

Cushing, William B. "The Destruction of the *Albemarle*."

Warley, A. F. "Note by Her Captain."

"An Interesting Letter—Recapture of the Point Smith Light Ship." *Daily Green Mountain Freeman.* May 22, 1861.

"A Brilliant Fight near the Mouth of the New River between the Gunboat Ellis and a Rebel Battery—Spirited Conduct of Captain Cushing, Who Blows Up His Vessel Rather Than Surrender It to the Rebels." *New York Daily Herald.* December 4, 1862.

"A Voracious Witness." *New York Times.* January 26, 1861.

Cushing, William Barker. "Outline Story of the War Experiences of William B. Cushing, as Told by Himself." *U.S. Naval Institute Proceedings* 38, no. 3 (September 1912).

Stewart, Charles W. "William Barker Cushing." *U.S. Naval Institute Proceedings* 38, no. 2 (June 1912).

"Experiences of the Massachusetts Eighth Regiment at Annapolis—Experiences of the Seventh Regiment at Annapolis." *Detroit Free Press.* April 27, 1861.

"He Built the *Albemarle*—Gilbert Elliott, of War Fame, Dies at his New York Home," *St. Louis Post-Dispatch.* May 11, 1895.

"Home Guards." *The Old North State* (Elizabeth City, North Carolina). November 2, 1850.

"Hostilities at Annapolis." *The Times-Picayune.* May 12, 1861.

"Late and Important News—Solicitude about Washington, etc." *Alexandria Gazette.* April 22, 1861.

"Lieutenant Simpson's Account of the Battle of Bull's Run." *Wheeling Daily Intelligencer.* July 27, 1861.

"Loss of a Gunboat—Special Expedition—Gallant Fighting—The Gunboat Ellis Blown Up." *Chicago Tribune.* December 9, 1862.

"Military in Pasquotank." *North Carolina Standard.* April 4, 1860.

"Naval Academy Midshipman FM Thomas Resigns." *The Baltimore Sun.* December 15, 1860.

"Return of the Star of the West; Her Attempt to Enter Charleston Harbor. The Damage Sustained by Her Landing of the Troops on Governor's Island, etc." *New York Times.* January 14, 1861.

"The Cutting Out of the Smith's Point Light Ship." *Glasgow Herald.* June 4, 1861.

"The Expedition Up Little River—Capture of a Rebel Fort—The Prize Schooner J. Munson & C." *New York Daily Herald.* January 28, 1863.

"The Ram *Albemarle*, a Brief History of How She Was Built, A Lesson in Perseverence—The Career of Her Constructor—A Cornfield Turned into a Shipyard—Great Difficulties Overcome—A Hazardous Undertaking." *Richmond Dispatch.* October 16, 1898.

"War Intelligence." *Brooklyn Daily Eagle*. May 21, 1861.

Winthrop, Theodore. "The New York Seventh Regiment—Our March to Washington—Dispatches from a Soldier, Killed before his Atlantic Assignment Was Complete," *Atlantic Magazine* (June 1861).

INTERNET

Higgenbotham, George B. "Rather a Monotonous Affair: An Irishman on the Union Blockade." USS *Grand Gulf*. July 1864. https://irishamericancivilwar.com/2013/07/07/rather-a-monotonous-affair-an-irishman-on-the-union-blockade/.

"Log Books of the United States Navy, 19th and 20th Centuries, USS *Jamestown*—Atlantic Blockading Squadron." Entries June 5, 1861–June 23, 1862. https://www.naval-history.net/OW-US/Jamestown/USS_Jamestown-1861-1863.htm.

"Milton Buckingham Cushing Person Sheet." RootsWeb. http://Freepages.rootsweb.com/~carrollrogers/family/ps01/ps01_041.htm.

"7th Regiment North Carolina Volunteers. 1st Organization." 7th Regiment North Carolina Volunteers. https://7thncvols.wordpress.com.

"21 September 1861: *Harper's Weekly* Reports on Forts Hatteras and Clark." The Civil War Day by Day. University of North Carolina at Chapel Hill. https://web.lib.unc.edu/civilwar/index.php/2011/09/21/21-september-1861/.

Detectives
A to Z